TRINITY'S CHILDREN

LIVING ALONG AMERICA'S NUCLEAR HIGHWAY

Tad Bartimus &
Scott McCartney

TRINITy's

CHILDREN

LIVING ALONG AMERICA'S
NUCLEAR HIGHWAY

Harcourt Brace Jovanovich, Publishers

New York   San Diego   London

The epigraph in chapter one is from *The Poetry of Robert Frost* edited by Edward Connery Lathem. Copyright 1930, 1939, © 1969 by Holt, Rinehart and Winston. Copyright © 1958 by Robert Frost. Copyright © 1967 by Lesley Frost Ballantine, Reprinted by permission of Henry Holt and Company, Inc.

The epigraph in chapter three is from *John Dryden: Four Comedies.* edited by L. A. Beaurline and Fredson Bowers. Copyright © 1967 by the University of Chicago. Reprinted by permission of The University of Chicago Press.

The epigraph in chapter four is from "BIG YELLOW TAXI" (Joni Mitchell) © 1989 HANSEATIC MUSIKVERLAG GMBH (GEMA). All rights administered on behalf of HANSEATIC MUSIKVERLAG GMBH (GEMA) for the U.S.A. Administered by INTERSONG U.S.A., INC. All Rights Reserved. Used By Permission.

The epigraph in chapter eight is from *The Killing of Karen Silkwood* by Richard Rashke. Copyright © 1981 by Richard Rashke. Reprinted by permission of Houighton Mifflin Company.

Permission for the epigraph in chapter ten was granted by the Albert Einstein Archives, The Hebrew University of Jerusalem, Israel.

The epigraph in chapter eleven is from *With Enough Shovels: Reagan, Bush, & Nuclear War* by Robert Scheer. Copyright © 1982 by Robert Scheer. Reprinted by permission of Random House, Inc.

Library of Congress Cataloging-in-Publication Data
Bartimus, Tad.
    Trinity's children: living along America's nuclear highway/Tad Bartimus and Scott McCartney.—1st ed.
       p.   cm.
    Includes bibliographical references and index.
    ISBN 0-15-167719-0
    1. United States—Military policy. 2. Nuclear weapons—United States. 3. Nuclear weapons—Social aspects—United States.
    4. Nuclear weapons—Social aspects—West (U.S.) 5. West (U.S.)—Description and travel—1981–   6. West (U.S.)—Social life and customs. 7. Interstate 25. I. McCartney, Scott. II. Title.
    U23.B37   1991
    355.8′25119′0973—dc20   91-21459

Designed by Trina Stahl

Printed in the United States of America

First edition
A B C D E

To Dixie Lee, who gave me roots, and the Colonel, who gave me wings

—T.B.

To Karen, for inspiration and for love

—S.M.

CONTENTS

vii

TRINITY'S CHILDREN

LIVING ALONG AMERICA'S
NUCLEAR HIGHWAY

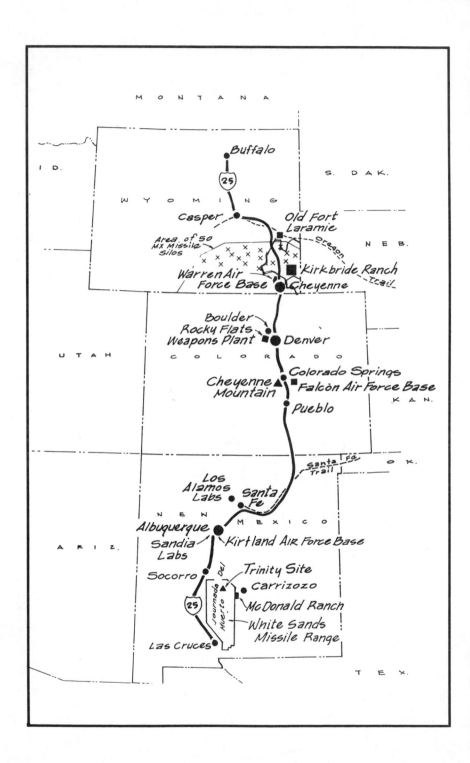

INTRODUCTION

More than a thousand miles of America's West stretch between the scorching New Mexico desert where the first atomic bomb—code-named Trinity—was exploded, and the windswept Wyoming high plains where the latest generation of nuclear warheads stand poised and ready under the sagebrush. In between, laboratories founded by the fathers of the atomic age now house scientists dreaming up new weapons that will be bigger and better and will produce more bang for the buck. In between, families cast aside by the government's need for their land fight on against Uncle Sam or just bemoan their parents' derailed careers and devastated lives. In between, factories that churn out nuclear weapons parts and employ thousands of people also contaminate our air and water with radioactive waste. In between, a general whose command post is buried in the womb of a granite mountain keeps vigilant watch over Soviet missiles while dreaming of fly fishing. In between, there are Patriot missiles and a "City of Secrets" and a glassblower in his sixties who perfected his craft while fighting with the Polish underground against the Nazis. He now uses his unique talent to create lasers for Star Wars. In between, a ranch wife's opposition to the MX missile silo planted in her backyard has grown into an international disarmament movement.

The people who work and love and sleep and pray in these places make up the story of *Trinity's Children: Living Along America's Nuclear Highway*. This book is a journey into the landscape and the soul of this restless and seldom-noticed slice of America. It is also an exploration of this nation's unique role in a fast-changing nuclear world. By exploring the lives of a handful of families over two generations, the book provides a study of human conflicts interwoven with modern science. It is set along Interstate 25, a concrete ribbon stretching from Las Cruces, New Mexico, to Buffalo, Wyoming. From Comanches to conquistadores to the cavalry to Star Wars, the vast crease in the country where the Great Plains embrace the Rocky Mountains has always been molded by the spoils of conquest and the quest for peace.

Much of what has happened here over the past half century occurred because J. Robert Oppenheimer, the head of the Manhattan Project, wanted to birth the world's first atomic bomb in the pristine beauty of New Mexico, his Shangri-la. Los Alamos became the Manhattan Project's pin on the map. Before Oppenheimer touched the mesa with his magic, it was nothing more than an elite boys' school tucked away in some magnificent mountains. Over the years, Los Alamos has drawn the heart of much of America's nuclear military to this still mostly empty section of the country.

Today, as we plot battles in the cosmos while trying to find security on earth, the warriors and wanderers are still coming to this clear-aired spot. Without fanfare or presidential announcements, a booming concentration of laboratories and military installations has grown up along I-25. Some of the people and places vital to the Nuclear Highway have come by choice, some by fate, some by accident. Many of today's homesteaders come for the same reasons that lured Coronado and Pike and Oppenheimer. They are giddy from being on the edge of the unknown, intoxicated with new discoveries, eager to get close to the moment of Creation, to find the vision to dream up new weapons they hope will never be used.

What they find is a region at ease with nature yet at odds with science, one built up by the machines of war yet touched by an aura of serenity. Here, Star Wars—the dream, launched by President Reagan, of a space shield made up of laser beams and rockets that would knock down and destroy incoming nuclear missiles—is taking shape in secret laboratories. Here, nuclear warheads are designed and deployed. Here, surrounded by one of the most beautiful and yet unforgiving landscapes on earth, beats the heart of the work that could save the world . . . or destroy it.

Today's questions take on new intensity. Government plants once cherished for their technological might and national defense importance may have been, in the past, winked at for their economic boondoggle. Now we know they are polluters and poisoners. The worst offender of the nation's seventeen main weapons factories and laboratories is located smack in the middle of the Nuclear Highway. The Rocky Flats arsenal has made nuclear weapons parts since the Cold War began. First hailed as a good neighbor in the 1950s, it has become a pariah to the nearly 1.5 million people of the Denver area. The dilemma of what to do with Rocky Flats—how to clean it up, how to pay for it, and what to do with its workers if it's closed—is at the heart of all questions in this fifth decade of the atomic age.

At a time when nuclear weapons plants, disarmament, and Star Wars are all vital topics, this book offers understanding of the people living beneath the headlines, folks who don't know one another and yet have so much in common.

This book is the result of hundreds of interviews conducted up and down the highway over four years, as well as extensive research in archives and records warehouses of documents dating back to the Manhattan Project. It is not a regional book, or a travelogue, but it is a journey. It is part love story, part oral history. It feeds off the emotion and excitement of its people and is paced by the whirl of technological changes. It is not a pronuke or antinuke book, but an exploration of the emotions and beliefs at work on both sides, and also in the middle. It is not a re-creation of Oppenheimer and the Manhattan Project, a discourse on nuclear disarmament and arms control, or a reconstruction of Star Wars' development. Rather, it is an exploration of how our history evolved and how we got to where we are today.

The book begins where it all began, in the desert of Trinity and the first atomic explosion, the empty place known to the Spanish as the "Journey of Death." It travels north, up the highway. It stops at towns trying to cash in on Star Wars, at cities such as Denver, trying to clean up the sins of its past megaprojects, at command posts such as NORAD's Cheyenne Mountain, at the silos where the creations from New Mexico are deployed. For now, that is the place where the nation waits for the next mile marker on its nuclear journey.

1

LIVING WHERE IT ALL BEGAN

My apple trees will never get across
And eat the cones under his pines, I tell him.
He only says, "Good fences make good neighbors."
ROBERT FROST

The sleek silver arrow hurled itself over Snaggletooth Peak, coming straight at her at nearly the speed of sound. Mary McDonald, one minute grooming her prized mare in the silence of a New Mexican desert ranch at high noon, wondered in the next when she would die.

Would it be with the first kick of a front hoof? Or would the nine-year-old quarter horse trample her, smashing her again and again against the steel pipes of the corral fence?

The F-15, one of the hottest jets in the U.S. arsenal, swooped over Mary's corral with a thunder that shook the valley. He was on her, this fresh-faced pilot who looked just like all the others over the years. How many of them had used her silver-sided barn as a landmark to turn for home?

Shit, Mary thought. No way out.

She was cornered, penned in by the Doc-Bar mare who was tied to the fence in the front, immobile in the rear, the hypotenuse of a triangle in the square corral. The horse was a testy animal in the calmest of times, bred for speed on one side and cutting on the other, and all her primeval instincts exploded in Mary's face.

When the horse reared and the first blow fell, the plane was already gone.

Mary grabbed what she could, clutching for some control in the sudden chaos. But the horse went wild. Dust was everywhere. Mary was pinned to the fence, no chance to get over it. "All I remember thinking was: She'll kill me! She'll kill me!"

The mare knocked her into the seven rows of rusty two-inch steel. Again and again, the horse pounded Mary's head into the fence.

"Me and her hit that sonofabitch with surprising regularity," Mary recalled.

The pain was immediate and excruciating. Mary's jaw was shattered into tiny pieces, almost as if a Sidewinder missile launched from under the wing of the F-15 had locked on and scored a direct hit on her left cheek.

She fell to the ground and tried to hide under a feed bunker, but the wooden trough offered little protection. The horse backed off a fraction, and Mary attempted to climb over the fence. But the mare hit her again, two thousand pounds of crazed flesh grinding her back into the dirt. Finally, the horse broke free and raced away. Mary's nephew Cameron, then nine years old, phoned for help. Mary waited an hour, slumped in the corral, half conscious, with Cameron pouring water on his aunt's crushed face, until her mother arrived.

Doctors put a pin in Mary's jaw, did what they could, and told her the cost to rebuild her face with plastic mesh and bone grafts would run $49,000. She didn't have the money. She said no.

Today, her inner ear is shattered, leaving her with little

sense of balance. Her cheekbone is gone too. The Air Force responded in what Mary calls typical fashion. It paid $7,500 to replace the injured horse, which had to be destroyed. But the Air Force refused to pay for a specialist in Albuquerque to fix Mary's jaw. She wasn't surprised. "They admitted guilt when they paid for the mare. They say they don't, but they did."

Mary now takes medication for her constant pain, pills to help restore her sense of balance. She talks with a lisp, slurring her words because her disfigured jaw doesn't move well. She's lost 40 percent of the movement in her legs.

Living next door to the White Sands Missile Range in south-central New Mexico proved almost deadly for Mary. For her family, for the other ranchers, a place that once looked so empty has now become too crowded. Good fences haven't made good neighbors because what goes on on the other side sometimes defies the laws of nature, and certainly of man. Fences can't hold in F-umpteens, or radioactive fallout, or stray missiles that end up in the manure next to someone's barn before some red-faced captain brings a crew to claim them and says, "Sorry about that, neighbor."

It wasn't that way when Michael McDonald, an Irish Catholic immigrant, settled here in the 1850s. The silence and the serenity of this wide open valley—so much nothing in the middle of nowhere—is one of the reasons Michael chose this spot. He didn't want to be hemmed in. The McDonalds found Texas too confining. Since they were among the first settlers here, they spread out from the west side of the Sacramentos, over the Oscuro Mountains and the Malpais lava flow, all the way to the Rio Grande. They claimed hundreds of square miles that would become part of New Mexico when statehood came in 1912.

Four generations later, silence is still what Mary McDonald loves to hear. Like the McDonalds before her, Mary grew up to appreciate the serenity and beauty of the place, the peace she found working cattle or tending horses, the innocence of a newborn calf, the satisfaction of doing chores and earning a living off a hard land. Some might question the wisdom of trying to ranch in the desert. But those who know the land know there is just enough here to make a living. Indians worship their land as their god and bind themselves to it by burying umbilical cords in the earth. They do it over and over again, with each generation. Mary is no different. The land is her soul; she is a part of it, intertwined and bonded by birth. Like the grasses and mesquite, the birds and wildlife, like the generations of McDonalds before her, Mary had to learn to make the most of what nature offered in this valley more than a mile above sea level. Take what the land gives, expect no more. Scratch a living out of the hard caliche. Find the wealth in the emptiness, where the sun beats down on cinnamon-brown rock, heating the air above the century mark.

The terrain is deceptive here, barely one hundred miles north of El Paso, a polyglot city of half a million. The land seems vacant. Even mesquite bushes don't crowd their neighbors. Yucca plants, with a beach ball of sharp, skinny green palms at their base and a large stalk reaching toward the fireball that is the sun, stand out on a tableau of boot-high salt grass. Water is so scarce and rain so seldom that dust swirls with each passing vortex of wind. Some years it's so dry that even the fecund mesquite withers and dies. Sounds are scarce too. Coyotes send out an occasional howl; a distant clatter of cattle can sometimes be heard, or the unwelcome call of a coiled rattlesnake. Most of the time, though, the place is so silent that a distant breeze rustling the tough, pale, scraggly grass disturbs like a boisterous patron in a hushed library. Cars pass through this part of New Mexico with the frequency of storms—few and far between. The silence is a reminder of the harsh environment, the delicate balance that nature has found in a treeless sweep of land. To a rancher, the silence is peaceful. To a visitor, it is unsettling.

To the east stand the Sacramento Mountains, where Snaggletooth juts out. There's also a ski resort, horse racing, people, and prosperity. To the west, mountains rise up and form a Berlin Wall, locking in the secrets of the other side. Over there, it's more dust and salt grass and mesquite. And something else. The few who venture up this way don't have much chance to see what goes on on the other side of this red-rock fence. The desert, the mountain, the sun, and the heat form a nature-made vault few Houdinis could crack.

The secrets that nature protects are the deepest secrets of the country's defense plans. From the first nuclear weapon to the latest Stealth fighters, Patriot missiles, and space lasers, this desert floor has seen it all. For the ranchers, living beside this Buck Rogers battle zone has been hard. For them, World War II never ended. They've fought one of the longest-running land disputes in the country. They've endured radioactive fallout. The land has been scarred by the secrets from the other side. So have the people.

Especially Mary McDonald, a forty-two-year-old woman trying to run a ranch alone. Tall and strong, Mary lives on McDonald land south of the small town of Carrizozo, struggling to work one hundred sixty head of cattle with her elderly parents and her nephew. She has learned the hard way that living in this land of secrets can be dangerous. But the changes in her life have not altered the routine of the anonymous warriors.

Several times a day, Air Force fighters and bombers foray out of their vaults to invade her world, violating the silence and serenity. Over the years, Mary McDonald has seen them all. F-umpteens with crew-cut kids at the controls. Some days there are just one or two. Some days there are at least thirty sorties. Round the clock they buzz her. Some game. She knows most of their maneuvers and many of their secrets— the secrets from the other side of the mountain, the secrets of Stealth airplanes, low-altitude warfare, and high-tech gizmos. The jets practice flying low and hugging the terrain, sometimes coming so close she can see the pilot, see his hands turn as he banks a $30 million airplane back to where it's supposed to be.

One day a B-52, a mammoth of a bird, popped up over a hill and was on a course straight for Mary's red-and-white pickup. She slammed on the brakes and thought it might hit her. All she could remember thinking was: There ain't a son-ofabitch alive who would ever believe this.

Years before the Air Force acknowledged that a "Stealth fighter" existed, Mary McDonald had a picture of it, a Kodak snap of an F-117, framed against a full moon, that looked like the silhouette of Darth Vader's childhood plaything. It might have been invisible to radar, but there it was, before her eyes, swooping over her house, making a racket. She called the Air Force to report the intruder, jet noise in the background on the tape of the call. The Air Force, under orders at the time not to acknowledge such an airplane's existence let alone verify that it was outside the bounds of the range, suggested it must be a commercial plane—a 737 whooshing in her front door and out the back at midnight. To Mary, the comparison was insulting, if only because the angular Stealth looks nothing like the much larger one-hundred-passenger jet. But secrecy was the order of the times. Scientists who went to Nevada for underground nuclear tests, which are conducted near the home base of the Stealth fighter, had to swear to the Air Force that if they saw an airplane while out there, they'd convince themselves they didn't see anything. It didn't exist, publicly. But Mary McDonald had a snapshot of the secret black bird.

She was privy to such privileged information because of what sits in her backyard, just across the mountains. There, the White Sands Missile Range, one of the largest army bases in the world, stretches forty miles wide and one hundred miles long, about one third the length of New Mexico. Jets are just some of the things that fly through the air here. Nearly every missile in the U.S. arsenal has been tested here. And now Star Wars has come to this desert. A giant laser capable of bouncing a beam off mirrors and into outer space is being constructed at White Sands. Scientists hope the beam will zap incoming nuclear missiles like Darth Vader's flyswatter.

That's Mary McDonald's backyard.

The problems here go back half a century, to World War II, when White Sands was called the Alamogordo Bombing Range. What began as a small drop zone for training bombers grew as planes became larger and faster and squadrons of pilots had to be quickly trained. More land was needed, so ranchers were told to move out. Some were curtly informed at gunpoint that the Army was leasing their land until the end of the war. The Army would pay rent, then return the land. They had two weeks to vacate.

In 1944, yet another secret weapon had to be tested. The generals considered detonating this gadget in the California desert, off the coast of Texas, in the San Luis Valley of Colorado, and in the desert of New Mexico. New Mexico was selected as the best site because it was so remote, the weather was favorable, and it was close to the secret laboratory where the weapon was being created. The original Stealth project. The Manhattan Project.

America's Nuclear Highway was born when the world's

first atomic bomb was carefully driven in parts from Los Alamos, New Mexico, through Santa Fe, down what is now Interstate 25. The core of the bomb made the trip in the back seat of a sedan and was taken to one of the McDonalds' ranches. Final assembly of the "active" parts occurred in July of 1945 in the ranch house of George McDonald, Mary's uncle. The house is just two miles from Trinity Site, a name chosen by J. Robert Oppenheimer. Scientists worked out of the adobe ranch house and even used its water storage tank for a swimming pool. Soldiers were housed nine miles away in what had been the house of Dave McDonald, another uncle of Mary's. Two months before the Trinity test, the Air Force accidentally attacked the scientists' base camp, dropping three hundred-pound practice bombs, which set the stables on fire and disrupted a poker game. Three days after that, the carpentry shop was mistakenly bombed. The elder McDonalds were barred from the land and didn't know about the damage at the time. Had she been there to see it, Mary, born four years after Trinity, hardly would have been surprised.

The sixteen-by-eighteen-foot northeast room of George's house was converted by the Army into a clean assembly room, vacuumed thoroughly of dust, its windows covered with plastic and sealed with tape. On a table covered with brown wrapping paper, two hemispheres of plutonium, warm to the touch and deadly only if ingested, were laid out with the other parts. The core of the Trinity bomb, perhaps the size of an orange (its measurements are still classified), was assembled on July 15, placed in a heavy box, and driven to ground zero, land that used to be McDonald land.

The instructions for the gadget read in part:

PICK UP GENTLY WITH HOOK.
PLUG HOLE IS COVERED WITH A CLEAN CLOTH.

12

PLACE HYPODERMIC NEEDLE IN RIGHT PLACE. CHECK
THIS CAREFULLY.

. . . BE SURE SHOEHORN IS ON HAND.

SPHERE WILL BE LEFT OVERNIGHT, CAP UP, IN A SMALL
DISH PAN.

No one warned the neighboring ranchers of what would
come next.

What happened at ground zero on July 16, 1945, at 5:29:45
A.M. MWT (Mountain War Time), changed everything. It ultimately ended the war, triggered the nuclear arms race, and
solidified New Mexico's role in the atomic age. From the
fires of Trinity in the desert the Spaniards named Jornada del
Muerto—Journey of Death—came explosive growth along
the Nuclear Highway, a slice of the country from southern
New Mexico through the Colorado mountains to the Wyoming plains.

Interstate 25 is the warpath of the atomic age.

Along its one-thousand-mile length lies an extraordinary
concentration of military and high-tech hardware. Much of
what's here is here because of Oppenheimer's decision to
build the first atomic bomb in New Mexico. It all goes back
to ground zero, to the McDonald ranch.

Dave McDonald was cooking breakfast before dawn on the
other side of the Oscuro Mountains, fifty miles from ground
zero. Searchlights to guide observation planes had been
waltzing across the sky, so he knew something was going on
over at the bombing range. When the nineteen-kiloton blast
went up, he thought a trainload of dynamite had exploded on
nearby tracks. It lit up the sky, and his house, as if a giant
flashlight had been turned on in his kitchen.

Frank Martin, who lived about twenty miles southwest of
Trinity Site, had received a strange warning from an army
lieutenant about a week before the test. "He said it was going

to be something really big, and he hoped to hell it didn't kill us all," Martin said.

The blast blew Martin out of bed. "You didn't have to be very smart to know that was something new."

Officially, the Army gave no warnings. After a forest ranger north of Silver City, New Mexico, broke word of the explosion to the Associated Press in Albuquerque, one hundred miles from ground zero, the Army issued an official release saying an ammunition dump had blown up. Few if any who lived near Trinity Site and saw the blast believed the story. It was visible as far away as Amarillo, Texas, and Los Alamos. The flash was so vivid that Georgia Green, a blind University of New Mexico student riding in a car to Albuquerque, asked her brother-in-law, "What was that?"

Raemer Schreiber, a Manhattan Project scientist who helped put the plutonium core in the Trinity bomb and the Fat Man bomb dropped on Nagasaki, said he and his colleagues went numb at the sight. "You know in principle what should be expected, but you can't imagine what it will be like. There was nothing in the black desert, then all of a sudden the sky and the mountains jump out at you. Then the heat and the shock wave hit you. My feeling was simply, 'We didn't goof.' Then afterwards, you started thinking about all the other things"—things like the death and devastation such a bomb could bring.

A mushroom cloud rose more than 15,000 feet from the desert floor, and winds carried it toward the northeast at 10 knots. Monitors had been stationed around New Mexico because of the danger of fallout—potentially harmful radiation carried in the cloud to cities and towns. About 150 troops were ready to evacuate towns if the radiation readings got too hot. Excess exposure to radiation can spawn cancers and cause poisoning. Buses were sent to Carrizozo, 110 miles southeast of Albuquerque, to remove its 1,500 people if necessary. The radiation levels reached no higher than 90 percent of what was considered allowable by the Army, so there were no evacuations. But there was fallout. Several hundred cows turned white, the hair on their hides bleached by the debris. Radioactivity spread 100 miles, with the highest levels found on Chupadera Mesa, 20 miles from Trinity.

The scientists were making up the rules as they went along. Initially they tried to calculate whether the atomic bomb they were building would ignite the atmosphere and destroy the world. That worry was discounted. Radiation exposure levels were another unknown. They knew the dangers, but the levels allowed were far higher than those permissible by today's standards. Minuscule pieces of plutonium carried on dust were yet another worry, because they did know that plutonium in human lungs could cause tumors. The Trinity bomb was not a terribly efficient explosion—it didn't use up all of the plutonium in the core. So tiny bits of "unexploded" plutonium were spread over hundreds of miles, carried on particles of desert dust. Plutonium has a decay half-life of 24,000 years: after 240 centuries it will be half as potent as it is now.

One government study of the Trinity test found that 815 people had either participated in it or visited the site between July 16, 1945, and January 1, 1947, when visits were curbed. Twenty-three people received exposures of between 2 and 4 rems. (An acronym for "roentgen equivalent man," rem is the unit in which radiation doses are measured. One rem amounts to about fifty chest X-rays.) Another twenty-two people received between 4 and 15 rems. At the time, 5 rems every two months was the allowable limit. Today, the Nuclear Regulatory Commission limits nuclear workers' exposure to 5 rems of radiation a year. By current standards, in other words, more than twenty people received a full year's dose at Trinity.

Soon after the blast, chain barricades with warning signs were placed around Trinity Site, which was visible from a passing road, but scientists took their wives and children on tours. The green-glass substance created when the fire melted the desert sand at more than 2,678 degrees Fahrenheit became a coveted souvenir—even though it was radioactive. It was dubbed Trinitite, and it was porous and grainy, almost like lava, when broken up into chunks. But right after the bomb, the desert had a smooth glass carpet of green Trinitite. Unaware of the danger of radiation, Frank Martin and his family trespassed across the green-glass desert floor, which extended for hundreds of feet. Rock dealers sold pieces of Trinitite, and a scientific supply house advertised the strange stuff nationally. El Rio Motel in nearby Socorro reportedly sold it as souvenirs. A Santa Fe bank gave Trinitite away to new customers. Even after officials decided wearing jewelry made of Trinitite was dangerous, and the remaining glass was scooped up and buried, small pieces continued to be found at ground zero; they can be found there today.

A better picture of the preparations and precautions that were taken in New Mexico, along with a more accurate account of the radiation levels, is now available. Documents locked away for decades as secret or classified were recently unsealed by the Department of Energy, which has set up a warehouse in Las Vegas for records on nuclear testing.

A June 20, 1945, memo to Oppenheimer and other senior staff from three officials revealed that even before Trinity, scientists were looking for ways to prevent dust-borne plutonium particles from spreading because of the danger of ingesting plutonium. Pouring concrete, gravel, asphalt, or even metal aircraft runway matting over the desert floor was considered, along with oiling or bulldozing ground zero. But those ideas were rejected as ineffective and likely to hamper test preparations. After all, the scientists were under intense pressure from the Army to test the bomb before President Truman's crucial meeting with Winston Churchill and Joseph Stalin at Potsdam, where the Allies approved plans for carving up Germany and Eastern Europe and the British and Americans drew up an ultimatum to Japan. Historians have noted that once Truman learned the bomb worked, he became much more forceful in the Potsdam negotiations and toughened his resolve. The Potsdam Declaration insisted on Japan's unconditional surrender. "The alternative for Japan," the declaration stated, "is prompt and utter destruction."

(The story is told that after Truman received word that the bomb worked, he and Churchill debated for several days whether to trust Stalin with the information. Finally, Truman told the Russian premier—who already knew. Truman, unaware that Stalin had spies in New Mexico, noted at the time that the Russian "showed no special interest. All he said was that he was glad to hear it and hoped we would make 'good use of it against the Japanese.' ")

Another memo, minutes of a conference with Oppenheimer and other top officials regarding countryside contamination, laid out criteria for weather conditions—wind not too strong, no rain, etc. One condition proved lucky for the McDonalds and their neighbors. "Wind not blowing over Carrizozo," it said. And another previously classified memo, written before Trinity by test director Kenneth Bainbridge, outlined options for covering up the radioactivity at ground zero after the explosion. Again, scientists considered sealing it with cement. Or burying it. Or even, incredible as it may seem, trucking it to the Rio Grande and dumping it in the river. In the end, the Army simply put up a fence.

But no fence could rein in the danger to civilians. One month after the explosion, low-level radiation was still found in the town of Bingham, twelve miles to the northeast. Officially,

17

the fallout pattern extended one hundred miles. But it went much farther—a Kodak plant in Illinois discovered that something had mysteriously fogged film.

For nearly half a century, scientists have fussed over radiation levels in and around Trinity Site, always insisting everything was safe but never quite ruling out trouble. Government studies over the decades, some of them classified until the 1980s, concluded that there was no apparent danger. A 1948 report found most of the radioactivity in the top two inches of soil. Cows purchased from New Mexico ranchers in 1948 still showed some gray bleached hair. They were trucked to the Schwartzman Packing Company in Albuquerque and approved for public consumption. The study also found radioactivity counts "not exceeding twice the background in the majority of cases"—background referring to the naturally occurring radiation from the sun. The study concluded:

> Easily measurable amounts of radioactive fallout remaining from the first atom bomb detonation are still found in an area some 10 miles wide and extending roughly northeast for more than 100 miles across the deserts of south-central New Mexico. The amounts of radioactive fission products to be found in any one place throughout this area are relatively small except at or near the detonation point. Here, enough radioactivity is still present to create a strong presumption of hazard to living things that remain continuously in the area.

There appeared to be no danger to Trinity Site visitors. But there was no guarantee.

"This finding"—that there was no significant hazard—"is gratifying indeed, but it would be rash to conclude in the absence of specific information, that now, no hazards associated with products of the bomb detonation exist in this area, the harmful effects of which may not appear for a number of years," the study said. Among other factors, low rain meant radiation wouldn't reach plant roots for a number of years, and scientists did not know how much plutonium was actually distributed through the area.

Years later, research continued to find radiation and plutonium particles in the Jornada del Muerto, but in low enough levels to be considered safe. In 1972, as once-a-year public tours of Trinity were established, a Los Alamos report noted that "encountering a rattlesnake during the tour presents a much greater threat than the radiation." A 1978 inquiry noted a lack of specific information on the plutonium fallout but said the area was "one of the significant plutonium contaminated areas in the United States, both in terms of quantity of plutonium deposited and area extended."

The 1978 research found that plutonium concentrations off the missile range amounted to only half the Environmental Protection Agency limit at the time. And a 1983 field investigation noted: "Even after 38 years, there are large areas (near ground zero) where vegetation is not growing."

Many of the ranchers who lived in the area in the time of Trinity have died from cancer, but no scientific studies were initiated. The ranchers wonder why, when the land around the Nevada Test Site has been extensively tested after hundreds of nuclear explosions, and compensation has been approved for families downwind, many of them in Utah, after lengthy litigation and congressional battles. Ted Coker, whose ranch near Bingham received one of the highest levels of fallout from Trinity, stood under the radioactive cloud. He died of cancer years later. But for Coker, and the others who died, there was never proof that Trinity was the cause or whether the cancer rates in New Mexico were out of proportion with what would be expected.

If there were many secrets from the other side of the mountain, Trinity was the biggest, the deadliest. Living with the Bomb became the heart of living along the Nuclear Highway.

Like the two hundred or so other ranchers around Alamogordo Bombing Range, Dave McDonald and Frank Martin believed that the end of the war meant a return to their land, a return to their livelihood. That's what the government promised; that's what they believed; that's what they planned for.

But the Army said it needed the land for another twenty years in the interest of national security and offered leases to keep it. The ranchers had no choice. They signed. And waited some more. A few spent the years working other acres they had, like the McDonalds. Some just hung around, taking low-paying jobs in Socorro and Alamogordo as roofers and night watchmen and struggling financially, despite the supplement of the government lease payments, until the day they could get back home.

In 1970, when the leases expired, the government told the ranchers that rather than giving the borrowed land back, it was condemning it. Keeping it. The buildings and the test ranges were permanent. As the weapons to be tested got faster, flew farther, and carried a bigger bang in an even smaller package, more acres were needed, not fewer. Who could be surprised? Beyond the real need for a giant test range, what army would ever retreat and give up ground it had already taken?

The ranchers wanted to be paid for their land, but condemnation is not the same as purchase. Under U.S. law, the Army can basically condemn what it wants in the name of national security and ultimately pay what it wants. And the Army decided that it had already paid enough—a total of $27 million over more than twenty years. Kind of like renting a house for two decades and then telling the owner he doesn't own it anymore. That arbitrary decision meant all the Trinity Site ranchers had no money to buy another spread somewhere else. They had lived off the payments, expecting the Army to fulfill the promise to return the land. They never got a lump sum. It ended up as slow torture.

Good fences don't always make good neighbors.

Overnight, families saw their wealth vanish. The ranchers sued, but courts held that the Army can indeed do what it needs to do in the name of national security. The taking of the land was legal, although maybe not right, not fair, not moral. It was one of those situations where the law couldn't distinguish between "legal" and "right."

Howard Wood's mother worked as a waitress to support the family, which lost 50,000 acres valued at half a million dollars or more. At age eighty-four, she ended up living in a public housing project.

Dave McDonald lives in the same low-income project, in Tularosa, New Mexico. At the county courthouse, his name is still on the deed to the acres the Army leased from him and then condemned. At age eighty-nine, he still pays taxes on 29,000 acres near ground zero. As far as he's concerned, they're still his because the Army never bought the land. The Socorro County records agree.

The Martins didn't have enough savings to pack up and move, so they got by on Frank's wife's salary as a Socorro schoolteacher. In the late 1950s, Frank opened an auto parts store with his brother-in-law. At age seventy-five, he still works there.

"We were just waiting around because they said they'd give it back," said Frank's son, James, now a state senator in New Mexico. "Dad and I always made plans over what to do when we got back on the ranch. . . . They lost a way of life. My dad was not happy selling parts. He'd been running

21

a ranch since he was twelve, because his dad had drowned then."

James Martin works for an aerospace electronics firm near White Sands that does research and development on weapons systems. "Isn't that ironic?" he said. "If you can't beat 'em, join 'em. You got to make a living. That's dang near the only thing we've got out here. . . . The one wish I have is that I could have had a ranching life. It's a helluva good life."

His is a story told all along the highway. If you can't beat 'em, join 'em.

But not G. B. Oliver. He's still fighting.

When his father set out to buy land for a family ranch in the 1940s, friends told him not to buy across the border because the Mexican government could take it away anytime. Instead, he bought 1,280 acres in New Mexico—and the American government took half of it away soon afterward.

Oliver blames the battle for his father's death. G. B. senior died of a stroke in 1972, one day after a heated meeting with a U.S. Army Corps of Engineers official.

"It's hard to believe what happened," Oliver said. "My dad said about the military that it was like watching a snake swallow a rabbit. They wrapped around us until they got us in a position where we couldn't do anything. Then they slobbered all over us and then they finished us off. . . . It killed Dad. He could not believe his government would do him like this."

G. B. junior and the other ranchers carried on a fight through courts and Congress, trying to get a fair price for their two million lost acres. They say their losses, in today's dollars, run between $25 million and $50 million. The battle has gone on so long it has been picked up by the second and even third generations of those who were escorted out by soldiers nearly fifty years ago.

"They can prove it was legal, but it was morally wrong,"
G. B. Oliver said. "In many cases, the law can't cover right
and wrong."

There have been hearings in Washington, studies galore,
and even congressional bills to compensate the ranchers. New
Mexico Republican senator Pete Domenici has called the
ranchers' plight the "most inequitable situation" he's seen in
two decades in the U.S. Senate. But sympathy hasn't yielded
a resolution. At a public hearing once, Domenici promised
compensation. "I hope you know we are very serious about
it and we are going to do something about it. . . . We want
to pass something next year and do it in a way that wraps
this up seven or eight or nine months thereafter so we can
go back to our normal living and not wonder when the government is going to do it."

That was November 15, 1983. Nothing has worked for the
ranchers, however, not even a sit-in.

In 1982, Mary McDonald and her uncle Dave, along with
a reporter and a photographer from the *Albuquerque Journal*
and a dog, sneaked through a gate left open at the White
Sands Missile Range and made their way in the dark back to
Dave's old ranch house. Mary and Dave had scouted a route
a few days earlier and had left a Coke carton to mark a crucial turn. Then, at 3:00 A.M., they led their small caravan
onto one of the most elaborately monitored pieces of property on earth.

They vowed to stay. Shotgun-toting Mary and eighty-one-
year-old Dave went to work putting up fencing and nailing
signs to posts:

> Road Closed to U.S. Army.
> Deeded Land—No Trespassing.

Dave did what any home owner might do after being away
for two decades. He puttered around the house. First he

23

replaced the front door and put Plexiglass over the windows. Then he cleaned out the fireplace and set up the andirons and wood they had brought. They'd hauled in one hundred gallons of water and enough food for two months.

"It's ours, by God," Dave said.

Armed guards discovered the McDonalds after sunrise. One suggested to Dave they'd drive him home and forget the whole thing.

"I am home," Dave said.

More White Sands guards arrived, along with federal marshals and even some army troops. The next day, an Albuquerque radio station, broadcasting live from the missile range, got a tip that soldiers and a helicopter were going to storm the ranch house. Within an hour, switchboards for the Army, the U.S. Attorney's office, and local politicians lit up with calls of support for the McDonalds. The Army backed down.

Mary and Dave's protest lasted four and a half days, until finally they agreed to leave after politicians promised compensation would be fairly negotiated. Mary knew it was time to give it up anyway. Dave was tired, unable to keep watch. And she was losing steam rapidly, running out of the amphetamines—"pocket rockets," she called them—that were propping her up.

But as always, the promises led nowhere.

In 1987, the ranchers lost again. A federal judge ruled that the law indeed allowed the Army to pay whatever it thought was fair for the disputed land. Two years later, a bill authored by New Mexico representative Joe Skeen offered money from Congress to the ranchers, who were assured that they'd be paid by the end of the year. But the bill died in committee.

At last count, there were fewer than a dozen of the original two hundred ranchers still alive and no immediate hope of compensation on the horizon. Descendants carry on the fight for themselves, their children, and the principle. They've seen Japanese-American internees compensated by Congress, and they hope for a similar justice. They also hope it comes before all of the original ranchers are dead.

And Mary hopes that someday the Army will pay to fix her jaw.

Bitter and brokenhearted, the McDonalds still dream of going back. Mary is particularly distrusting and angry. She fights often with colonels and generals, with politicians, even with fellow ranchers over the best course of action. She cusses and one time ended up in a fistfight while arguing the ranchers' case at a hearing. She tape-records every conversation she has with a government official.

She chain-smokes Salems and guzzles Riopan Plus when her ulcer flares, as if the antacid were water from a desert oasis, as if it could put out the fire in her heart as well as in her belly. The pain from her jaw, and her lost battles, have worn her down. She tried to move away once, to Phoenix, but lasted only three months before she went home to "her mountains" and the silence and peace of her family's land. Out of anger, she talks about sneaking back out to the off-limits ranch house—a "Stealth protester"—and making another stand.

"If we go home, we'll keep it. I don't care if they kill us."

2

BOMB TOWN, U.S.A.

*It is difficult to say what is impossible, for the dream of yester-
day is the hope of today and the reality of tomorrow.*
    AMERICAN ROCKET PIONEER ROBERT H. GODDARD

*Thank God that when those Scuds came in, the people of Saudi
Arabia and Israel, and the brave forces of our coalition, had
more to protect their lives than some abstract theory of deterrence. Thank God for the Patriot missile.*
    PRESIDENT GEORGE BUSH, *February 15, 1991*

Interstate 25 shoots off of Interstate 10 on the south side
of Las Cruces, forming a drunken Y on maps of southern
New Mexico, then rolls up and down hills as it heads north
out of town. Las Cruces is caught in a no-man's-land where
New Mexico fades out and Texas gets off to a slow start.
Even the radio can be schizophrenic. If you set the dial to
92.3 FM, you hear an Albuquerque country station at the top
of the highway hills, which fades to an El Paso rock station
down in the pits. It's the Eagles meeting the Judds at Ele-
phant Butte. Crosby, Stills, Nash and . . . Cash. Reba
McEntire singing "Satisfaction."

The airwaves here are filled with ads that might appear
familiar to a lot of people just passing through. Turn on the
TV set, and a round-faced, middle-aged CEO looks straight
at the camera for an honest pitch: I run the company, and I

look trustworthy, and this is what we offer. This CEO was a space hero, known worldwide. One Christmas he read from the Book of Genesis to a distant, captive world. "In the beginning . . ." He definitely had flair, and he knew how to get a message across.

Later, this CEO ran an airline. "We earn our wings every day," he used to say. He took to TV before Iacocca, before the squeaky guy who liked his shaver so much he bought the company. The astronaut-turned-CEO sold Eastern Airlines, the way any pitchman would sell soap. For a while, at least, it worked.

Now Frank Borman lives in Las Cruces, New Mexico, on the Nuclear Highway. And why not? To some this place is a future boomtown, one that will take off with Star Wars and space business. Frank Borman, who says he came here to join his son's business after leaving Eastern years before its bankruptcy and liquidation, sells cars in Las Cruces. "Frank Borman on Dependability," the ads begin. It's not "We earn our wings . . ." but kind of "we kick the tires every day." You'll find dependability at a Borman dealership, he promises. Who would doubt him? This guy read from the Bible while completing the first orbit of the moon in 1968. "In the beginning, God created heaven and earth . . ." Frank Borman, astronaut. A guy with the Right Stuff.

Now he sells Hyundais (and Fords) in Las Cruces, New Mexico. You never know what—or who—you will find along the Nuclear Highway.

The road to the White Sands Missile Range hooks into I-25 north of Las Cruces and turns east through a mountain pass. Like billboards touting the next tourist trap, signs that this place is different begin to pop up. On one hill there's a giant radar station. Others have observatories. A tiny sign announces a NASA facility. There's another for the turnoff to Lincoln Laboratories, the secretive high-tech company tied to the Massachusetts Institute of Technology (MIT). Laser beams, next right. Space experiments, hang a left.

And there's the Star Wars Deli, a hole-in-the-wall country kitchen with plastic tablecloths, cheap chairs, tacky Indian souvenir headdresses, sand clocks and salt-and-pepper shakers, and pictures of local interest, such as the once-top-secret Stealth fighter and the still-very-secret YF-22, the next generation of fighter jet. For all its Naugahyde charm, the Star Wars Deli seems schizophrenic: a tourist-trap greasy spoon with a yuppie menu featuring vegetarian pizza and turkey-and-avocado sandwiches, a favorite of scientists and engineers who work down the road.

Inside the gates, the White Sands Missile Range looks superficially like any other dusty Army outpost in the desert: a couple of nondescript brick buildings, a truck yard, a cafeteria, and a headquarters with a flagpole. Considering it is the biggest test track in the free world, or so the military brass used to boast when there was a clear distinction between the free world and the Communist world, a visitor is stunned at how few buildings there are at White Sands. Out here there are nearly as many miles as people. White Sands stretches over 3,200 square miles; it provides jobs to 9,500 people.

Just inside the gate is what is affectionately known as Missile Park, where every generation of rockets and missiles tested here and deployed finds a place of honor beside the road. From a small sounding rocket called Tiny Tim to today's nuclear and conventional supersonic monsters, the folks at White Sands plant their unarmed missiles in the sand the way a proud gardener plants daffodils.

No missile planted in the garden is as famous now as the Patriot surface-to-air missile, the star of the Persian Gulf War, which intercepted some 90 percent of Iraq's clumsy, yet terrifying, Scud missiles. The Patriot earned its wings here, proved that it might work. The cheers for its Scud-busting performance, which allowed Israel to remain out of the war and helped hold together the Arab-American coalition against Iraq, reverberated through the White House and all the way back to the southern New Mexico desert.

Behind the missile park and some barbed-wire fences is the Range Control building, a two-story shoe box encased in concrete and steel to prevent enemy ears from eavesdropping on the computers inside. At White Sands, Range Control is where the action is. Nothing happens on all those square miles without Range Control giving the OK. This is where you take the pulse of the place. This is the nerve center, the brains, the eyes, the ears.

This is also the biggest video arcade in the world.

In the basement of the Range Control building, three men sit at a computer console decked out like the cockpit of an airplane. Each has a red joystick. One man radios to the control tower at Holloman Air Force Base, forty miles away, for clearance to take off. When clearance comes, throttles advance, the stick gets pulled back, and the planes take off. A button is pushed, and the wheels retract. From a seat in the basement of Range Control, each is flying an old pre-Vietnam F-100 fighter jet on a predetermined circular racetrack pattern. To the men in the building, it's all a video game. They are sitting in cushioned chairs, armed with joysticks, staring at video screens. But out on the range, real airplanes are flying, under the arcade's remote control. Each man has a red-and-green horizon scope in front of him, just like in a cockpit. Each has an altitude gauge and an airspeed indicator. And each is a target. (Old military jets now end up here, rather than the scrap heap, to be blown to bits by experimental weapons.)

One floor above in the Range Control building, another team

of experts tracks the airplanes on radar screens that use bright colors to trace the routes. Rather than just blips on the screens, the planes create overlapping lines of red, green, and purple as they race over White Sands. When the first target is in a safe spot, a range controller gives the OK to fire the first missile.

From there, the computers really take over. The Patriot missile system—the most sophisticated the United States has deployed—waits one second, then another, and then fires its first two-thousand-pound volley toward the airplane at supersonic speed.

Now there are three airplanes in the air, and one armed Patriot missile. The only human playing the game is the flight safety officer, who holds a small green box with two red buttons. Pushing a red button would destroy the million-dollar missile before it got to its target. Should the supersonic missile stray off course, toward a nearby ranch or one of the two commercial aircraft corridors that pass near White Sands, the flight safety officer would destroy it. It's a job that gets more nerve-racking all the time. As missiles fly faster and faster, the time it takes them to reach the target, or the ranches, can be measured in fractions of seconds. The data coming from the missile—the telemetry—get more complex with each generation. Computers process the numbers radioed back at nanosecond speeds, giving the flight safety officer as good a picture of the missile's performance as is computerly possible. Millions of bytes of data. Millifractions to process it. Seconds to decide whether to push the red button. Arrgh! The game gets more dangerous as the weapons get bigger, stronger, faster. The missile range, of course, hasn't become much bigger recently. Big as it is, the top brass at White Sands say the weapons are outgrowing this test track. For now, White Sands relies on the experimental weapons staying on course, its computers, and the quick finger of the flight safety officer with his green box.

With the missile in flight, eyes turn to video monitors in Range Control that are tracking the drone F-100. Without noise, or warning, the remote-controlled airplane and the computer-controlled missile converge on the monitor, and the missile scores a fiery direct hit. Debris falls across the desert. The arcade masters cheer. The red line on the radar trails off parabolically toward the bottom of the screen. *Adiós*. The man with the joystick down below leans back to relax and watch what happens to his comrades.

Range Control gives the second missile the OK to launch, and the Patriot system takes over again. One second. Two. Three. Fire. *Boom*. The target plane is destroyed. The boys at the controls cheer again. Finally, the third missile destroys the third plane.

Score: Missiles 3, Drones 0. Put in another million dollars, and play the game again.

This exercise took place at White Sands when the Patriot was an antiaircraft system. Before the Persian Gulf War, the Patriot was upgraded from an antiaircraft weapon to an antimissile weapon simply by perfecting computer codes in its system—an outgrowth of Star Wars development. A program troubled by cost overruns and concerns about whether the darn things would actually work, it got a second wind in the late 1980s with the military spending boom and the new technologies the boom produced. The Patriot uses the next generation of radar—phased array radar, which is really an array of many, many radars working together to pinpoint positions—to zero in on its supersonic target. Without the advanced radar and computers, the system couldn't react fast enough to missiles. Critics likened the task to shooting a bullet with a bullet. But in 1986, the improved version of the

Patriot intercepted a U.S.-made Lance missile at 26,000 feet. Still, there were nagging concerns over whether the Patriot could really knock down incoming warheads. That had never been done before in battle. And the Patriot cost so much it was tested against a missile only once.

But all the doubts disappeared in a contrail and a blast when Saddam Hussein launched a Soviet-made Scud toward United States forces in Saudi Arabia and the Patriot knocked it down. The historic event, on January 17, 1991, was by chance captured by television crews, who didn't know at first what they were filming. The intercept startled the world and made the Patriot an international celebrity. It was a triumph for U.S. technology that was hailed as a vindication for years of defense spending. And it was a victory cheered roundly back at White Sands, where all Patriot testing and training takes place. The darn thing really did work. Post-war analysis, however, showed all was not perfect with the Patriot. Fifty-one of fifty-three Scuds fired over Israel and Saudi Arabia were indeed engaged by the Patriot, but missile debris and Scud parts still caused injuries and damage to populated areas. One Patriot missed its Scud, and another time a computer glitch prevented the Patriot from firing at a Scud headed for an Army barracks near Dhahran, Saudi Arabia. That Scud killed twenty-eight Americans.

White Sands averages more than twenty "missions" a day and more than two "hot firings" each day. In a hot firing, a missile, or other weapon, is actually launched. Many of the missions here involve live ammunition, like shooting at targets towed behind airplanes. F-15s play electronic warfare games, one against the other. An entire European battlefield has been constructed in the north end of the range, complete with railroad bridges and enemy runways to be bombed. During some tests, military police block state highways 70, 54, and 380 in the area. Ranchers north and west of the missile range are sometimes evacuated for larger tests.

The drone system can handle airplanes and tanks, up to a dozen at a time. It can move a column of M-47 tanks across the desert of White Sands better than Patton, or Atari. It can fly airplanes two hundred feet apart and synchronize them to within one second. Try that on your Microsoft Flight Simulator. Soon supersonic drone aircraft will fly over White Sands. And helicopters. And pretty soon the whole battle will be played out by remote control. Real hardware, real bullets. Real airplanes, tanks, and missiles in real battles, not just simulations. But no humans—they're safely tucked away in a basement. Already, this is the largest system of its kind in the world.

People at White Sands joke about it, chuckle at the concept, and admit that what goes on here would drive any Nintendo junkie crazy with envy. Range Control is the ultimate Ms. Pac-Man, or Space Invaders. Super Mario Bros. take on the Communist world in the ultimate showdown. Death rays at twelve paces.

"Guys just love this," one White Sands expert admitted. "It's nice to have a job where you can play video games."

It wasn't always that much fun, however. Established toward the end of World War II as the White Sands Proving Grounds in order to test rocketry the Army had been working on since 1943, the missile range has seen its share of duds and misfires over the years. Some rockets sailed off to attack enemy lands such as Colorado and Mexico. (One rocket narrowly missed a Mexican mining company's gunpowder and ammunition dump south of Juárez.) Some ended up in ranchers' corrals. Others never got much past the launch pad. Some weapons, like the ill-fated Sergeant York antiaircraft gun, got the ax in part because of testing done at White Sands. Sergeant York kept missing, and was canceled.

33

The range takes its name from White Sands National Monument, a one-hundred-square-mile deposit of fine white gypsum sand. The sands of this quirk of geology form dunes that continually shift with the wind, sometimes exposing artifacts from Spanish or Indian peoples. They can be seen from space, and when they are compacted, they can form a super-hard surface. Space shuttle Columbia landed on a gypsum runway at White Sands Missile Range in 1982.

Long before space shuttles, the Army was a vital part of the history of the Southwest. Through this area passed the original Spanish Camino Real—the Royal Road—connecting Mexico City, the capital of the new Spain, with Santa Fe, the capital of the new Mexico. The Camino Real, which followed the Rio Grande, laid out the path for I-25 and the Nuclear Highway. Cavalry General Stephen Watts Kearny, whose federal troops annexed New Mexico bloodlessly in 1846, continued on to California after the annexation and laid the first wagon road to the West Coast down through the Jornada del Muerto and what became the missile range, and then west through Arizona.

In 1862, Colonel Christopher "Kit" Carson was ordered to Fort Stanton, located on the Chisholm Trail southeast of Carrizozo, to hunt Mescalero Indians in the mountains and valleys surrounding the future missile range. Geronimo, the Mescalero Apache chief, had much of his home territory here. Billy the Kid was captured and jailed in the area, only to escape. Sheriff Pat Garrett, who lived on what is now missile range land, tracked him down and shot and killed him. A Wild West legend for having killed the Kid, Garrett himself died violently in a gunfight near here in 1908.

Then there's the legend of Victorio Peak. A small bump on the map of the missile range, Victorio Peak is a rocky mound, littered today with creosote bushes, rattlesnakes, and bullet-pocked military targets. On top, rusted steel bars bolted to weathered timbers guard a four-foot-square opening. Some four hundred feet below lie either one hundred tons of gold bars worth more than $1 billion or one of the wildest hoaxes of the Wild West. It's a puzzle whose solution has eluded treasure hunters and presidential aides, a treasure so great people have died for it, a legend so compelling even the U.S. government has dug for it.

All because of a traveling quack foot doctor named Milton Earl "Doc" Noss.

After a 1937 hunting outing on the peak, Noss reported finding gold bars "stacked like cordwood," along with twenty-seven skeletons, Wells Fargo chests, and Indian artifacts. He claims he carried some out through a narrow crevasse that led to a cavern inside Victorio Peak. When he, his stepson, and a few others tried to enlarge the passageway with dynamite, the whole thing caved in, burying the treasure and the truth.

Noss, whom G. B. Oliver and other area ranchers knew only as a shyster and a storyteller, was killed in a 1949 gun battle with a partner over Noss's failure to turn over a share of the alleged bars. The partner, Charles Ryan, had invested $28,000 in Noss's "treasure" and was later acquitted on self-defense grounds. Noss died with $2.16 in his pocket. Since then, his family has raised more than $500,000 from eager investors in an effort to find the gold.

If there ever was gold in Victorio Peak—and historians discount the possibility—or if there still is, where it came from is itself a mystery. Although New Mexico's history begins with the Spanish explorer Coronado's search for gold, no mine capable of producing one hundred tons was ever found in the southern part of the state. Some said Noss might have discovered a secret stash of the Mexican emperor Maximilian, or Padre Felipe La Rue, a missionary said to have discovered a rich gold deposit and hidden it from Spanish soldiers and church authorities. Some said the Apache chieftain Victorio, for whom the peak was named, hid his spoils in his headquarters. And some said that even though Noss might have fabricated the whole thing, there could still be a stash of gold in Victorio Peak—a secret U.S. booty from World War II, hidden at the missile range under cover of the Noss tale, sometimes referred to as "Patton's Gold."

In 1958, Air Force Captain Leonard V. Fiege claimed he stumbled on gold while deer hunting on Victorio Peak (military personnel are still permitted some hunting on the range). Fiege passed a lie detector test and his claim set off a "top secret" search of the peak by army and U.S. Treasury agents in 1961. The Army at first denied the search, but acknowledged it a year later. Military police patrolled for trespassers and treasure hunters, and a steel door was placed over the new shaft that had enlarged the old crevasse.

Descendants and associates of Noss and Fiege, who claimed the treasure was theirs by inheritance or investment, cried foul. Rebuffed in their efforts to get onto the missile range and fearful that the Army had already made off with what was there, they tried to contact higher authorities.

It wasn't until the 1973 Watergate hearings that the legend heated up again. Former presidential aide John Dean recounted Attorney General John Mitchell's and White House staffer John Ehrlichman's interest in the treasure tale. It had been brought to their attention by famed attorney F. Lee Bailey, who represented some relatives of Noss and even produced a gold sample for the governor of New Mexico.

In 1977, the Army agreed to recognize six claimant groups and allow a two-week search, led by Florida treasure hunter Norman Scott. Ground radar readings indicated there was a cavern four hundred feet down, right about where Noss had said it was, but the dirt and debris of the cave-in was too much for the expedition. They couldn't reach the cavern. An attachment to a 1989 defense spending bill, slipped in by Representative Joe Skeen, authorized another search, but Noss descendants have to pay the Army's costs.

White Sands spokesman Jim Eckles said the Army insists it never took any gold and firmly believes there is no treasure. The Army did bulldoze passages and place steel doors over mines, he said, closing all entrances to discourage treasure seekers from trying to slip onto the often dangerous missile range. Security has been kept tight in the area, the southwestern part of the missile range, because vital weapons are tested there, he said. A recent hike to the top of Victorio Peak with Eckles revealed all kinds of debris from F-15 strafing runs and other scars of mock combat.

Whether Noss's descendants and other claimants ever get into that Victorio Peak cavern, and whether they find any gold, or evidence gold was once there, depends now on their ability to raise cash. They may have an advantage over other treasure stories in the Southwest (of which there are many), because most talk about some general area where the Lost Dutchman's Mine or some other bounty might be. This is the only one where people say the treasure is right there, in that spot, down that hole.

In this area of colorful history, the Army officially opened the proving grounds in July of 1945. Just three months later, three hundred railroad cars of captured World War II German V-2 parts (and captured gold bars?) arrived at White Sands. With the help of 125 German scientists who had surrendered to the Americans and were brought to New Mexico in 1945, including Dr. Wernher von Braun, soldiers and scientists assembled V-2 rockets for testing. The V-2 had terrorized England toward the end of the war, and Hitler, not unlike Saddam Hussein in this instance, had bet that V-2 missile strikes could turn the tide his way. In fact, historians have observed that Hitler shrugged off German development of an atomic bomb in favor of concentrating on the V-2.

The first V-2 at White Sands was fired on April 16, 1946, and this test was far from any armchair video game. The blockhouse was crowded, and because there wasn't enough room at the window, people rushed out the blast door for a look as the rocket lifted off. But those who got outside quickly wanted back in—the V-2 had turned around just three miles up and was headed back at them. People outside collided with those still trying to get a look, and the test ended in mass confusion. The V-2 crashed to the east of the block-house, far enough away that no one was hurt.

With the captured V-2s, American scientists learned how to use explosives to separate stages on rockets. By 1951, a total of sixty-seven V-2 fuselages—46 feet long and 5½ feet in diameter—had flown at White Sands. V-2s set altitude and velocity records. One of the V-2s was the first man-made object to penetrate outer space. The captured V-2s gave the United States a big jump in rocket construction and testing. And the V-2s helped lead to the development of the United States' large missiles to ferry warheads, men, and satellites into space: Redstone, Nike, Atlas, Titan, and Minuteman. A scientist familiar with the V-2 design and technology would note that modern weapons are based on the same principles.

Today, White Sands is more than just a giant launching pad or shooting arcade. Scattered within its boundaries are some of the most secret and sophisticated experiments in the military. They end up here because it is remote and secure— the same factors that brought Oppenheimer and the Trinity test here more than four decades ago. There is so much money and so many acronyms, so many agencies and so many weapons, that probably no one person knows everything that goes on there.

In one part of the range the Army has a Vulnerability Assessment Laboratory. It doesn't sound real impressive, but "they do a lot of secret stuff there that they don't show too much," one White Sands insider said. What they work on are "counter-countermeasures." The other side may know our weapons, and we may know their countermeasures, but we don't want anyone to know our counter-countermeasures.

Elsewhere, tests are run on the next generation of non-line-of-sight weapons—firing a missile that could duck over the other side of a hill, find the enemy, and attack on its own. Then there are smart munitions and bomblets—cluster bombs that can be released over a column of tanks, then find the targets on their own and attack from the top, where current tanks are more vulnerable because their heavy armor is on the sides. Another facility, also very hush-hush, tests the radar cross-sections of new aircraft and missiles—how invisible the Stealth weapons really are.

Add to all that dozens of radars, observation points, and all kinds of instrumentation at White Sands, and you have one of the most sophisticated military test facilities in the world, as well as one of the most highly surveyed pieces of real estate anywhere. It's no surprise that as soon as the U.S. military buildup in the Persian Gulf began, the Pentagon ran to White Sands to further test its weapons, its strategies, its counter-counters, Stealths, missiles, and whatevers in the desert.

Using conventional explosives, the Defense Nuclear Agency can simulate the blast effects of an eight-kiloton nuclear explosion, more than 60 percent of the yield of the Hiroshima blast. In fact, the Army can just about produce the power of a small nuclear explosion in the battlefield now with conventional arms, such as a bomb that sprays a fine mist of fuel for miles, then erupts in a conflagration that literally sucks molecules out of soldiers. The Army's Nuclear Effects Directorate has a solar furnace forty-five feet high and one hundred feet long in the southwest corner of White Sands that can create thermal radiation bursts similar to a nuclear explosion. With that, the military can see how electronic circuits, transistors, and other missile components will weather the nuclear environment at about 5,000 degrees Fahrenheit. On the east side of White Sands, SDI, the Strategic Defense Initiative, has begun constructing the Ground-Based Free Electron Laser, another Star Wars device to zap lasers into outer space. But the project ground to a standstill with cuts in the 1991 budget. The future of the billion-dollar GBFEL is in limbo.

Another SDI-related program already has been tested at White Sands. The High Endoatmospheric Defense Interceptor—HEDI for short, and the faster, smarter, stronger Patriot—is a missile that can seek out and destroy incoming intercontinental nuclear warheads as they reenter the atmosphere. It's a ground-based antiballistic missile—a concept that treaties tried to eliminate more than twenty years ago. With the 1972 Anti-Ballistic Missile Treaty, the U.S. and the U.S.S.R. agreed to the MAD doctrine—Mutual Assured Destruction. If one nation had a defense against nuclear weapons, it might be tempted to launch an attack, figuring it could survive nuclear retaliation and conquer. Without ABM systems, however, retaliation is the deterrent to attack. The MAD threat kept us at nuclear peace for more than four decades.

Now ABMs are back. The Pentagon says one hundred rockets could be deployed at a single U.S. site without violating the ABM treaty. The warhead of the super-speedy HEDI missile would use an infrared seeker and maneuvering rockets to zero in on the nuclear weapon in the upper atmosphere, then destroy it with a burst of pellets. All within fifteen seconds of launch. The $383 million program, which had its initial test flight on January 6, 1990, is designed to pick up the stragglers that get through other space-based Star Wars systems and to protect against low-level launches from off-shore submarines.

James Wise grew up a science fiction nut, anxious to read about whatever futuristic fantasies he could find. Today, he handles many of those sci-fi dreams he read about as a high school kid. "In science fiction, some things that exist only in people's minds will be facts someday. I have a personal relationship to that particular fact," he said.

Wise is a technical director at White Sands, a bureaucrat in charge of much of the operation. Trained by Georgia Tech as an engineer, he came to the missile range in 1955 after working on "special weapons" for the Army—that's military talk for nuclear weapons. Now some of his most powerful weapons to test are beams of light, right out of the pages of his teenage fantasies.

The missile range, he believes, doesn't stand a chance of going out of business no matter how much peace breaks out around the world. The United States will always be testing new weapons and will always need a place to do the testing. Budget cutbacks have already forced the Army to shoot less and measure more, Wise said. But no matter how sophisticated computer simulations become (and experts can simulate just about any kind of war you want on computers now), there will always be some who want to see the fiery explosion, want to see the thing, whatever plane or missile or gun or laser it might be, actually work. They have to hear the boom. As Wise said, "I believe you can do a lot of testing by computer simulation, but I do not believe we are smart enough to ever rely on total computer simulation."

Many believe testing has already outgrown White Sands. But there's too much political opposition to take new lands for the missile range, and no chance a bigger tract of land

41

could ever be acquired in the United States. White Sands will be the test range, probably forever. And it will keep attracting sci-fi fanatics who find the supersonic speed of the work and the Buck Rogers aspect of its toys exhilarating.

But someday the range may change from a testing track to the site of real weapons, where, for example, real space guns are based. In fact, that change may have taken place already.

In a remote part of the range, not far from the area where missiles are supposed to land, sits the free world's most powerful laser. There aren't any banners or billboards calling attention to the site. Just a few arrows and: MIRACL, NEXT LEFT.

Mid-Infrared Advanced Chemical Laser. At first glance, Miracl looks like a giant model of human intestines made out of fancy pipes. The pipes and mirrors sit on a million-pound concrete bench, which floats on pistons. At its top is a turret-like telescope contraption called a beam director: it aims the laser beam. On the front of the beam director are six black stickers in the shape of airplanes and missiles—these signify targets killed, just as a World War II fighter pilot put a rising sun on his plane for each Japanese airplane shot down. Imagine: shooting down a speeding airplane with a beam of light.

While politicians, academics, and philosophers debate the merits of Star Wars, cut the budgets of some projects, and scale back others, this laser beam has already shot down and killed those six airplanes and missiles, drones flown to test the laser. Miracl could probably knock out a satellite in space, but officials say they don't know for sure because the United States has yet to test it there. No East-West treaty prohibits tests of antisatellite weapons in space, but the Soviets have conducted no known antisatellite experiments since 1982, and the United States has shied away, hoping to maintain that East-West restraint. Despite the lack of testing, however,

Miracl could be an operational weapon right now against targets in the atmosphere above the Nuclear Highway, or even in space. The six black markers of experimental kills signify that Star Wars is already here, that we can now shoot down missiles with beams of light in the real world, not just in computer simulations and science fiction.

A laser (the word is actually an acronym taken from *l*ight *a*mplification by *s*timulated *e*mission of *r*adiation) is a machine that puts molecules in an excited energy state, causing them to emit light of a precise wavelength in an intense, narrow beam. The type of beam is determined by the substance being "lased."

In the case of Miracl, the machine is basically a fancy rocket engine. A gaseous oxidizer and a fuel mixture are burned in the combustion chamber to produce fluorine. Deuterium, a gas, is injected into the flow to produce excited molecules of deuterium fluoride, which give off light. Presto, a deuterium fluoride laser.

From the maze of pipes and mirrors, the beam from the Miracl laser goes to a Beam Transfer Area—a switchyard that can direct the laser several different ways. There's a carbon dump if you don't need the beam, there's a hazardous test site nine hundred meters away where you can zap tin cans on the fence if you want to, and there's the beam director—the turret-like telescope that swivels and can send the beam to zap missiles. The beam director is so sophisticated it can focus past infinity, scientists claim. Not that it needs to—infinity is far enough, they add. (Eckles, the public affairs specialist at White Sands, says he brought a CBS television crew out to the Miracl laser one time. They looked at the pipes and tanks and mirrors and stuff and said, "That's not a laser." When he took them up to the beam director, which really is nothing more than a telescope, the producer exclaimed, "Now that's what a laser looks like." Millions of TV viewers one night saw the beam director and were told it was the laser.)

Laser technology dates from 1960. Miracl, which has been around since the 1970s, was simply a program to see if a deuterium fluoride laser could be made so powerful that it could become a weapon. With Miracl, the power is set by the amount of chemical fed in: it is the free world's most powerful laser because it has the biggest tank farm of chemicals and it can burn those chemicals very, very quickly. At full power, Miracl can run for only half a minute with its existing tank-farm capacity. It costs $4,000 per second to operate. (For comparison, the entire federal government's costs are about $3,800 per second.)

Miracl was actually abandoned in 1983, then resurrected under the Strategic Defense Initiative. Two decades ago, the Navy wanted to see if beams of light could be used to protect ships from incoming projectiles or kamikaze planes. It worked, but the laser machine was so big that it could never fit on a ship. Understandably, the Navy doesn't much care for something that doesn't fit on a ship, so it abandoned the program.

When Reagan's SDI came along in 1985, the idea of using beams of light received new life. Lasers have a big advantage over antimissile rockets like Patriot, HEDI, and their cousins—speed. Nothing can travel faster than the speed of light, so nothing could outrun a laser. And since the beam can be continuous, nothing can fire faster than a laser. One beam rapidly targeted across the sky could do the work of hundreds of HEDI missiles. Someone somewhere in the Pentagon remembered Miracl, and the program was off to a giant head start over other Star Wars competitors. Today, as funding for and interest in Star Wars dwindles, the Miracl laser remains perhaps the only operational SDI weapon.

Of course, the military doesn't call Miracl a weapon—which

might escalate the arms race. And as weapons go, Miracl certainly has its shortcomings as it's set up now. You can't move it, you need a week's warning to get it ready, and it only works for thirty seconds. So officials are careful to call it a "potential weapon." That may be only a matter of semantics. As football coaching legend Darrell Royal used to say, "Potential just means you ain't done it yet." Six kills on the front show that Miracl has indeed done it.

Using available light, scientists know the beam director can track satellites hundreds of miles away, but they say they don't know for sure if that means they could do the reverse—send a laser beam toward those satellites. The atmosphere can distort the beam, break it up, and send it off course. But that's a problem that is being worked on, according to Gene Frye, manager of the high-energy laser facility.

"We're trying to develop it into a contingency antisatellite weapon," Frye said. "We have to see if it has that capability—but we think it does. Nobody wants to advertise it as a [antisatellite] weapons system. But logically, you can see it developing into that."

Technologically, Miracl really isn't all that special—it uses mid-'70s science for its most important functions. But it is the most powerful thing the United States has got, and it exists, which in the realm of SDI cutbacks gives it a tremendous boost over other beam programs. It may not be ideal, but experts say it could be functional . . . should we ever want to use it as a weapon, of course.

Through 1990, Miracl was undergoing a $20 million upgrade with advances designed to steady the beam so it could target satellites. The improvements were approved by then–Defense Secretary Frank Carlucci after heated internal debate within the Pentagon. Carlucci's decision, made in the waning days of the Reagan administration and reported by

Aviation Week and Space Technology, an industry publication known in defense circles as "Aviation Leak," signified a shift in Star Wars philosophy, from a purely defensive shield to an offensive threat capable of attacking satellites. In a land war, an early goal is to knock out the other guy's radios, phones, and other communications. By the same strategy, satellites would be early targets in an intercontinental nuclear war.

Carlucci's 1988 decision to upgrade came after the commander in chief of the U.S. Space Command, General John L. Piotrowski, stated publicly that the Soviets have large ground-based lasers capable of damaging or destroying American satellites. Piotrowski said the lack of a U.S. satellite killer is a "grave detriment to our national security" and that an American laser is needed to deter Soviet aggression and make possible more research on the damage Soviet lasers might do. *The New York Times* reported in a front-page story on the Miracl upgrade that Piotrowski played a key role in securing the new capabilities for the New Mexico device.

To date, the military has sunk some $800 million into the top-secret laser facility at White Sands. The whole operation there employs four hundred people and includes a fifty-foot-diameter spherical vacuum chamber—about half the size of a space shuttle cargo bay—which can simulate the void of space. A pipe can carry the Miracl laser beam into the stainless-steel vacuum chamber. The military uses the chamber to place dummy warheads or other targets in a space-like environment and then see what happens when they are zapped by a laser. How powerful must the laser be to damage or destroy them, especially if they are rotating as nuclear missiles do in flight? How much damage would a Soviet laser do to U.S. satellites? SDI tests on nagging questions such as those continued in the vacuum chamber long after the Berlin Wall came down and East-West tensions eased.

Before Miracl could actually be used on a satellite in space, approval would have to come from the President. For now, Miracl sits silent in the desert—out of sight and out of controversy. But it's there if we want it or need it.

Full-scale battles by remote control. Shooting down airplanes with video games. Running target practice on a peak that may be filled with gold. It's all here at White Sands. And so is the future: death beams in the desert.

3

CITY OF SECRETS

For secrets are edged tools
And must be kept from children and from fools.
JOHN DRYDEN

Through most of New Mexico, I-25 follows the Rio Grande, hanging close to the only water readily available in the desert. Like so many of our once-great rivers, the Rio Grande is more like a big ditch, largely dammed and tamed in southern New Mexico, a chain of reservoirs cut through the valley. The Nuclear Highway passes through little ranching and farming towns, such as Truth or Consequences, which was called Hot Springs until the town became smitten with a television show and changed its name. Heading north, the same direction the Spaniards traveled and the missiles fly, the road parallels the Jornada del Muerto and the missile range. It's about 240 miles from Las Cruces to Albuquerque. Travelers can't see much of the missile range and the secrets that, from the west, as from the east over by Mary McDonald's place, are protected by mountains. Other than the curious

"T or C," the only town of note is Socorro, a dusty Old West college town northwest of White Sands.

Socorro has its share of Nuclear Highway projects, of course. Few are left out in this slice of the country. At the New Mexico Institute of Mining and Technology, the art of digging gold and uranium and oil from the ground has been yielding to projects that can be carried out only in the seclusion of the desert. Today, the barren mountains that ring New Mexico Tech's campus are littered with bomb shelters and laboratories and bunkers for staging explosions. Booms can be heard regularly as students stroll to the cafeteria. One of the institute's most sophisticated projects has the wonderfully bureaucratic title of Terminal Effects Research and Analysis—it means how to kill better.

TERA is so hush-hush even the school that gives it a home doesn't know much about it. It tests explosives and weapons systems, and it works in coordination with the Center for Explosives Technology Research, which finds ways to kill tanks. Stopping tanks is one of the toughest counter-countermeasure problems of the modern battlefield. After rockets and missiles got so good at stopping tanks, tanks found a new countermeasure: draping their sides with "reactive armor" that will explode when hit and disperse the incoming missile, keeping it from penetrating the tank's inner cocoon. That idea has been refined in the U.S. M-1 Abrams tank to a shell of layers of materials, including nonradioactive uranium, with layers of air in between. The layers disperse the rocket's force before it can do much damage. To counter those countermeasures, some of the best antitank weapons now consist of long rods of depleted uranium that can be fired at very, very fast speeds. When the heavy rod hits the tank, it has enough force to pierce through the reactive armor and spray the soldiers and their systems with very hot droplets of molten metal. It's not a pretty sight.

49

The Pentagon created a stir in the late 1980s when it said the United States believed the Soviets had an armor that could counter our counter-countermeasure—a tank that could withstand our hot rods. The stir reached New Mexico Tech, where the task at hand is to find a metal or some sort of weapon that can pierce the Soviet tank. Tank technology is a constant case of one-upmanship.

CETR borrows techniques developed for nuclear weapons programs and uses finely tuned explosions to create new substances. Different matter can be fused together with these special explosions to create new alloys. (For a time, CETR was getting its fancy explosives from Los Alamos, one of the two nuclear weapons labs up the road.) Some of the alloys might form new projectiles capable of piercing the next generation of armor, or even become the next generation of armor capable of stopping the next generation of antitank slugs. Not all these new alloys are for killing and destroying. Some can be used to build and benefit, yielding engineering and technological breakthroughs. Some of these new substances can withstand intense heat and could one day form the skin of a space plane. Some new substances created at CETR might transmit electricity with less resistance. Some might form super-strong cutting tools. This is a campus that literally rocks with ka-booms, some of which involve several tons of high explosives.

On the other side of I-25, to the west of Socorro, scientists have planted a garden of giant antennas, shaped like huge satellite dishes, that listen to deep space for sounds of intelligible life, hunt for clues to the beginning of the universe, and survey the Milky Way and distant galaxies. It's called the Very Large Array, or VLA, and these high-tech tulips, each roughly the size of a three-bedroom house, are planted here because they can hear without distortion out in the desert. There are twenty-seven dish-shaped antennas, each about eighty feet in diameter, that move on twenty miles of tracks. It is the world's most sensitive radiotelescope. Passing along the highway, there's no telling what you might find out here.

Heading north, I-25 leads right into downtown Albuquerque. Albuquerque is a typical southwestern city in many ways, brimming with broad, straight streets, struggling with a multicultural population, and giddy from years of rapid growth. The city is actually a giant shallow bowl, fenced in by mountains to the east and a high mesa to the west. The fancy neighborhoods are up in the heights, up toward the mountains, up where there's a forever view; the poorer neighborhoods are down below in the valley, where houses crowd together and neighbors can gaze straight into one another's windows.

But Albuquerque is different from Phoenix and San Antonio and Houston. It is a city that is driven by defense dollars, one where the military, and military weapons, provide more employment than any other industry. It is a city that, like so many of us, grew up with the Bomb. And it prospered with the Bomb. It still does. A recent headline in the local newspaper proclaimed that despite cutbacks in defense programs that wreaked economic havoc on some cities, weapons work was still Albuquerque's "Golden Goose." This is, after all, the only city on which the United States has accidentally dropped a nuclear bomb. Whenever a debate crops up about the ethics of nuclear weapons work, or the environmental hazards—such as the groundwater contamination—the weapons work produces, the downside is always discounted in Albuquerque. No matter how grim the weapons work gets, there is always a silver lining—the Bomb provides thousands and thousands of jobs, and where would the city be without it? The Bomb is part of the pocketbook of Albuquerque, part of its history, its heart, and its soul.

It's also part of its soil.

In 1990, a Department of Energy study of radioactive fallout found higher-than-expected levels of plutonium in nine soil samples taken from Albuquerque locations. Plutonium, the nuclear fuel of the bomb dropped on Nagasaki and still a key ingredient in today's thermonuclear weapons, doesn't occur naturally. Nature doesn't produce it; man does, by bombarding uranium with neutrons. So the plutonium that was found came from atomic weapons work. No doubt about it.

The plutonium was discovered in such small concentrations that it posed no health problem, officials agreed. The concentrations were only one tenth of the level that would trigger an EPA cleanup. Most of the contamination was found two to six inches deep in the soil, in older parts of the city. And small amounts of plutonium outside the body usually aren't automatically harmful—you have to ingest it before it can kill you.

What caused it to wind up in Albuquerque soil was a mystery, officials said. Fallout from the Trinity test was thought to have blown away from Albuquerque. Some fallout probably came from the Nevada Test Site, where nuclear weapons were exploded aboveground in the 1950s and 1960s. In fact, twenty-four of the thirty-three sites tested in Albuquerque showed plutonium levels consistent with areas downwind of atmospheric testing.

But those nine other sites had much higher levels. And they were not places you'd think of as being in the line of plutonium fire: Rio Grande Park and the Rio Grande Zoological Park, for example. Roosevelt Park, a median on Ridgecrest Street, and other areas in different quadrants of the city. Even University of New Mexico land had higher levels.

DOE ruled out various theories. There weren't any problems or mistakes in the testing; it couldn't have been from Trinity, or an accident, the government report said.

But there was another theory: The research-grade plutonium found at the nine sites came from wartime experiments
in the 1940s in which plutonium entered the sewer system,
scientists theorized. It could have gotten concentrated in
sludge and was then used by the city as fertilizer. Most of
the contaminated areas were city lands or street medians.
Unknowing landscape workers could have taken the sludge
and sprayed it to fertilize grass growing in the desert climate.
Raw plutonium, dumped in a sewer system, ultimately fertil-
izing grass on street medians. This truly is the Nuclear
Highway.

"We do not have any proof of that, but it is a scientific
speculation," Gene Runkle, supervisory health physicist with
the DOE's Health Protection Division, said in news reports
of the plutonium contamination.

"Things were not handled the same as we do today," he
said.

Driving up I-25 here puts you right in the heart of the City
of Albuquerque. But if you fly, you land smack in the heart
of the City of Secrets, home to a concentration of the nation's most advanced research, home to the nerve center of
the nation's nuclear weapons, a place literally littered with
curious-looking contraptions.

To the untrained eye, a simple act such as landing at Albuquerque International Airport is routine. If you land toward
the west, you fly through a pass in the Manzano Mountains,
turn to the north, then back to the west for touchdown. It's
a bit more interesting than landing at one of the mega-depots
like Dallas or Atlanta, but still pretty routine.

Yet to the educated eye, that landing over the mountains
and down into Albuquerque is something more—a bird's-eye
peek at some of the most sensitive work in the American
military: the City of Secrets. The airport is one of the few

major commercial jetways that shares runways with a full-scale U.S. Air Force base. Albuquerque International is actually within the confines of Kirtland Air Force Base, and Kirtland, a huge tract of land in the right-hand armpit of the intersection of I-25 and Interstate 40, is in some ways the nucleus of the Nuclear Highway.

Here at the airport is a city within the City of Albuquerque, a sprawling complex that employs thousands of people who can tell you little of what they really do. Part of their job description is keeping secrets, because they work on some of the most highly classified guns, bombs, airplanes, and lasers in America.

On some days, a traveler with a window seat might see a C-130 transport parked in a remote corner of the airfield, ringed by jeeps with machine-gun-armed sentries. Barricades warn the curious to stay away. The guards' fingers are clearly by the triggers. Soldiers can be seen gingerly removing a payload from the plane onto pallets and then to a truck. Sometimes the convoy goes up toward the mountains.

Other days at Albuquerque International, there might be a B-1 bomber parked on the runway opposite the passenger terminal. Attack helicopters squat on the tarmac like overgrown grasshoppers, alongside Military Airlift Command transports, the workhorses of the Air Force.

On most days, a frequent flier's glance toward some of the buildings here at the City of Secrets will yield a look at a row of unmarked tractor-trailer rigs, each cab brimming with antennas. The innocent eye might not know that these gleaming eighteen-wheelers are lined with bulletproof armor and equipped for special missions. The typical vacationer might not give a second glance to the adobe-colored three-story square building. Few even notice the huge mirrors, or the long high-speed sled track, or the concrete bunkers etched into the mountains, or any of the other novelties that can be seen from a Boeing 737.

But they all have a place along the Nuclear Highway.

At the edge of the main east-west runway sits the world's largest trestle built entirely of wood — no bolts, nails, or screws. The top of the trestle is level with the adjacent runway, but this giant Tinkertoy constructed of 6.5 million board-feet of lumber actually extends down twelve stories into the arroyo, beyond sight of most airline passengers. To test for survival in a nuclear war, the Air Force bombards the trestle, and whatever objects it parks on top of it, with electromagnetic pulses — the same kinds of pulses produced by a nuclear explosion that kill normal electronic circuitry. That's why it has to be made entirely of wood: metal beams or bolts would distort the EMPs, as they are called. The EMP bombardment comes from a pair of 5-million-volt pulsers. On some days, there's a B-1 bomber, or a new plane for the President, parked there, being checked out to see if its electronics will keep working in the middle of a nuclear war.

The one place a tourist can visit at the City of Secrets is the National Atomic Museum, which has an amazing assortment of warheads and bombs on display, from Fat Man to the huge early H-bombs to today's football-sized weapons of genocide. It also has an almost humorous scrap heap out back of obsolete Atlas missile parts and other space junk.

There is much more to the City of Secrets. This is a place where scientists play games with the fastest computers in the world. The game is "What does it take to destroy the world?" Laboratory researchers compete against one another to find the best way to blow up the enemy.

In yet another of those nondescript concrete megaboxes near the airport runways, scientists explore the secrets of infinite energy — nuclear fusion. They use the free world's largest X-ray machine for dual purposes: sometimes they zap nuclear weapons components with radiation to see if they'll survive in the "hot" environment of a nuclear war long enough to explode themselves; sometimes they try to fuse two atoms to unlock the secrets of energy to see if they can create limitless electricity in the laboratory. The same machine does both. In nuclear weapons work, there's almost always that silver lining.

If the astute window-seated traveler looks back to the east, he or she can see concrete bulkheads dotting four small mountains, an exclusive neighborhood built up to its edge. Inside those bunkers there are nuclear warheads. Lots of them. When a KC-135 airborne fuel tanker crashed and exploded one night in those hills, the residents immediately thought one of the bombs had gone off. Shoot-to-kill signs protect the perimeter. When a soccer ball goes over the fence in the Four Hills neighborhood, it is not retrieved.

There's probably not another neighborhood like Four Hills anywhere in the country, even in the world. Picturesque and exclusive, it sits high above the city, with a glorious view of the valley, the airport, and the string of pearls lined up in the sky to land. It is quintessentially Albuquerque — a little adobe here, some ranch-style homes there: a Century 21 kind of neighborhood. Retirees and housewives take their 10:00 A.M. jogging-suit walks through the hilly streets. Homes on the edge of the development have military fences in their backyards, sturdy chain-link property-line markers adorned with stern warning signs. Four Hills is built right up to the back of what some say is the largest single nuclear weapons storage vault in the country.

Beyond the fence sit four hills of the Manzano Mountains, the hills that give the neighborhood its name. Concrete double doors pock the sides of the hills — the same kinds of doors the world watched laser-guided bombs smash through in Baghdad missile storage depots. At the base of the four hills of the Manzanos is a ring of triple chain-link fences topped with barbed wire. For the military, a triple chain-link fence with barbed wire is as good as a billboard screaming "Nuclear Weapons Inside Here! Right Here!" There is also a pale Air-Force-green headquarters building — the home of the 3098th Aviation Depot Squadron, the caretakers of some four hundred or so nuclear weapons estimated to be stockpiled in the hollowed-out hills.

The Air Force always issues the same statement when the question comes up: they can "neither confirm nor deny" the storage of nuclear weapons inside the hills. But everyone in the neighborhood, in fact most Albuquerque residents, thinks they know what's inside those doors. They assume the fences mean only one thing. As journalist David H. Morrissey of the *Albuquerque Journal* wrote: "The presence of nuclear weapons underneath the Manzano Mountains has been one of Albuquerque's most talked-about 'secrets.' "

Since the Air Force will neither confirm nor deny the existence of nuclear weapons inside the Manzanos, they certainly don't talk about how many of the contraptions are there. Nuclear weapons reference books have said the Four Hills dump includes everything from air- and ground-launched cruise missiles to 1960s-era Titan II warheads to Minuteman III warheads and probably more than two hundred plain old nuclear bombs — the kinds dropped from airplanes or lofted by artillery guns. Recently, when treaties with the Soviet Union have ordered reductions in nuclear forces, the warheads from the deactivated missiles apparently often end up here. Four Hills is said to be the Air Force's largest warhead storage facility — which by some counts may make it the largest in the world. Even those who work around Kirtland joke about the nukes, just like the residents. One department at a government facility located within the Kirtland confines even said that the military allows agencies to store old files in unused weapons storage caverns. Security may be a little excessive, but what a great place to mothball all those old press releases!

And despite the Air Force's tight lips, the official history of Kirtland Air Force Base would seem to spill the frijoles. In the early days of nuclear weapons, the bombs were assembled and stored in igloo-like structures down south of the runways in an arroyo. But "during the late 1940s and early 1950s, a secure storage area for special resources was constructed around a small range of Manzano Mountains foothills," the Air Force history says. "Operational functions at Site Able, as the storage area was known, began on April 4, 1950, under the Army's 8460th Special Weapons Group."

"Special weapons" is the military's wonderfully understated term for nuclear weapons.

Richard and Mary Carter retired to Albuquerque from New York and bought a ranch-style home with a circular drive and desert landscaping in Four Hills. In their backyard runs the sturdy fence with warning signs. It seems best not to breach it.

To the Carters, who watch truck convoys head up to the hills from time to time, the nuclear warheads are not a worry. "Sometimes at night a whole flood of lights will come on out there, and you wonder what's going on," Mrs. Carter said. But most of the time it's just a bold jackrabbit or a wandering coyote.

"We heard mention of the weapons when we bought this house. . . . Maybe if we were younger we would have thought about it more before we bought, but at our time in life, it's not a factor for us."

"If it's there, you have to believe it's safe," said Carter, an anesthesiologist from Schenectady. "And it's OK with me. Someday they might need it.

"The good thing about it — and this was a factor when we bought the house — is that there is so much clear area behind the house. And you know that nobody is going to build up against us. You can be sure of that."

Airplanes lifting off from the nearby runways would certainly be considered a greater hazard, like the KC-135 tanker loaded with jet fuel that did crash one night adjacent to the Four Hills neighborhood, killing the crew. And it's doubtful that the Air Force still flies around Kirtland with huge nuclear bombs hanging gingerly in the belly of an airplane, like the one that accidentally fell out of a B-36 on May 22, 1957.

Thankfully, the nuclear components of the Mark 17 hydrogen bomb didn't go off. The story didn't come to full public light until 1986, when the *Albuquerque Journal* used the Freedom of Information Act to dig up old military documents mentioning the drop. Some of the details remained classified, but crewmen recounted the horror — and humor — of the moment.

It seems the ten-engine B-36, ferrying the nuclear bomb from Biggs Air Force Base in Texas to New Mexico, hit some rough air at 1,700 feet as it was coming into the airport — Albuquerque International, a.k.a. Kirtland Air Force Base. The navigator, who had to climb around the bomb before landing to set a large pin that secured the shell, grabbed a lever to steady his balance in the turbulence. It was not a good lever to grab. The switch released the twenty-one-ton behemoth, which apparently was just resting in a sling. (A Mark 17 is on display at the National Atomic Museum, but there is no mention of the accident.) The bomb crashed through the closed bomb bay doors and landed four and a half miles south of the control tower. Some in the crew thought the bomb had taken the navigator with it. One crewman yelled, "Bombs away!" The plane, suddenly twenty-one tons lighter, lurched about a thousand feet higher in the sky.

The navigator scampered back to his seat, "whiter than any sheet you ever saw," radio operator George Houston said in 1986. "I didn't touch anything. I didn't touch anything," the pale lieutenant was said to have exclaimed. The plane dutifully informed the control tower that it had, well, dropped a nuclear bomb.

Conventional explosives in the bomb detonated on impact in the uninhabited area, but there was no nuclear blast because not all the weapon's parts were in place for it to be armed. Also, the conventional explosives have to be triggered in a precise way to set off the nuclear chain reaction. The explosion killed a cow and gouged a crater 12 feet deep and 25 feet wide. Minor radioactive contamination was noted; there were no human injuries. The Mark 17, 24.5 feet long and 5 feet in diameter, was the first thermonuclear weapon to be carried aboard an airplane. It was estimated to have a nuclear explosive yield of 10 megatons, or more than 600 times the power of the Hiroshima bomb. That bomb may have been more powerful than any warhead in the current U.S. arsenal.

Kirtland has a lot more to do with nuclear weapons than just storing (and occasionally dropping) them. Scientists and military folks here like to say they are involved from cradle to grave — inception to deactivation.

Inception begins with Sandia National Laboratories, one of the nation's three nuclear weapons labs. Sandia is ensconced behind the fences of the Air Force base, but it is actually operated by the Department of Energy, the agency in charge of nuclear weapons research, development, and production. (Congress specifically didn't want the Pentagon in charge of the whole ball of wax.)

One of New Mexico's largest employers (the whole Kirtland complex is the state's largest employer), Sandia primarily works on the arming and firing parts of the bomb — the devices that ready it for explosion and set the detonation in progress. The two other labs, Los Alamos and the Lawrence Livermore national laboratories, have responsibility for designing the actual nuclear part of the warhead. If a nuclear bomb were a hand grenade, Sandia would be in charge of the pin.

Sandia has been involved in almost every nuclear weapon and warhead since the end of World War II and has been in on every nuclear test the United States has had since Trinity. Sandia scientists apparently came up with the firing design that created the "enhanced radiation" artillery shell — the infamous neutron bomb that kills people through intense radiation but limits damage to buildings. They developed a nuclear weapon that digs deep into the earth before it explodes, allowing it to toss an airfield into the heavens. They worked on a nuclear warhead that was maneuverable after it reentered the atmosphere from space — similar to a cruise missile, except that it could be fired across continents by ballistic missiles.

To do all this designing and development, Sandia has actually helped lead the technological charge in this country. To manufacture "hardened" computer chips — specially made microcircuits for bombs and military gear that could withstand the radioactive environment of a nuclear war — Sandia was first to develop a "clean room." Special filters and ventilation systems keep out dust, dirt, and microscopic junk that could contaminate minute microelectronic circuits. The Sandia design invented here in 1961 was used in clean rooms throughout the world. Sandia scientists lend their expertise to other weapons systems besides nukes, such as coming up with systems that can teach computers to work like nerve cells and actually "see" targets — recognize targets in a video picture. There are even robot contraptions like the Honda four-wheelers called "Fire Ants," which boogie across the desert, sneak up on the enemy, and destroy tanks by remote control. And Sandia scientists are working on a giant gun capable of launching small satellites into space. Now they are taking some of their weapons expertise to industry: they've invented robots to clean up environmental hazards, new metals and microchips, and an array of high-tech goodies that are now declassified because of relaxed Cold War tensions. Only recently have the labs opened up, dropped some of the security restrictions, and invited companies to see what's sitting on the once-classified shelves.

Sandia remains solely responsible for the safety of nuclear weapons. The people who come up with the system to fire the things also have to make sure that they don't fire accidentally. That safety role carries over into transporting nuclear weapons, storing them, taking them out of the planes and silos, and testing them from time to time. So Sandia scientists have been known to send a truck with a nuclear materials canister into a wall at eighty-four miles per hour. (The canister survived, the truck did not.) The Department of Energy handles every shipment of a nuclear weapon — or of weapons materials — through Sandia. Those trucks parked out by the tarmac at Albuquerque International are actually "Safe-Secure Trailers." They are escorted from weapons plant to weapons plant to military base, etc., by a pair of Chevy Suburbans with darkly tinted windows and machine-gun-toting guards. Couriers get six weeks of training at Sandia. Nuclear protesters sometimes try to follow the square-rig trucks with bright stripes but no commercial markings. They sometimes play a cat-and-mouse game. The DOE even checks with police for warrants on the protesters' cars, according to a DOE report that was mistakenly faxed one day in March 1990 to governors' offices around the country. Oops.

Sandia also plays a big role in the game of simulating nuclear explosions. Ever since weapons tests went underground in the 1960s, the government has looked for better and cheaper ways to test and punish weapons parts. Now, as a treaty limiting underground tests looks as if it could come over the horizon in the next decade, Sandia has just about perfected ways to do all the testing in laboratories and on computers. They can zap weapons parts with simulated lightning bolts, for example, to see how they'd survive a direct strike. They can bombard them with X-rays, shake them to heavy g-forces, and put them through just about everything imaginable in a nuclear war.

Inside one giant buff-colored building, Sandia has constructed a machine so powerful it can consume fifty times the entire electrical generating capacity of the *entire world* in a matter of seconds. It's called the Particle Beam Fusion Accelerator II (it's the second generation), and it uses all that juice to direct ion beams down the spokes of a one-hundred-foot-wide wheel, all focused toward a tiny target area about the size of a penny. When the target gets zapped, there is so much energy it's similar to a hydrogen bomb explosion. The goal is to create fusion — the nuclear reaction of the stars and of thermonuclear bombs — in the laboratory. Already scientists can use PBFA II to study the physics of thermonuclear weapons without exploding a nuclear device under the Nevada desert. New designs and new materials can be checked out to see what gives the best bang. Or they can simulate the effects of a nuclear explosion on an electronics package. And beyond that, if they can achieve fusion in the laboratory, then they may be able to create a nuclear power plant that could produce electricity through fusion. Today's power plants use fission — splitting atoms, as with the early atomic bombs. Fusion forces atoms together, producing vastly larger amounts of energy from various forms of hydrogen, which is in limitless supply, and with less radioactive waste. That's the irony of nuclear weapons work — there's always a silver lining.

At Kirtland, Sandia isn't the only nuclear game in town. The City of Secrets is host to myriad agencies and outfits related to nuclear weapons. The Pentagon's database on the nuclear stockpile — the status of every warhead: Where is it? Is it ready to be fired? Broken? In repair? — is kept here. So is the Joint Nuclear Accident Coordination Center, a round-the-clock organization of nuclear firemen. They are to nuclear weapons accidents what daredevil firefighter Red Adair is to oil well fires. You won't find much mention of it in the literature Air Force spokesmen and spokeswomen hand out to reporters and authors. But if you just drive around Kirtland, which is 22 percent larger than the District of Columbia, you can find the Interservice Nuclear Weapons School, where the military sends soldiers who will be handling the darn things. There they get taught which lever to pull and which one not to pull.

The Air Force also has its own "national lab" devoted to much the same kind of high-tech weapons research that goes on at Sandia. It was called the Air Force Space Technology Laboratory until recently rededicated as the Phillips Laboratory, in a consolidation of military research facilities. The lab here became a "Super Lab" for the Air Force. It's been around since the 1960s and, Miracl laser aside, is credited with using a laser beam to shoot down a drone aircraft at Kirtland in 1973.

More recently, the Phillips Lab has been successfully bouncing laser beams off satellite-mounted mirrors in key Star Wars experiments. They say it all works.

Lasers are the bread and butter of Star Wars, and a crucial part of lasers is the glass vacuum tubes necessary for the various contraptions scientists dream up. It's not all new skills and new talent — glassblowing is a crucial part of SDI. Czeslaw Deminet, seventy, originally from Poland, was a master glassblower who married his Old World talent to Star Wars research. During World War II, he fashioned bombs for the Polish underground. With ten patents to his credit, Deminet created glass tubes and chambers for lasers and other projects until his 1989 retirement, which was postponed from 1985 until a replacement of his caliber could be found. Deminet did such things as fashion a piece of glass to expose krypton to liquid hydrogen in a vacuum and produce liquid krypton — for SDI laser experiments, not Superman. He also fashioned an elegant glass swan for a visitor's children.

"There's no way you can make this by machine. It's technology that's four hundred years old, and today, without glassblowers, you wouldn't have lasers," he said.

Inside a superhardened building encased in steel and concrete to prevent curious Soviet eavesdropping, Air Force experts use an array of supercomputers to calculate new kinds of nuclear explosions, simulate nuclear war, map out Star Wars scenarios, and come up with key measurements and equations for all kinds of high-tech cruise missiles, smart bombs, and Stealth aircraft. Supercomputers are so prevalent that New Mexico even has a network where high school kids can log on and use the mighty machines for elaborate science fair projects, or just for the experience.

There are more Cray supercomputers in New Mexico, an Air Force computer expert once said, than anywhere else. They're here at the weapons center, they're across the street at Sandia, they're at Los Alamos up the highway, and they're at "underground places nobody knows about."

All told, it is possible, even probable, that New Mexico has the most extensive nuclear weapons research, management, training, and testing facilities and organizations in the world. No wonder unescorted Soviet citizens still aren't

allowed here. This is the nucleus of it all. A City of Secrets.
The city provides jobs, enhances education, drives growth
and development. Had the atomic bomb not come to Albuquerque in the 1940s, the city wouldn't be as vibrant as it is
today. Albuquerque has its "Golden Goose." Everyone seems
to cash in in some way. Hispanic entrepreneurs get government contracts to design tiny metal parts and electronic circuits for new nuclear weapons. Pueblo Indians win
multimillion-dollar contracts to fabricate sheet metal for the
military. High school kids, some of them the sons and daughters of Ph.D. scientists working inside the labs, some of them
the offspring of recent Mexican immigrants, get to play with
the world's fastest supercomputers. The price that has to be
paid is living with nuclear bombs in your backyard, or plutonium in your soil, or toxic chemicals leaching into your
groundwater from some high-tech Sandia experiments. Albuquerque seems to share the basic irony that has dogged
nuclear weapons work over the past fifty years — there's a
price that has to be paid, but there's always a silver lining.

4

BOMB BABIES WORKING INSIDE THE LABS

Don't it always seem to go
That you don't know what you've got
Till it's gone
They paved paradise
And put up a parking lot.
   JONI MITCHELL

Heading up I-25 out of Albuquerque in the winter is like making a pilgrimage to the God of Snow. If you don't have skis strapped to the roof of your car, you're an infidel among true believers. In the northbound lanes, which lead to Santa Fe and Taos, skis of all sizes are mounted on everything with wheels, modern attack spears atop Trojan Toyotas. This sixty-mile stretch of America's Nuclear Highway is an autobahn for schussboomers who cruise at eighty miles an hour uphill and even faster coming back. When the government raised the speed limit to sixty-five in 1987, the first sign was changed here, and Governer Garrey Carruthers personally got up in a cherry picker and made the switch.

Speed, after all, is a big part of what skiing is all about. Children who grow up skiing compete at ski races. And in ski racing, the difference between victory and defeat comes down to units of time not comprehensible by the human mind — fractions of seconds, milliseconds, microticks of electronic clocks. How long is one hundredth of a second? Zip, it's long gone. The human hand and the human eye are far too slow to judge winners with stopwatches. Light beams and computers are the tools of choice. Precision at world championships and Olympic competitions is essential. Those who can do it — pick the winner — possess a special talent and a rare skill.

Allen Church is one of the experts. A ski nut who grew up in the mountains of northern New Mexico, Church found himself spending hours at his two daughters' ski races. What Little League is to most of American suburbia, ski racing is to those raised in the enchanted mountains near Santa Fe and Taos. Gradually, Allen Church began to officiate at ski races. He had expertise in that field — he knew a lot about timing, about measuring millis and micros. From schoolgirl races in the Taos Ski Basin, Allen advanced through the small world of ski race timing to bigger and bigger championships. Now he is one of the leading ski race timers in the world. He was at the Olympics in 1980 at Lake Placid and in Calgary in '88 on behalf of the International Ski Federation.

Balding, with thick gray eyebrows and a relaxed, friendly, athletic air about him at age sixty-two, Church came by his ski race timing expertise in a curious way. He is a timing expert for nuclear bombs.

To trigger a nuclear explosion, one needs to make things happen at incredibly precise moments — the same kinds of fractions of millifractions of seconds found on the ski slopes. To make an atomic bomb like the device tested at Trinity and dropped on Nagasaki, one needs to place a sphere of high explosives around a plutonium core and set off the explosives so that they symmetrically squeeze the plutonium. Mix in a supply of neutrons, and it will go boom. There's more to it, of course, but that's the gist of the gadget. The explosion has to be perfect, or the chain reaction won't happen, the atoms won't split, and the atomic energy won't be released. If the timing isn't right, if every part of the high-explosive sphere doesn't go off at the same millisecond, you get a very messy dud that would scatter unexploded plutonium all over the place. And to trigger a thermonuclear weapon — a hydrogen bomb — the configuration and the timing are even more elaborate. It's all a matter of timing.

"There is some exchange of information," Church says of his hobby and his job.

Firing hydrogen bombs is not what he set out to do when he was young and thought he wanted to be a veterinarian. A struggle with organic chemistry forced that dream aside, so he went to Hollywood and tried acting, even appearing in a few movies. He was drafted into the Army during the Korean War, worked in field artillery at Fort Sill, Oklahoma, and fixed radar at Fort Bliss, Texas. Once out of the service, he went to Stanford University and studied electrical engineering. He was recruited by a company — well, not a real company — doing some pretty special engineering work. The organization was back in his native New Mexico. His older brother already worked there. It seemed like a good fit.

Allen Church knew about the existence of this organization long before the rest of the world did. His grandfather had been the founder of an exclusive boys' school in northern New Mexico, a place for wealthy East Coast and Midwest industrialists to send their sons for a rigorous education in the wilderness. Allen's father was a teacher at the school, who married the boss's daughter. But the school was to be dismantled, the family displaced.

The Manhattan Project took over the Los Alamos Ranch School and never gave it back. The Churches were forced off the mesa by the atomic bomb. While some in the area speculated wildly about what was going on atop the Pajarito Plateau, including a bizarre tale that a submarine base was being built there, the Churches basically guessed what was going on. Ferm Church, Allen's Harvard-educated father, recognized Ernest O. Lawrence, a nuclear physicist he had previously met. Ferm and his wife, Peggy Pond Church, got to know some of the scientists and recognized their work. Before the war was over, Ferm even sent a physics textbook to his eldest son, Ted, in college, with paragraphs on nuclear fission theory circled.

Fate was working against the Los Alamos Ranch School and Allen's grandfather, Ashley Pond II, almost from the start. Ashley was a city boy from Detroit who knew some of the top people at the big car companies. He had been a sickly child, and following an almost fatal case of typhoid in 1898, Ashley was sent out West for his health, to New Mexico. For a time, he lived among cowboys on working ranches, and he fell in love with the landscape and the life. He founded his first school in the bottom of a deep, wide Mora River canyon on the east side of the 13,000-foot-high Sangre de Cristo Mountains.

Like so many before him, Pond was enchanted by this land of beauty and mystery. He followed in the footsteps of Coronado, who believed his seven cities of Cibola were always just over the next scarlet hill, burnt red at sunset. Coronado and his fellow Spaniards christened the mountain range the Sangre de Cristo — the Blood of Christ. Centuries of artists have agonized over capturing their light on canvas, and renegades from some of America's wealthiest families have found a serenity in New Mexico when it eluded them everywhere else.

Thus Pond was not unique when he settled near the Sangre de Cristos, thinking he had found paradise. But he hadn't.

A flood came through the canyon in 1904, wiping out the school and almost sweeping away Pond's daughter, Peggy.

Pond convinced some of his Detroit auto friends to invest in a tract of 32,000 beautiful Pajarito Canyon acres known as the Ramon Vigil Land Grant. The Detroit industrialists wanted an exclusive club for their friends and fellow tycoons, a retreat in the wilderness managed by Ashley Pond. But Ashley, daydreamer that he was, never quite got the club off the ground. He kept wiring for more money from Detroit, building and dreaming but never drawing the customers needed, until finally the investors' patience wore thin.

"Mr. Pond, while he is the nicest fellow in the world and with the nicest family [that] would help most materially in making the ranch attractive and cheerful to visitors, had not the business talent and managerial capacity to conduct the affairs of such a club as we hope to develop along efficient, economical lines," wrote Harry Joy, the president of Packard Motor Car Company, in 1916. The scheme was abandoned.

That year, Ashley Pond found a farm near the Ramon Vigil land that was atop a high mesa overlooking the Rio Grande valley. It was a perfect setting for a school, and there certainly was no danger of flood. Even then, the high mesa born a million years ago in the eruption of the Jemez Volcano was staked out because of its security. "A more isolated spot could hardly be imagined, but isolation was an important part of my father's plan," Pond's daughter Peggy later wrote. In 1917, only five years after New Mexico became a state, Pond opened the Los Alamos Ranch School, beginning with only a three-story log lodge, which became the heart of the school. It flourished for twenty-five years, although Pond himself, the idealist who was never one for administration or details, hired a director, A. J. Connell, to run the school. During World War I, Ashley went overseas for the Red Cross but continued to serve on the school's board of directors. He maintained that kind of grandfatherly relationship with Los Alamos until his death, in 1933.

Connell was an Irishman born on Saint Patrick's Day, who also came to New Mexico for his health. He shared Pond's love of the outdoors but was a more practical man. He ran a rigorous program to toughen boys, many of whom were sent to the school to strengthen weak bodies and young minds. They wore scout-like khaki uniforms with bandannas. Shorts were the only pants allowed — even in the bitter winter. Flannel shorts were required at ice hockey and at dress-up events, such as graduation and formal evening dances in the lodge with a Santa Fe girls' school.

Each day, the wake-up bell rang at six-thirty, signaling outdoor calisthenics, breakfast, room cleaning, and inspection before classes. There were chores around the farm, horseback patrols through the wilderness, marksmanship, and music. Each boy was assigned his own horse. School life was patterned after the Boy Scouts, an organization dear to Connell. The ranch school was a largely self-sufficient community. Although dormitories, the lodge, and maintenance buildings took up only a few acres, the school owned 880 acres for the students to roam over and had a joint-use agreement with the U.S. Forest Service for many thousands more. Food that couldn't be raised on the property was shipped from Santa Fe on a narrow-gauge railroad that came only as close as the Otowi Switch (pronounced Oh-toe-wee), near the Rio Grande, which was twelve miles away down two lengthy, treacherous hills. No roads were paved, provisions had to be trucked up, and rain, snow, and thunderstorms were serious problems. Even on good days, the thirty-five-mile one-way trip to Santa Fe took one to one and a half hours.

In 1921, Connell hired Fermor S. Church right out of Harvard to be a teacher — a master, as they were called at the school. He graduated from college with a degree in illuminating engineering, but geology was his love. He was, ironically, the first scientist to arrive at Los Alamos. Three years later, Church married Peggy Pond, a dreamer herself, who shared her father's love of horses and wilderness. Peggy, who had first come to the Pajarito Plateau with her father at age ten, had gone off to an eastern boarding school and Smith College because her father's school was open only to boys. And Connell was basically a chauvinist who wouldn't allow women to teach or help run the academy. He believed boys were sent to Los Alamos to get away from their mothers' influence. The director's prejudice reportedly extended even to horses — legend had it that Connell wouldn't allow mares at Los Alamos.

Peggy was the first faculty wife allowed on the mesa. As she said later in her book *The House at Otowi Bridge:* "I was rather pleased with myself for having outwitted my father, who had been so unfeeling as to plan his school for boys and not for girls." She and Ferm spent their honeymoon at a cabin in the pines, riding to the top of a mountain or down to a wide valley for day trips. When school was in session, Peggy rode alone, exploring canyons filled with purple asters and hills blanketed with piñon and ponderosa pines. Even after her first son, Ted, was born, in 1925, Peggy continued her solitary forays. For almost twenty years the family, which expanded to three boys, lived a simple life close to nature at the ranch school. Photo albums reveal young, lanky, smiling boys frolicking in the Rio Grande.

By 1940, the school was flourishing, with a peak of forty-seven students aged twelve to eighteen. Los Alamos grew to more than twenty buildings. The school produced business executives, scientists, and artists — high achievers all around. Author Gore Vidal — known then as Gene — was a student in 1940. Sportsman Bill Veeck and John Crosby, the founder and director of the Santa Fe Opera, were alumni. Los Alamos alumni served at the top of American Motors, Sears Roebuck, the Santa Fe Railroad, and Quaker Oats.

Shortly after Pearl Harbor, headmaster Lawrence S. Hitchcock, a major in the Army reserves, was called to active duty, and Ferm took his place. World War II brought other immediate changes to the mesa. By the following May, an airplane was seen circling over the ranch school. No one understood it, but it was an omen. That spring, a huge windstorm toppled ancient trees — another omen. Then, in November, the surveillance began making sense. The military was scouting a site for a secret project.

The military came to New Mexico for many of the same reasons other wanderers had, including Pond. The Army wanted isolation; the scientists required a beautiful, stimulating setting. The military searched for such a site, needing also good transportation and an adequate water supply for a town, along with available labor and a mild climate. They looked at places around Los Angeles, but decided that was too populated. They explored Reno, Nevada, but it didn't have any air service. New Mexico, however, had convenient transportation because all TWA flights to the West Coast stopped in Albuquerque to refuel, and the Santa Fe Railroad came through. It was inland enough to be out of range of the Japanese, should they threaten the West Coast. And it offered a radiance in the landscape that would be acceptable to the sophisticated scientists — some said prima donnas — who would be stationed at the secret place.

Having narrowed the selection to New Mexico, Army officers then scouted several sites, including the town of Jemez, straight west of Santa Fe. But the Army brass, along with project director J. Robert Oppenheimer, found Jemez unacceptable because of a lack of water and buildings. Oppenheimer had an ace in the hole, a place nearby that might be perfect.

A man of diverse appetites and a varied cultural background, Oppenheimer was also an avid outdoorsman who, like so many others, discovered New Mexico early in life. He'd been sent to the mountains for his health. But unlike thousands of other boys, who left the Sangre de Cristos behind when they were healed, Oppenheimer kept a piece of himself in the blood-colored hills by purchasing a small ranch on the Pecos, which was his haven.

"My two great loves are physics and desert country," Oppenheimer wrote to a friend before the war. "It's a pity that can't be combined."

Now they were. Funny how fate had fused together lives on the mesa. Oppenheimer remembered the boys' school he had seen while horseback riding. The generals thought that might be just right — there were buildings and dormitories, water and roads. The Los Alamos Ranch School was close to what everybody was looking for. Climate could be harsh at 7,300 feet above sea level. The Albuquerque airport was one hundred miles away; the railroad fifty miles. Good enough. They took it.

Peggy Pond Church wrote later that she was glad her father never lived to see the day when the U.S. government came to seize his beloved school. The military told Connell the site was needed through the end of the war. (It was appropriately, if not sarcastically, labeled on an Army survey map the "Los Alamos Demolition Range.") A letter from Secretary of War Henry Stimson to Connell dated December 7, 1942 — one year to the day after Pearl Harbor and just five days after Enrico Fermi achieved the world's first nuclear chain reaction at the University of Chicago — notified the school it was to be condemned for the war effort.

"You are advised that it has been determined necessary to

the interests of the United States in the prosecution of the War that the property of Los Alamos Ranch School be acquired for military purposes," Stimson wrote.

Lieutenant General Leslie R. Groves, the military mover behind the Manhattan Project, wrote in his 1962 recollection, *Now It Can Be Told,* that he thought the school's owner, a nonprofit corporation, was receptive to a wartime shutdown because Connell was having trouble finding teachers during the war. The school was "very happy indeed to sell out to us and close down for the duration — and, as it turned out, forever," Groves said. ". . . Its owners could have made considerable trouble for us . . . by causing too many people to talk about what we were doing."

There may be some revisionist history in the general's recollection. Connell wasn't hostile to the idea of allowing the military *temporary* use of the school, Ferm and Peggy said in their booklet for the Los Alamos Historical Society, *When Los Alamos Was a Ranch School.* But he did call it a "great blow" when he announced the closing to parents. The school was not overjoyed at the thought of closing down — and no one wanted Los Alamos to close permanently.

Faculty and staff had until February 8, 1943, to vacate, but bulldozers and mechanical ditchdiggers were already moving in. The Christmas holiday was canceled and classes were accelerated so that the remaining school year could be completed by the deadline. On January 21, the last four diplomas of the Los Alamos Ranch School were awarded — one to Ted Church. That was the day before the condemnation papers were filed — and sealed for national security purposes — at the Sandoval County Courthouse. Ferm Church kept a copy of a February 17, 1943, letter from a War Department official, J. M. Harman. The bureaucrat was either naive or deceptive:

"I have been much impressed by the School tradition and

atmosphere, and would like very much to continue as much of the same as possible, until such time as, I hope, the School may be reconstituted,'' Harman wrote.

But almost from the start, the seizure of the ranch school appeared permanent. The Army didn't want a lease; it wanted to own the property. The school refused to sell, so the Army condemned it over the school's objection.

The condemnation papers, dug up by the Los Alamos Historical Society, include an inventory of what was taken. The list paints a picture of what life was like at the ranch school. It also shows that the Army appropriated everything, right down to the combs, brushes, and candlesticks. The inventory runs ninety-six legal-sized pages, and includes:

1 BRASS LAMP

1 DEER HEAD AND SKIN

1 OWL, MOUNTED

BEAR SKIN

7 AMERICAN FLAGS, 3 × 5, COTTON

RIFLES

1 ASPARAGUS KNIFE

1 CHEVROLET SEDAN, AND TWO TRUCKS

57 SADDLE HORSES [LISTED BY NAME, COLOR,
    AGE, AND WEIGHT – ASHLEY WAS BLACK,
    21, 1100 POUNDS]

3 WORK HORSES

70 SADDLES

53 NAVAJO SADDLE BLANKETS

SHEEPSKIN HOUSE SLIPPERS

BOYS UNIFORMS, SWIM TRUNKS, PAJAMAS,
    ATHLETIC SOCKS

1362 GLADIOLA BULBS

184 YO-YO STRINGS

————

The Army said it would pay $335,000 inclusive for the fifty-four buildings, the athletic socks, the Navajo blankets, and the 880 acres. But the ranch school foundation fought for more and won another $60,000 in federal court for fair market value plus interest. On August 23, 1943, the Los Alamos Ranch School officially became a casualty of war.

"We played the game and hid the soreness in our hearts, going on with our lives as best we could," Peggy wrote later.

Given his intellect and his science and engineering education, Ferm probably could have gone to work for the Manhattan Project and its offspring if he was interested. But he didn't want to get involved. That was industry, and he was a teacher.

He worked as a substitute teacher in New Mexico public schools for a while, but he couldn't get a regular job because he didn't have the class hours in teaching courses required for state certification. He got a teaching job at a private school in California and took Peggy and Hugh, the youngest, out there for Hugh's sixth-grade year. But the family didn't like California much — no changing seasons — and headed back to Taos. There, in the summer of '44, Ferm started his own school — a tough task with a war on — in Taos. It was called the Los Alamos School, and it was backed by the same foundation that had owned the ranch. Allen, who had gone off to private school in California when the ranch school closed, came back for his senior year at his father's school. But the academy graduated only one class and closed in the summer of '45. Allen is the only surviving graduate. The two others were killed in a car accident.

Perhaps the school failed simply because of its name. In the summer of 1945, Los Alamos became synonymous with Hiroshima and Nagasaki. A frightened parent wrote to Church: "New Mexico is far too dangerous for my boy." When Fermor wrote to parents to announce the school's closing, he explained: "Not the least of our handicaps came with the revealing of the 'Los Alamos Secret' and the consequent identification for most people of the name Los Alamos with atomic destruction." The name Los Alamos was the key, Allen said. "It painted a picture in people's minds."

Handsome, gentle Fermor, a stickler for detail, went to work for the Philmont Scout Ranch, then for the Kit Carson Electrical Co-Op in Taos, and worked his way up to office manager. He and many of the office staff resigned following a clash with one of the elected directors. Fermor later got a position with an Albuquerque engineering firm, surveying power lines in northern New Mexico. He enjoyed the work because it kept him outdoors. After retiring, he lived a casual life and maintained friendships among the powerful and wealthy he'd known through the ranch school. But he never went back to teaching, which was his first love, and he never quite recovered from losing Los Alamos, never quite got it all back together. He even advised his youngest son, about to go off to college in 1950, to maybe seek some other career than education. In the twenty-fifth anniversary booklet for his Harvard class, Fermor Church listed his occupation simply as "ex-schoolmaster."

Ironically, Fermor became active in an environmental group with some Los Alamos scientists. He was one of the founders of New Mexico Citizens for Clean Air and Water, and was the group's treasurer and newsletter editor for several years. Ferm Church, resentful of the lab's coming, became an environmental activist alongside the scientific descendants of J. Robert Oppenheimer. "He was resentful of the lab coming, and now here we are with a common interest in clean air and water, and working quite effectively together," said John Bartlit, a Los Alamos chemical engineer

79

and longtime chairman of the group. "There was no tension at all. They [Fermor and Peggy] were so committed to the movement. That overrode everything else."

Born in the first year of the century, Fermor Church died at the age of seventy-five.

Just as the Army never gave up White Sands, the desert of the Journey of Death, neither did it give up Los Alamos and the mountains of the Blood of Christ. Like the ranchers, Ferm Church died a displaced person. The quest for control of the atom meant, always, the taking of land, never retreating. The genie was out of the bottle. Los Alamos had lost its innocence. It could never again be a serene boys' school with ponies and picnics. As Allen Church says now with a wink: "It turned out to be a bigger project than anybody thought."

After the ranch school was closed in '43, Ted enrolled in Harvard for one semester, then transferred to the Massachusetts Institute of Technology on a Navy scholarship program. He was assigned to a troop transport ship in 1945 and made one round trip to the Philippines after the war.

In 1947, Ted came back to New Mexico for a job interview — at Los Alamos. The circle closed. The interview was arranged by a family friend, Dorothy McKibbin, the Santa Fe–based office manager for the Manhattan Project, who'd befriended many of the scientists. Ted wanted to get back to New Mexico, and he wanted a job in science. The only thing around New Mexico was nuclear science. He had offers elsewhere — RCA, Philco, Bell Telephone — but none seemed as intriguing as the work at Los Alamos. He wanted to be involved in the application of atomic energy to peaceful means — part of the silver lining. He recalls thinking the employment would be temporary. He put aside whatever feelings he had about the loss of the school and signed on with the scientists who had displaced his family.

If you can't beat 'em, join 'em.

They offered him a choice of working at the Los Alamos lab or at the newer branch of the lab in Albuquerque, called Sandia. He picked Sandia.

"I chose not to go back to where my home had been. It was so different. It was not the place we called home."

Ted stayed at his "temporary" job at Sandia until he retired in 1990, at the age of sixty-five. He started off working on the electronics of radars and microwaves, miniaturizing circuits. As bombs grew more powerful, they also shrank because their insides got tiny. Ted led the electronics program until 1969, then oversaw product testing equipment, and in 1975 took charge of the flight instruments department — telemetry. Seven years later, he shifted gears from trying to deliver bombs to trying to make them safer. He was put in charge of mechanical testing — shaking and shocking weapons to scrutinize their construction and design. "You make it, we break it," Ted said. In 1987, he initiated a program to search out hazards at Sandia. "They wanted someone who knew where all the ghosts and skeletons were, or could find out," he said.

The switch to the safety side of weapons, although not sought out, was welcome. In 1970, Ted had formally become a Quaker, although he and his wife had been attending Friends' meetings for eighteen years. His parents were doing some work with the Quakers in Santa Fe, although the family had grown up Episcopalian. Quakers have a pacifist religion, and for someone making nuclear weapons, that can pose an ethical dilemma. Being accepted by the Albuquerque Friends Meeting took a lot of understanding.

"Some folks always had a problem with me and what I do — what they think I do," Ted said. "Friends have a saying, though: Better to be in the world than out of it."

The perception on the outside of a weapons lab can be that of a secret hideaway filled with crazed Dr. Strangelove warmongers hankering to see mushroom clouds. That's not the reality. Soul searching goes on inside the labs: Are we doing the right thing? How can we make these things safer? Ted's Quaker faith forces him to respond to the real world: Nuclear weapons are here. What can I do to help? Can I help make them safer? Can I help ensure they'll never be used? Better to be in the world than out of it.

"I think there was a recognition on my part that getting the world to peace is much more complicated than other people think. . . . There were times when Friends were asking if I'd leave [Sandia], and I'd think: Well, if I were to leave, somebody else would come along. Being a Friend, it might be helpful for me to stay and make a long-term contribution. Not necessarily in making changes today in what the lab does, but maybe in the philosophy — conveying values that I, as a Friend, have. . . .

"As long as nuclear weapons exist, they demand a response from me. Many engineers and scientists just say, 'It's up to the politicians.' But I feel engineers and scientists have a responsibility to help the public understand."

Allen joined Ted at Sandia after the Korean War. He began with the "power supply group" — those were the days when high tech meant transistors, not computer-chip circuits. For a while, he and Ted worked together. Now he supervises a group in the arming and firing systems division at Sandia. When there's a new warhead idea to test, a weapon to check, Allen provides the hardware and system to fire it. His people are the ones that hook up the tests underground in Nevada.

Allen the pragmatist complains about environmental and safety regulations that, sometimes with a good deal of absurdity, require labeling of minute pieces of toxic substances, like tritium, and transportation of tiny parts by certified hazardous substance carriers. While his brothers may wrestle more with the moral questions of their work, Allen the realist shrugs. "People say, 'What about all those crazy people who work with nuclear weapons?' I say we're not crazy. I find people here to be very sincere; they take it with a great deal of responsibility. I'd rather be a part of it than leave it to someone else."

Hugh, the youngest Church son, graduated from Taos High School in 1950. He had polio his senior year (he still walks with a limp) and enrolled at the University of New Mexico, where he studied physics and meteorology. From there, he earned a master's at UCLA in meteorology, got married, and joined the United States Weather Bureau, now the National Weather Service, in Washington, D.C., in 1956.

"I always thought I'd like to work outdoors, to be a rancher. But my physical handicap prevented that," he said.

As it was with all the others, the magnetic, emotional attachment of New Mexico beckoned. In 1957, he joined Sandia, which by now had four thousand employees and was deeply involved in testing nuclear weapons in Nevada and in the Pacific. Weather forecasting had become a vital part of the tests for predicting and minimizing the fallout and blast effects. Hugh shuttled between tests in Nevada and the Pacific, until treaties banned atmospheric tests and forced the blasts underground. It looked like a meteorologist's job might disappear underground as well, but Hugh became involved in aerospace nuclear safety work — Apollo 13 had a nuclear power supply. Lately Hugh has gotten more involved in studying the characteristics of particles in the atmosphere — how beams of light, or infrared rays, are transmitted. That's a crucial factor in Star Wars systems, missile guidance, and detonation monitoring. And Hugh has been involved in ozone studies and air pollution, as well as working with the Defense Nuclear Agency on "nuclear winter" — a possible consequence of nuclear war in which smoke from weapons blasts and fires would encircle the earth and block out much of the sun's energy.

"I thought a lot about whether I wanted to work on nuclear weapons programs," Hugh said. "You wonder why you have to be working with weapons of destruction when there's so much else to do out there. But I believe the deterrence aspect has kept us out of war for so long. You make every effort to make sure things aren't used in the wrong way. And there's comfort in having somebody even-tempered handling it.

"We all go through these questions. I wrote to Ted when I was considering working here and said, 'Hey, how do you feel about it?' He said, 'You have to wrestle with that yourself.' He wasn't going to tell me what to do."

Like Allen, Hugh mixes his hobby and his profession. For six years he was the chairman of the Albuquerque-Bernalillo County Air Quality Control Board, which sets policy for a strict vehicle inspection and maintenance program, and a ban on fireplace and stove wood-burning on some winter nights. The combination of weather patterns, mountains, fireplaces, and hundreds of thousands of cars and people can leave a brown smog over Albuquerque. Under Hugh, the board began requiring gas stations to sell oxygenated fuels — which are spiked with ethanol or similar additives so that the gas burns cleaner — during the winter months, when the brown smog is worst.

"I'm always interested in what the air does," Hugh said.

So the environmentalist-scientist finds himself working on pollution problems while at Sandia — adopting the Quaker attitude of being in the real world, working on the real problems. He notes that his work at Sandia doesn't contribute to making bombs. He believes Ted's shift to safety-related issues, away from electronics and the actual wiring of the bombs, was a response to his religious faith and his beliefs.

The pacifist-scientist, the environmentalist-scientist, both dealing with the real world in their own real way.

"Was that his way of resolving the conflict? I think so," Hugh said of his brother. "And for myself, I don't directly work on weapons — I do meteorology."

Hugh's son wears his hair long and his ideals on his sleeve, Hugh said. He has worked for a public information research consumer group, has studied graduate-level physics, and is participating in a joint U.S.-Soviet astrophysics project at Columbia University. He loves physics, Hugh said, but swears he'd never join a nuclear weapons laboratory.

"It's OK to be an idealist — like my son. But you also have to be a realist," Hugh said. "The questions when working with any weapons are always difficult. But that's where the jobs are."

Peggy Pond Church was an idealist too. As a little girl on the Pajarito Plateau she had run wild through the woods, riding horses into the mountains and befriending Indians. Once, she buried her childhood treasures in a secret hole. An arrowhead. Some beads. But the child's link to the land was severed when her life became intertwined with that of another, Oppenheimer, who had also cherished youthful memories of the land, the place artist Georgia O'Keeffe once called "the Far Away — a beautiful, untouched lonely-feeling place." Peggy never could go back to retrieve her treasures. Los Alamos had become too ugly, she said.

Instead, she became one of New Mexico's most celebrated poets. Although not an activist, she wrote of her opposition to nuclear weapons and nuclear work. And she hated Los Alamos for what it stood for and for what it had done to her family.

Peggy had written poetry since 1933 — the year her father died. At Los Alamos, she had a tiny cabin with a view of a gorgeous canyon, where she created her poems. With her home lost to the nuclear age and her husband stringing power lines across the Southwest, Peggy lived in Taos, Berkeley, and Santa Fe, and stepped up her writing. She wrote and wrote, in journal after journal. They were romantic poems about the wilderness she grew up in and the changes that had come to her land. They were loving and caring, sweet and simple. She ended one poem in memory of her husband with this:

The sound of the wind in the pines was always
your favorite music.
As we scattered your ashes the wind lifted
some of them in a light cloud;
the rest mingled instantly with the weathered fragments
of volcanic ash at the cliff's base.
On the way down among the anonymous grasses
one of us found an arrowhead,
obsidian, perfect in shape,
a word joining then with now
and all our own past with forever.

Peggy was an insecure writer who would put away a poem after one rejection notice and never pursue its publication again. But many of her verses were accepted. Peggy's poems were published in the *Atlantic Monthly* and the *Saturday Review*. She had eight collections published, and in 1984, at the age of eighty-one, she received the New Mexico Governor's Award for excellence and achievement in literature and was named a "living treasure."

Beyond the beauty of New Mexico and its people, ancient and contemporary, Peggy Pond Church used her poems to vent her rage at the nuclear age. Her verses point out some of the problems she had with physics and science coming to

New Mexico, with the militarization of New Mexico. She said she never drove past the high security fences of Los Alamos without tears in her eyes. She used to tell friends that she wished the volcano that created the Los Alamos mesa would erupt again. She wrote in *The House at Otowi Bridge,* her loving book about Edith Warner and her teahouse near Los Alamos, about how she felt at Christmas the year of the bombing of Hiroshima and Nagasaki:

> *I could hardly bear to think that such destruction had been rooted in the heart of our once sacred world, that the man who put the bomb together just before it was dropped over Hiroshima had lived for a while in my own house where the wisteria still flowered against the window and the apricot trees I planted when my children were tiny had only just begun to bear fruit. Whenever I went to the little house by the river I found myself pouring forth streams of condemnation against those who had usurped our places on the plateau.*

In another poem called "Endangered Species," she wrote:

> *The weapons he has invented must destroy him.*
> *Out of each violated atom he himself shall let loose*
> *the fire of his own annihilation.*

So it was with great irony that Peggy Pond Church's sons grew up to carry on the work of Oppenheimer and the scientists on the mesa. "Little did I dream," she wrote, ". . . that all three of my sons would find their life work in fields connected with atomic energy. . . . I suppose no generation has grown up to live in a world so changed from that of their own childhood."

87

Her sons say their chosen careers caused Peggy Pond Church a great deal of distress, although she grew to accept their involvement. She possessed that rare combination: a poetic soul tempered by a good dose of common sense. She was feisty, outspoken, and uncompromising, but she mitigated her antinuclear sentiments out of respect for her sons' positions, and she didn't take part in protests, although those who knew her had no doubt that she wanted to be more active. When the boys would discuss their work, it was never in the context of weapons, but always electronics or meteorology.

"Sort of deep down inside, maybe we knew she was right. She had an idealist's approach, but it's a real world," Hugh said.

"It distressed her highly, the fact that we all ended up working in the military-industrial complex," he added. "In deference to us, she was not an active antinuke. Clearances have been revoked for stranger things."

Said Ted: "She would blurt out that her sons work at the bomb factory. We'd say we don't produce a thing."

Perhaps it was fate that Peggy Pond Church became friends with a neighbor she had run into at the end of Camino Rancheros in the hills of Santa Fe. Perhaps such friendship might not have been possible had Peggy not come to accept the inevitable in this part of the country. The woman was French, Françoise Ulam, the wife of mathematician Stanislaw Ulam. Stan and Françoise had been among the first landing party of Manhattan Project scientists after Peggy was evicted from her home, and it was Stan who, with Edward Teller, cracked the secret of the more powerful hydrogen bomb that is still built along what is known as the Teller-Ulam configuration. Perhaps once the women might have been enemies, but, widowed, they became friends. They would converse at the grocery store, attend Santa Fe parties, live the life of intellectuals in a community of artists and scientists, including Georgia O'Keeffe.

"She was terribly distressed and distraught about what had been done to her territory," Françoise said. "At first, she didn't like those awful people who had destroyed her school and her land. But from getting to know some of the people, she realized it wasn't a question of black and white, good and evil. She admitted she liked some of the people at Los Alamos. . . . There were definitely barriers because of the history, the intrusion of the physicists, and also the moral scruples, I suppose."

While they didn't agree with her views of nuclear weapons, Peggy's sons did share the family's sense of loss at being evictees. Today, the Churches still lament the loss of the school, still consider themselves victims of the war effort, still complain about family furnishings and collections never returned, and wonder what life might have been like had Oppenheimer never seen their land. They've gotten over whatever bitterness there was, they say; time and the passing of generations tend to dull emotions. There was never any possibility of getting Los Alamos back after the war, they note, because the lab clearly had to be made permanent. The name Los Alamos now stood in history as one of destruction and annihilation, and the beautiful mesa was now a bulldozed mess of barracks and laboratories.

"After they raped it, who wants it back?" Hugh said.

"We were displaced persons just like the refugees in Europe," Peggy said in a 1985 interview. "We didn't know what to do, where to go; my husband had lost his life's work. This man with an engineering degree from Harvard wound up building power lines all over New Mexico, never to teach again. . . . I try not to sit in judgment on the world. But I don't go back to Los Alamos now because it's so ugly I can't stand it."

The Church family embodies the conflicts of America's Nuclear Highway. Ferm and Peggy the idealists; their sons the realists. It's the same struggle — ideals versus reality — that many of the Manhattan Project scientists debated among themselves. Even Oppenheimer wrestled with it. It carries through arguments over the arms race, over nuclear weapons treaties, and now over the Strategic Defense Initiative, Star Wars. Do we strive for the ideal, or do we deal with the reality? Why can't the two coexist? Why must we choose sides?

Toward the end of her life, Peggy grew more and more reclusive. Always a rugged outdoorswoman who ordered clothes from L. L. Bean and captured rainwater to reuse it, she grew frail and complained about her health. Her eyesight diminished, making reading and writing difficult. She wanted to donate the family photo albums to the Los Alamos Historical Society, and she seemed in a hurry. Hedy Dunn, the director of the historical society and a friend, said Peggy kept pestering her to come get the albums.

"She wanted to clear the decks," Hedy said.

Frustrated by her failing health, a virtual prisoner in her own house, Peggy Pond Church typed up her own obituary. A member of the Hemlock Society, she took her life at age eighty-two.

"It has long been my belief that in old age when the body fails we should be permitted to lay it down at a time of our own choosing and allow the spirit to go free. To a poet death is another phase of life. . . . Those who know my books will know I have already said all there is to say."

5

LOS ALAMOS LOST

In some sort of crude sense which no vulgarity, no humor, no overstatement can quite extinguish, the physicists have known sin.

J. ROBERT OPPENHEIMER, *November 25, 1947*

The road to Los Alamos off I-25 skirts the center of Santa Fe, then follows an ancient trail across the Rio Grande and up the steep face of the mesa. It's the same trail the pueblo Indians used, the same trail the Spanish used, the same trail Ashley Pond used, the same trail J. Robert Oppenheimer used. Roads are better now. Pavement came in years ago, and now the route is under construction again. Widening, rebuilding, improving. Bigger trucks, more cars, more people clamoring to get to the top of the hill.

Commuters to the million-year-old mountain 7,300 feet above sea level whiz along now, making in forty-five minutes a trip that used to take hours, if the radiator didn't boil over and all the tires held. Drivers cross the river in White Rock Canyon and zoom through a curious place in history without a second glance. Parallel to the four-lane speed bridge is an abandoned one-lane trestle spanning 150 feet across the shallow Rio Grande. It's the Otowi Bridge, what's left of it. Boards have fallen in the water; weeds and bushes block both ends. Once that rickety span was the gateway to Los Alamos, to the scientists and their secrets. In those days, Edith Warner, the Otowi railroad station mistress, lived at the bridge and ran a tearoom. Over coffee and cake there, many Manhattan Project geniuses found refuge from their awesome task. But the restaurant was demolished to build the wide modern bridge. The old road that conveyed so much history, that provided the path for the first atomic bomb to leave the mesa and change the world, was abandoned and left to rot away.

Along the new road, protesters from Santa Fe, the center of the small but vocal antinuke community in New Mexico, have sprayed fluorescent orange messages to the commuters. Concrete barriers lining the road warn DOE KILLS, referring to the Department of Energy, which oversees the national laboratories and nuclear weapons research and production. The vandalism detracts from the natural beauty along the thirty-five-mile drive to Los Alamos. But so do the concrete barriers, the multilane roads, the compact cars zipping to the labs. Nature's gifts — the rich blue skies and ten-thousand-foot peaks that have lured artists to New Mexico for centuries — clash with man's gift: concrete and graffiti. They symbolize how the scientific work that draws men and roads and protesters has tampered with nature in this slice of the country.

It's not as difficult to get to Los Alamos as it once was, but even the drive up the new road is tough — steep, winding, sometimes slow even for the sports cars driven by pony-tailed Ph.D.s. Los Alamos's seclusion was always its allure. That's why the Tewa Indians settled atop the mesa in the fourteenth century. (The Tewas were eventually expelled by European invaders. Their descendants still live below the mesa in the San Ildefonso area.) The mesa was a tough place to reach, an easy place to protect. That's why Ashley Pond, seduced by the seclusion, the security, and the magnificent landscape, put his school there. That's why Oppenheimer and the U.S. Army seized it for their clandestine laboratory. Some land is prized because it has water, valuable minerals, access to oceans, or sacred symbolism. The Pajarito Plateau had almost no water, few resources, and little significance. But it was fiercely fought for down through the centuries because of its strategic significance: it was safe.

When the Army moved in with its trucks and ditchdiggers, only the fifty-four ranch school buildings — half of them houses — were at Los Alamos. A few top Manhattan Project recruits moved into faculty housing, but most early arrivals bunked at neighboring ranches (putting them in Santa Fe was considered a security risk). They were scattered on the flatland below the mesa, and life there was hard, especially in the winter. Commuting was a bumpy, time-consuming hardship. From the start, Los Alamos had a housing shortage, a problem as serious as getting good labs and an adequate water supply. Oppenheimer initially suggested that the ranch school offered instant housing for the thirty or so scientists he guessed he needed. His estimates proved to be ridiculously low, so the Army set out to build housing for three hundred. But even before the ranch school students departed, construction crews had swelled the population to a small town of fifteen hundred.

The crews quickly erected quadriplex apartments in early 1943. The second wave of recruits got somewhat better accommodations, in what were known as Sundt Apartments. They were named for the construction firm that put them up, M. M. Sundt Company, and notable for their lack of heat. (None of the original Sundts are left at Los Alamos, but some younger siblings, "Latter-Day Sundts," are still used.) That first spring, major pieces of borrowed equipment — items such as a cyclotron from Harvard and two Van De Graaff generators from the University of Wisconsin — were installed at Los Alamos, and research began in earnest.

The people who went to Los Alamos disappeared into a post office box. Their official address was P.O. Box 1663, Santa Fe, N.M., a stealth address. More than a hundred children were born with P.O. Box 1663 as their place of birth. Few visitors reached the mesa, and trips to Santa Fe were strictly regulated by the military, which controlled the road and kept vehicles in a guarded motor pool. Those denied the shopping trips relied on hundreds of catalogs that came addressed to residents of P.O. Box 1663. Those lucky enough for furloughs in Santa Fe, when asked where they were from, invariably answered: "Post Office Box 1663." The responses always drew peculiar glances.

The mesa technical areas were ringed with barbed wire. The road was sealed by a guard tower. Agents patrolled with dogs. Outgoing mail was censored by military specialists. Army security agents worked as bartenders at La Fonda Hotel in Santa Fe, eavesdropping on any loose lips. (Despite all the security, two spies — Klaus Fuchs and David Greenglass — were passing secrets to the Russians through Santa Fe, but the Army didn't uncover them until 1950. Their spy-ring contacts were alleged to be Ethel and Julius Rosenberg, who were executed for treason in 1953.) Famous names were disguised and occupations were never mentioned — everyone was an engineer. "Henry Farmer" was really Nobel Prize–winner Enrico Fermi, an Italian physicist who initiated the first atomic chain reaction. Niels Bohr, a Danish scientist and another Nobel Prize winner, became "Nicholas Baker." Recruiting support staff was difficult because nonscientific workers were asked to depart for an unknown place for an unknown purpose. Families and friends had to be kept in the dark about the recruits' whereabouts. P.O. Box 1663 — that's where they were.

Los Alamos still uses that same box number.

New arrivals reported to 109 East Palace Avenue in Santa Fe, the project's office. (It is now a curio shop catering to coyote-crazy tourists.) They were greeted by Dorothy McKibbin, who became a friend and confidante to many of the most famous Manhattan Project participant/prisoners. As Santa Fe office manager, Mrs. McKibbin, the single parent of a young son, calmed nervous and wary travelers, issued security passes, and made sure everyone and everything got to its proper place. She was the front door of the Manhattan Project, the tenuous connection to the outside world. Twenty-seven couples were married in the living room of her old adobe house beside the Santa Fe Trail.

Fuller Lodge, the glorious three-story log building constructed for the ranch school in 1924, became the project's mess hall, and its classrooms were converted to a PX and other shops. On the south side of a pond, named none other than Ashley Pond by the ranch school, green laboratory buildings sprouted. Roads were nameless and unpaved. Buildings were thrown together as "temporary" structures. There was only one telephone line when the project began in 1943, courtesy of the U.S. Forest Service; there were three by 1945. All long-distance calls were monitored. An infirmary handled the sick until a hospital was established in 1944, and a dentist arrived that year, along with a laundry and cleaning concession. The living was primitive — sometimes water got so low that residents had to check the level in the wooden water tank near Fuller Lodge before turning on the shower. Families fought over maids; some items were in short supply, like diapers and children's clothes.

There was a dichotomy in some of the hardships — the choices are almost never simple at Los Alamos. Scientists wanted better roads up the mesa, for example, but the distrusting General Groves, the Army's man in charge, liked the treacherous conditions because they discouraged travel. Highways were improved as it became more difficult to move equipment and supplies safely up the hill. But the few phone lines off the mesa were never augmented by extras; it made it easier for the Army to monitor calls.

Relations between the scientists and the Army were uneasy. The Army had wanted the civilians commissioned into its ranks, but they balked, insisting on "scientific autonomy." Oppenheimer fought for an open scientific community, where data and discoveries would be shared with colleagues — a university-like atmosphere with the academic freedom the bomb builders were accustomed to. Groves wanted none of that. He believed limiting access to information made it easier to protect that information. Oppenheimer won. Los Alamos had weekly colloquiums to pass along progress and ponderings among the scientists. But Oppenheimer, a master at organization and motivation in the laboratory, increasingly found himself battling the bureaucracy, a situation partially attributable to typical Army red tape, only exaggerated by security concerns. In one snide memo, Oppenheimer fought hard to requisition one nail, to be used on a wall in the director's office for a place to hang his soon-to-be-famous porkpie hat. In the end, he won his battle and got his nail. "They didn't know how to handle civilians," scientist Raemer Schreiber said in an interview, "and we didn't know how to get along with the Army."

The other major complaints were over the low salaries doled out to some of the world's greatest minds, who had given up outstanding academic positions to shiver and suffer on a hidden mesa in northern New Mexico, working on a world-changing project from 7:30 A.M. until late in the evening six and seven days a week. One scientist pointed out to Oppenheimer at a meeting that plumbers got paid more than physicists — three times more. Oppenheimer, with a wit so quick and a tongue so tart that his remarks offended many, could always put the question in proper perspective with a single sentence. (When asked once why he didn't continue with nuclear weapons work after the war, he replied, "You can only fry an omelet once.") This time, Oppenheimer simply told his underpaid charges that plumbers did not know the importance of the project they were all working on; the scientists did.

That's what made the Manhattan Project succeed. The hardships strengthened the sense of urgency to create a weapon able to win a war that already had raged in Europe for three years. As Oppenheimer and Groves set about creating a small city atop the mesa, Japan was battling U.S. forces island by island in the Pacific. Hitler won a string of conquests in the first two years of the war, and by 1943 the Germans occupied most of Eastern Europe and France. For many of the scientists at Los Alamos, the war was a personal tragedy. Some were Jews who subsequently lost whole families in the Holocaust. A large number were refugees from their native lands who fled to Britain and America to escape the Nazis. So as work began at Los Alamos — work they believed had to turn the tide, and turn it before the Germans unlocked the nuclear secret — the scientists had a sense that they could finally strike back. There was an amazing collection of brilliant minds, some drawn by the fight against the Nazis, some by the excitement of their colleagues, some by their own consciences or curiosity, and most inspired by the dynamic Oppenheimer. Atop the mesa, there was an excitement that could be tasted, could be worn. Everybody there shared the anticipation of being one of the chosen few to witness the creation of a new world. As Schreiber said: "It was a magnificent opportunity to do something very important."

"The morale of the fellows was not high for the first few

97

months, naturally, but after that it rose, and I have never seen such *esprit de corps* in a scientific group. It has been a real pleasure to watch this particular set of fellows mature into the competent physicists they now are," Robert R. Wilson wrote to Princeton colleague H. D. Smyth on November 27, 1943.

The project had its disappointments as well as its eurekas. Three types of bombs were considered. One was a uranium gun that would shoot one plug of enriched uranium into another to cause the chain reaction that splits atoms, liberating the incredible energy that binds the atom together. The second was a plutonium gun, which worked on the same theory. And the third was an "implosion device": instead of smashing two pieces of material together, a sphere of explosives would be set off around one lump of plutonium, compressing it and forcing the chain reaction and the nuclear explosion. The idea of implosion was first proposed by thirty-six-year-old Seth Neddermeyer, an experimental physicist.

From the start, the scientists were most confident that the uranium gun would work, but they were intrigued by the potential for more power from the other two. In fact, Wilson noted in a 1984 oral history with Los Alamos lab staff that the necessary physics to make the uranium gun bomb was known even before 1943. But the implosion idea, thought by some to be a better bet for a nuclear bomb anyway, presented a complicated, challenging physics problem. It was too good to pass up.

The fascination with bigger booms goes back long before the Manhattan Project, long before the nuclear arms race. Through the ages, man has always wanted the biggest stick, or sword, or cannon, or rocket, or bomb, or nuclear bomb, or thermonuclear bomb, or cruise missile, or space laser. What runner doesn't want to go faster? What physicist doesn't want to push the envelope with new discoveries? The Manhattan

Project was not all that different, and Los Alamos is no different today.

In time, the scientists decided to focus their work on the uranium gun and plutonium implosion ideas. Oppenheimer also discarded a theory Edward Teller presented for a super-bomb — a thermonuclear bomb in which one nuclear explosion would be used to set off an exponentially more powerful explosion. Such a bomb might be capable of devastating wide, wide areas, Teller said. But Oppenheimer gave the super-bomb a low priority because it would take more time. America needed a bomb to use against the Germans and the Japanese, and it needed it fast.

Work continued on the plutonium implosion idea, but the tough part was getting the perfect sphere of explosives, and getting it to go off just right. Predictions were that a plutonium core that collapsed inward would be more efficient and produce a bigger blast using less of the precious material, which was in very short supply. Technically, it would be a better bomb — if it worked. But each part of the sphere surrounding the plutonium had to explode at the correct instant, with exactly the right force, so that the explosive force would go inward — not outward — and the plutonium would be uniformly compressed. It was an engineering riddle: how could you manufacture a hollowed-out basketball of explosives and get it to explode toward its center? When the explosives riddle was solved, they were ready for the Trinity test.

Confidence was high among the scientists. But in keeping with a kind of intellectual black humor that pervaded the Manhattan Project, this verse was making the rounds shortly before Trinity:

> *From this crude lab that spawned a dud,*
> *Their necks to Truman's ax uncurled,*

99

Lo, the embattled savants stood
And fired the flop heard round the world.

Scientist Joseph McKibben, who with Kenneth Bainbridge and George Kistiakowsky had spent the night sleeping under the Trinity plutonium implosion bomb to "guard" it, threw the final switch and then had to run out from his bunker to throw some other switches ten seconds after the explosion. It was no flop, and McKibben says he knew instantly that the war was over.

"I knew we had two other bombs, and I felt sure we would use them and they would bring the war to an end. It was obvious that was what was going to happen," McKibben said.

Confidence in the uranium gun bomb was so high that it was never tested. It had already been shipped in pieces out of Kirtland Air Force Base in Albuquerque to the South Pacific. Known as "Little Boy" — it was thought by some to have been nicknamed for the slender Oppenheimer — it was a $10\frac{1}{2}$-foot-long cannon almost $2\frac{1}{2}$ feet in diameter, which shot a bullet of uranium into three rings of uranium in the nose. It weighed 9,700 pounds. After Trinity, the nuclear components of the "Fat Man" plutonium bomb, a shorter, rotund bomb said to have been nicknamed for the rather beefy General Groves, were sent over the Otowi Bridge, through Santa Fe to Albuquerque, then to Tinian in the South Pacific, where they caught up with the casings and other parts.

Back at Los Alamos, scientist Leo Szilard circulated a petition protesting the bomb's impending use. Colleagues had argued for a demonstration that would shock the Japanese into surrender. But the military was not convinced that such a show of force would work, and a dud would be a great morale boost to the enemy. Edward Teller, the co-inventor of the hydrogen bomb and later a major architect of Star Wars, delivered a rationale to Szilard in a tart letter that prophetically laid out U.S. strategy through the long Cold War.

First of all let me say that I have no hope of clearing my conscience. The things we are working on are so terrible that no amount of protesting or fiddling with politics will save our souls. . . .

But I am not really convinced of your objections. I do not feel that there is any chance to outlaw any one weapon. If we have a slim chance of survival, it lies in the possibility to get rid of wars. The more decisive the weapon is the more surely it will be used in any real conflicts and no arguments will help.

Our only hope is in getting the facts of our results before the people. This might help convince everybody that the next war would be fatal. For this purpose actual combat-use might even be the best thing.

. . . I feel I should do the wrong thing if I tried to say how to tie the little toe of the ghost to the bottle from which we just helped it to escape.

There were other reasons, of course, to use the bomb. Hundreds of thousands of U.S. troops were waiting in the South Pacific to invade Japan. Even if that assault was successful, it would have involved a slaughter of atomic proportions. And, inevitably, there had to be justification for spending $2 billion on the atom bomb program. Many scientists at Los Alamos came to believe that dropping both types of bombs was an administrative decision rather than a military necessity.

Oppenheimer, who uttered his famous quotation from the Hindu scripture *Bhagavad Gita,* "Now I am become Death, the destroyer of worlds," upon the Trinity explosion, personally argued for restraint. Groves fired off a terse reply to an Oppenheimer message sent three days after Trinity.

Dear Dr. Oppenheimer: I have received your teletype dtd [dated] July 19, 1945, and have discussed its contents with some of our Washington associates. Factors beyond our control prevent us from considering any decision other than to proceed according to existing schedules for the time being.

It is necessary to drop the first Little Boy and the first Fat Man and probably a second one in accordance with our original plan. It may be that as many as three of the latter in their best present condition may have to be dropped to conform with planned strategic operations.

On August 6, 1945, the untested Little Boy uranium gun bomb was dropped on Hiroshima, causing an explosion with a force equal to 13,000 tons of dynamite. (Today's thermonuclear weapons make Little Boy seem like little more than a Saturday Night Special. Then again, today's most powerful conventional bomb packs the punch of only 5 tons of TNT.) The temperature at the site of the explosion was estimated at 5,400 degrees. Victims were burned up to two miles away. Estimates of deaths, although they have never been conclusive, total more than 200,000. Of 76,000 buildings in the city, 48,000, or 63 percent, were totally destroyed. Only 6,000 escaped damage.

Three days later, Fat Man, the Trinity copy, was dropped on Nagasaki. It was as big as a one-person underwater diving bell, about five feet tall, with an explosive yield later estimated at 22,000 tons of TNT. The steep hills of the city confined the larger explosion, so Fat Man actually caused less death and destruction than Little Boy. Total deaths were estimated at 140,000.

Japan had not yet agreed to U.S. surrender terms, and on August 10, the day after Nagasaki, Groves reported that he had a third bomb — the second Fat Man — ready to leave New Mexico August 12 or 13. But President Truman ordered the bombing stopped. On August 14, Japan gave up.

Whether two bombs were needed has been one of the imponderables. Looking back, was it necessary to build the implosion bomb? Once built, did it have to be used? What would have happened if the Manhattan Project had stuck to the uranium gun only? Would the United States have had the bomb a year earlier? Robert Wilson said in his oral history that questions such as those have always bothered his conscience.

. . . Had we made a bomb sooner, you know, that would have saved — that really would have saved millions of lives. It's a terrible thing to think about, but, whenever I have a guilty conscience, my one is for having worked on a bomb that killed so many people, but the other is that I worked on a project that didn't kill enough people soon enough. It could have saved millions. Literally millions. A year earlier, and although those invasions of Tinian and all those expensive things, the Japanese that were killed, the Germans that were killed, the Jews that were killed. It just boggles your mind. Had we been more alert, had we concentrated more, and decided not to do the plutonium, and concentrate on one thing, we might have done it faster.

Question: Just gone right out on with the gun?

Wilson: Well, that's Monday morning quarterbacking, of course. But, I do have a conscience, sometimes, and usually a bad conscience, and I had it during the war because we weren't working hard enough. And we were working like people obsessed.

What happened next was crucial, not only to the future of Los Alamos but also to the future nuclear arms race and to history for the next fifty years. Los Alamos originally was established as a temporary community. Once the war was over, it was no longer needed, so top physicists began making plans to return to their universities. Oppenheimer's office aided in job placement. It was time to move on. The work was done. Some denounced what they had done, saying that to a scientist, one of the great tragedies is when such a monumental, historic, brilliant breakthrough — an entirely new understanding of nature, with endless potential — results in mass mutilation, death, and destruction. Oppenheimer said the physicists had known sin. He felt the scientific Shangri-la had become the Devil's Den, the curse of Los Alamos. Now there were other omelets to fry, ones that didn't reduce the creators and explorers to tears at the thought of what they had done.

But the Army wasn't sure it was finished with Japan when the surrender came, and the world was still a turbulent, dangerous place. So a stockpile of bombs was needed. And since improvements could be made in the size of the boom as well as in the safety of handling the bomb, work proceeded on nuclear weapons at Los Alamos. A debate began in Washington over who would oversee atomic research, capabilities, and weapons. Debates in Washington are never measured in milliseconds or microseconds; there was no immediate answer. No one seized the day, so Groves and the Army said: "Carry on."

Oppenheimer, a strong voice for international control of nuclear weapons, urged his staff to scale down. But he also recognized that they would not disappear altogether. He wanted out of the bomb-making business and thought manufacturing should be transferred to the government or private industry, not to civilian scientists or the University of California at Berkeley, which has been the contractor that operates Los Alamos for the government since the war. On August 20, 1945, just a few days after the end of the war, Oppenheimer issued a memo to division and group leaders, saying that the lab should slow down but not stop. "No steps should be taken which commit the Government of the United States to an abandonment of work on adequate weapons, or to a 'crash' development thereof," Oppenheimer said.

The lab was in turmoil. Scientists wanted out; General Groves insisted that everything continue as before. "My own frank opinion is that it is truly unrealistic to 'carry on as usual' as the General wishes," Kistiakowsky said in a September 4, 1945, memo to Oppenheimer. "Could it be explained to him that the result of this policy will be a complete disintegration of the Project in the course of the next few months (not that I object to it, but I feel that he ought to appreciate the situation)?"

Like most of the senior scientists, Oppenheimer resigned his Los Alamos position; he would return to Berkeley. On his last day, November 16, 1945, Oppenheimer accepted from Groves a scroll of appreciation to the men and women of Los Alamos. He was as blunt as always in his acceptance speech, tempering the festive occasion with a "profound concern" and reiterating his call for control of nuclear weapons and for a united world. "If atomic bombs are to be added as new weapons to the arsenals of a warring world, or to the arsenals of the nations preparing for war," he said, "then the time will come when mankind will curse the names of Los Alamos and Hiroshima."

With the future of the lab in doubt, Norris Bradbury, one of the remaining senior scientists, took over as director. Struggling to maintain a quality staff and wrestling with the uncertainty of Los Alamos's future and its role in the nation's defense posture, Bradbury turned to Groves for direction. On January 4, 1946, a major general whose expertise was in construction, whose claim to fame before the Manhattan Project was that he had helped build the Pentagon, laid out U.S. nuclear policy in his own letter to Bradbury.

> . . . *Unfortunately, no legislation has been passed, and certain forces are at work the effect of which has been to delay any legislative program.*
>
> *It has therefore become necessary for me to make definite plans, despite the fact that this will commit to some extent at least any future control body. Our wartime effort was to end the war. Everything was sacrificed to that objective. We counted on suitable legislation being passed promptly at the end of the war. We should not count on atomic bomb development being stopped in the foreseeable future.*
>
> *The Los Alamos site must remain active for a considerable period. . . .*

The decision was made by default, perhaps because there was never a chance to stop a nuclear arms race, to put the genie back in the bottle, or, as Teller said, to tie the little toe of the ghost. And perhaps Oppenheimer and the others were wrong. Perhaps weapons capable of obliterating a city in seconds helped to maintain greater world order, kept the Cold War cold, and eventually resulted in the era of George Bush and Mikhail Gorbachev. That's the trouble with the work at Los Alamos: the question that nagged at those pioneers in 1945 remains today. Some of us come home from work wondering if we served a client well, or did our best with a malcontented employee, or got the bricks straight on the wall. At Los Alamos, scientists wonder if their efforts will help save the world. Or destroy it.

As Los Alamos carried on, work began on bigger and more efficient implosion bombs, and the "Super," Teller's dream of a thermonuclear device that would use the energy of a plutonium implosion bomb to fuse atoms together and release incredible energy rather than merely splitting atoms apart. At the time, there was little debate whether pursuing the Super meant escalation of the infant nuclear arms race. Another decision by default. Bradbury needed challenging projects to retain good scientists. He even talked about additional Trinity tests to try out new ideas—beyond the scientific implications, such explosions might be fun for the workers.

The world kept changing, dashing whatever hopes there were among the scientists of keeping the genie restrained. The Soviets seized control of Czechoslovakia in the winter of 1948, and Communists maneuvered into power in Hungary. Berlin was blockaded the following summer. Communist forces won out over Nationalists in China in 1949. The Soviets exploded their first atomic bomb in the summer of 1949—nicknamed "Joe I," after Russian premier Joseph Stalin. Within a month, the U.S. stepped up production of uranium and plutonium. Policymakers forged ahead with the hydrogen bomb. On January 31, 1950, Truman announced in favor of proceeding with its development. *The New York Times* that year published a booklet called "We Are Not Helpless, How We Can Defend Ourselves Against Atomic Weapons." It cost ten cents and included a guide to recognizing a nuclear blast, along with a map of destruction if a bomb was dropped on top of City Hall in downtown Manhattan. Fallout shelters were identified in towns across the country.

Los Alamos could hardly be considered temporary now. In fact, the newly established Atomic Energy Commission affirmed the course Groves had laid out. In 1948, it decided to drop questions of abandoning Los Alamos, and by 1951, a building program totaling more than $100 million was under way. What army ever retreats?

The work at Los Alamos has not been without its hometown tragedies. By the end of 1946, thirteen workers had died—seven of them from construction accidents, one from a smudge pot explosion, and three from accidentally drinking chemicals. There were also two radiation deaths—prominent scientists killed when experiments went awry.

Harry Daghlian was working alone the evening of August 21, 1945, just a week after the end of the war, when he accidentally dropped a block of tamper material used to reflect neutrons into the nuclear assembly. The block fell on an almost complete assembly, and the plutonium "went critical" at once, starting the chain reaction and giving off intense amounts of blue radiation. Daghlian died less than a month later.

On May 21, 1946, Louis Slotin, the leader of the critical-assemblies group, was standing next to two pieces of plutonium propped apart by a screwdriver. The screwdriver slipped and the two pieces fell together, bathing the room in warm, blue radiation. Slotin was able to knock the pieces apart, and his body absorbed much of the radiation. He died nine days later. Seven others in the room were overexposed, but they survived thanks to Slotin. Raemer Schreiber was one of the seven. He knew right away that Louis Slotin had taken a lethal dose.

"It didn't do anything to me but scare me to death," Schreiber said. "After that, the Slotin accident, there was an absolute edict: No more hand assembling of fissile material."

Even though its secret was out of the bag and Los Alamos was readily identified as the nation's atomic bomb lab, it remained a closed community, encircled by barbed wire. Basic physics research continued, along with weapons work. And the exploration of nuclear power to do other things—move mountains, power rockets, drive submarines, generate electricity—began as well.

The lab outgrew its mesa, so a bridge was built to another one, and the lab moved. A town, looking like any old suburban American town, sprang up in the vacated area of the original lab, where the ranch school had been.

Los Alamos was opened up in the 1960s to people "outside the fence"—those without top-secret clearance, just plain folks. The barbed wire retreated to surround the labs themselves. The outer guard post became a Mexican restaurant.

Today, Los Alamos is a company town of 18,600, one of the strangest in America. No other town has such a high concentration of Ph.D.s. No other town is filled with nondescript buildings labeled nothing more than "Tech Area 46" or "Tech Area 55." Only the triple fences, video monitors, and machine-gun-equipped guards offer a hint of the town's true purpose. When a group of security-badged men race back to the Kentucky Fried Chicken to retrieve a stack of papers left behind after lunch, a visitor can only speculate as to what secret plans capable of tipping the uneasy balance of world affairs might have been left to the Colonel.

There's not much left to remind residents or visitors of the Manhattan Project era. Original laboratories are gone. The icehouse where the first plutonium cores were initially assembled is still there, but it's the chapter house of the Red Cross. The ranch school's Fuller Lodge is a community center that offers aerobics for the elderly and noontime lectures in Jungian psychotherapy.

The town is as homogeneous as any suburb, perhaps more so, but it is also a place of contradictions. It is surrounded by beautiful natural scenery, yet below the vistas is a decidedly ugly town, devoid of trees or flowers or even fresh paint, filled with plain-Jane buildings of 1950s and 1960s concrete functionalist architecture. Touted as being on the cutting edge of technology, Los Alamos appears frozen in time, keenly reflecting the utility of its scientist residents. Recently it voted to pay for a new library. That was a necessity. But an expanded historical museum and a better science museum were both voted down—luxuries the town decided it didn't need. Besides, such attractions might lure more visitors, and they're not wanted.

"It is a logical, conservative, frugal town—not style-conscious or color-conscious," said town council member Nancy Bartlit, who has spearheaded drives to update and beautify Los Alamos. "People just don't want Los Alamos to be discovered. Maybe it's part of the dichotomy left over from that attitude of being a closed community, when so many activities were secret."

But people who do venture in will see signs of sophistication not easily found elsewhere in America. Visitors to the lab's small science museum, which is open to the public, might think the glass-enclosed display of a Cray 1-A, Model 4 supercomputer, one of the fastest and most technically advanced in the world, is just a model. But it's not—it's the real thing, discarded as obsolete junk like some used chemistry beaker because there are now even faster Crays. Some universities and researchers would scream for any supercomputer. Los Alamos is probably the only place with a supercomputer already under glass in a museum.

In 1976, Los Alamos got the first supercomputer Seymour Cray built. Cray 1-A, Model 4 was delivered in 1977. The lab helped Cray get started and continues to be one of his biggest clients. And Cray, perhaps predictably, moved his new computer company to Colorado Springs—a day's drive up the Nuclear Highway from Los Alamos—when he split with the original Cray Research Incorporated. Los Alamos has the biggest stockpile of supercomputers in the world. They are used to help design nuclear devices by handling calculations on the nuclear reaction down to the nanosecond and beyond. "Cross-calculations" done by hand for Trinity are handled now by these computing mammoths.

Today, 7,700 people work at Los Alamos, more than 1,500 of them Ph.D.s. That's double the size of the lab in 1969. Nuclear weapons technology accounts for 53 percent of the work. Two thirds of the weapons in America's nuclear arsenal come from Los Alamos designs (its rival, Lawrence Livermore National Laboratory in California, which was established for Teller in 1952, accounts for the other one third). The nuclear devices in the W-80 cruise missile warhead, which is only 31.4 inches long and less than a foot in diameter and weighs only 290 pounds, in the W-85 on the submarine-based Pershing II, and in the W-78 on the Minuteman III ballistic missile were all created on the mesa.

Those who run the lab like to say their task is to take on any project in which science can make a difference. Those at Los Alamos in 1945 were sometimes ambivalent and uneasy when science made a difference. And employing that curious reasoning laid out by Teller and others so long ago, deputy director Frank Finch mentions to visiting dignitaries and reporters that "our primary mission is nuclear deterrence"—through nuclear proliferation.

Many who work here struggle with the moral questions of thermonuclear weapons—weapons of genocide, they have been called. Others refuse to work on weapons programs and stick to the many nuclear-energy-related projects or pure science: chemistry, biology, computer science, geology, etc. That the lab carries on basic scientific research not directly related to weapons is one legacy of Oppenheimer. On the other hand, some of the scientists hunger to make the biggest boom, to find new ways to shape and change nuclear explosions, to be the side with the biggest gun. They even pine for the days when testing was aboveground and the creators got to see just how impressive their packages were. Others rationalize that there are strategic advantages of having a better warhead: you can give up old warheads at the superpower negotiating table, sign new treaties, and still have just as much boom in your back pocket, just as much force to offset the other guy's, just as many megatons to destroy the enemy and the world.

Old-timers at the lab complain that it has lost its spunk, the sense of adventure that helped carry it to new discoveries. Bureaucracy stifles creativity and threatens the kind of pure scientific research cherished in the old days. The spirit of Oppenheimer has been replaced with a corporate culture that considers scientific larks a waste of time. Joe McKibben, whose scraggly hair and bushy eyebrows make him look as if he came right out of central casting when the call came for a "mad scientist," spends hours running calculations on a Macintosh personal computer at his home in the Los Alamos suburb of White Rock. Since his retirement, he says he's had weird thoughts about particle theory, how the world is put together, basic theoretical physics. What he's thinking about could have something to do with "cold fusion"—the highly controversial and widely rebutted theory that a fusion reaction could occur at room temperature. Maybe there are particles out there that haven't been discovered yet. As McKibben says, "The fact that *you* can't run one hundred yards in ten seconds doesn't mean that it can't be done."

"In a sense," he says, "I got out in time. I'd get fired for doing this at work now, wasting my time. A lot of decisions on whether a certain piece of research is done are not made by people here who understand but by someone in Washington who doesn't."

Some retired administrators tell stories of bureaucrats set up to do nothing but answer calls and inquiries from Washington. Sig Hecker, the director of the Los Alamos National Laboratory, the man who holds Oppenheimer's post, agrees that Los Alamos is a far more formal place than it was back in the Manhattan Project days. Funding is different, government involvement is different. "They didn't have thirty audits at one time," he quips.

Los Alamos does other things besides design nuclear bombs. About 22 percent of the lab's work is non-nuclear defense-related: conventional weapons, antisubmarine warfare, intelligence, and the Strategic Defense Initiative—Star Wars.

Star Wars is big business here. Before it ever had catchy names and worldwide concern, SDI was actually under way here twenty years ago, a decade before President Reagan opted to launch a multibillion-dollar program to invent a space shield against incoming nuclear warheads. Much of the research that led to Reagan's decision was done here with work on beams of light, beams of particles, and, of course, supercomputers. One of the ironies of SDI is that the foundation for it comes out of nuclear weapons programs. There's a certain satisfaction for the scientists in figuring out new ways to destroy the things they created.

Lawrence Livermore, where Teller holds court, also is a leader in SDI research. It was Teller who persuaded Reagan that SDI was possible and should be pursued. Teller's role, not surprisingly, has been controversial. Some in his lab have charged he hyped data and exaggerated results just to get Reagan to go for the idea. Unlike the decision to proceed with the H-bomb, the SDI decision has been intensely, publicly debated. By pursuing the idea, does the United States escalate the arms race? Does it increase the possibility that nukes might be used in the first place? And then there's the nagging question of whether the darn thing is even possible. Despite Reagan's enthusiasm for a shield and the Bush administration's continued support for the idea, the military concedes we'd probably never be able to get all the incoming nukes. Is it worth the billions?

Los Alamos is pioneering lasers and particle beams that can be fired at nuclear missiles, destroying them in space. These beam weapons probably have a long-term future in the weapons business. It's a safe bet we'll always want faster, better weapons, no matter how peaceful the world may appear. It's also a safe bet that no weapon can travel faster than the speed of light. As far as we know, *nothing* can travel faster than the speed of light. Planes and missiles can already outrun the speed of sound several times over, but not even the F-umpteen can go faster than the speed of light. It's the universal speed limit, one of the few rules physicists can't violate. And if the Los Alamos beam weapons can travel at the speed of light, nothing can outrun them. Their day in the U.S. military arsenal will undoubtedly come.

That day may not be very far off, either. Los Alamos scientists have already fired a Star Wars gizmo—a neutral particle beam (NPB)—in space. And it worked.

The experiment was called BEAR, Beam Aboard Rocket, a not-too-subtle reference to the Soviet mascot. An NPB machine generates a beam of particles, such as hydrogen atoms. The beam stays straight as it moves through space because it has no electrical charge and is not influenced by earth's magnetic fields. In BEAR, an NPB machine was fitted atop a refurbished nuclear missile and launched from the White Sands Missile Range 120 miles into space. It fired 340 pulses in about 6 minutes and landed 55 miles up the range, toward Mary McDonald's ranch. Jubilant scientists compared the BEAR test with the Trinity test, because they believe it proves that Star Wars, the whole idea of which is to create a system that can shoot down nuclear missiles in space, can be made to work. "In every one of our predictions, we were on the money," said Richard Burick, program director for NPB research at Los Alamos. "It was an extremely successful experiment."

A huge NPB ground test facility was built at Los Alamos during the Star Wars building boom of the late 1980s. A much larger BEAR is slated to be launched into space by January of 1992, followed by an orbital demonstration of neutral particle beams, called Pegasus, which probably will include zapping targets. Pegasus is scheduled for 1994 or 1995. Whatever debate there is over Star Wars, development and testing march on. The Grumman Corporation already has a contract for Pegasus. An NPB system could probably be deployed before the end of the decade.

Ironically, NPB is based on a Soviet invention, made available through scientific literature. Los Alamos has taken the technology a lot further, though. And American experts even demonstrated the BEAR for a Soviet delegation. "They loved the name," Burick said. The Los Alamos team ran the beam for the Soviets for an hour. They'd brought along one of the co-inventors of the technology, and, Burick said, "It knocked his socks off."

Los Alamos and Boeing are also well on their way to building another Star Wars laser—this time on the ground. The earth-anchored laser is politically attractive for SDI—it removes some of the stigma of putting weapons in space. Such lasers may also help SDI skate through compliance with treaties banning ballistic missile defenses.

Already at White Sands, construction is under way on GBFEL, the Ground-Based Free Electron Laser. Despite funding cuts, inventors are confident a laser will be based at White Sands. Research on free electron lasers actually began in 1978 at Los Alamos. Scientists found that if you strip an electron from light particles in the beam, it will be much more manageable in the atmosphere. Now neutral—that is,

115

without an electrical charge—the beam can move through the atmosphere without distortion. Normal laser beams are hard to use from the ground because the atmosphere breaks them down and sends them off course. GBFEL hopes to skirt that problem.

Scientists already have great confidence in the physics of the free electron laser and are perfecting such a contraption's engineering. The goal is to fire the beam from White Sands and bounce it off satellite-mounted mirrors in space so it zaps incoming ICBMs, preferably while they're still on their way up—before they scatter their multiple warheads. (In the nuclear weapons business, that's called MIRVing, and it's a lot tougher to destroy the bombs after they MIRV. Because the missiles move so fast, a Star Wars system would have only a few minutes to get the job done before warheads would be raining down on the United States.) Scientists hope they can prove it will work by 1994, when White Sands will have a completed laser.

Just as some aspects of nuclear weapons physics research were spun off into SDI projects, and advances made by the National Aeronautics and Space Administration in the space program contributed to launching the high-tech revolution, so Star Wars will yield new advances for use closer to home. Neutral particle beams, for example, can be used to zap plutonium and other nuclear materials, either to take the place of reactors to create tritium or to break down the substances into safer forms. That could help with the radioactive waste storage problem, because the leftovers to be warehoused might not be as dangerous.

And free electron lasers hold the potential for amazing medical breakthroughs in treating disease, as well as for computer technology advances. Scientists believe free electron lasers might someday replace X-rays for killing cancer tumors, or might be able to destroy viruses, as in AIDS. A free electron laser may eventually etch circuits on microchips that would be far smaller than today's circuits. That would allow smaller, faster, more powerful computers—even putting a Cray on a single chip. Today's popular PCs use a main chip with circuits engraved at 1-micron size. Advances in the works with lasers will take that down to about 0.2 microns. The Japanese are way ahead of the U.S. here, but with a free electron laser, circuits could get as small as 0.05 microns, and the U.S. could make a quantum leap in high technology. Marry that with new parallel-processing computer techniques, and the possibilities are mind-boggling. For the military, such computing power could revolutionize submarine warfare and other computer-based applications. Computers could even be created that would be powerful enough to reliably run a Star Wars system—one of the major stumbling blocks to SDI. And, says Sid Singer, a Los Alamos administrator for SDI programs, "there are other applications I can't talk about."

Beyond Star Wars, the lab is scurrying to find its niche in the new world, the post–Cold War days of perestroika and glasnost. Defense cuts have already hurt. The question of the lab's permanence has been revived. Do we really need new nuclear warheads?

Sig Hecker, an Austrian-born scientist and ski fanatic who runs Los Alamos, the $1-billion-a-year lab, says that the day to shut down hasn't yet come, and probably never will. "It still appears this country will have a nuclear deterrent as its primary defense for decades to come," Hecker said in an interview.

The genie can't ever go back in the bottle.

"There are thousands of companies that take care of planes and tanks and guns. But there are only three labs." Hecker

117

was referring to Los Alamos, Sandia, and Lawrence Livermore. "We see what we do as changing, but we don't see [the nation] dropping anything drastically."

Although nuclear weapons research and development has been shrinking since 1985 and may continue to shrink, it will probably never disappear, because that would make the nation more vulnerable to surprise attack from an enemy's new weapon—as Japan was in 1945. Dick Slansky, the head of Los Alamos's famed Theoretical Division, which over the years has been the most prized place to work, says there are still dynamics of nuclear explosions that aren't understood. The labs remain at the forefront in big science research, and science can make a difference in improving the environment, medicine, and the economy, as well as in moving war to new levels.

"That's our heritage," Hecker said. "We tackle the big problems. . . . The challenges are absolutely immense and endless, because technology is not slowing down."

The bottom line is that there may be some retrenching at Los Alamos with the advent of peace, but never a retreat. "We do expect to offset the decline in defense [money] with an increase in non-defense," Hecker said.

One project concentrates on making nuclear weapons safer. That's comforting and disturbing at the same time. Weren't they safe in the past? The answer from the administrators and scientists working with the warheads is that you can always get safer. In 1990, Defense Secretary Dick Cheney issued orders to the Army not to move the W-79 nuclear artillery shell because a computer analysis—and actual tests—found that it was likely to explode accidentally. Small artillery shells are based on the same implosion design as the Fat Man. The concern was that if a shell fell off the back of a truck and landed a certain way, a volatile fuel could blow up, triggering the conventional explosives surrounding the plutonium core.

Mary and Dave McDonald at Alamogordo, New Mexico.

A U.S. Air Force F-117 Stealth fighter, trained in southern New Mexico, after a run on Iraqi targets.

The McDonald ranch house, where final assembly of the Trinity bomb core took place.

Hoisting the Trinity bomb.

(courtesy of White Sands Missile Range)

The world's first nuclear explosion.

Pieces of Trinitite found at ground zero.

(courtesy of David Breslauer)

Rancher G. B. Oliver at the White Sands Missile Range fence that divides his land.

A Patriot intercepts a Lance missile at White Sands, September 11, 1986.

Ken Renegar
outside the
Star Wars Deli
in White Sands.

A view of the Sandia/Kirtland complex from the Four Hills
neighborhood. In the distance, a commercial jet lands on a runway
at Albuquerque International.

The four hills of the Manzano Mountains in Albuquerque, where nuclear weapons are reportedly stored.

A B-1 bomber atop the all-wood trestle at Albuquerque International, home of Kirtland Air Force Base and Sandia National Labs.

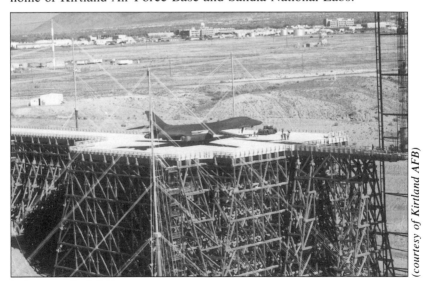

An unmarked truck used to transport nuclear warheads, components, and materials on interstate highways.

Master glassblower Czeslaw Deminet fashions a device for Star Wars research at the Air Force weapons lab in Albuquerque.

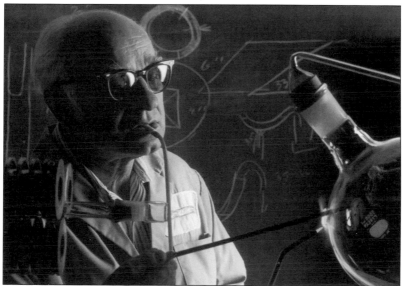

Master Sergeant Art Mangham with
a Cray-2 computer at the Air Force weapons
laboratory in Albuquerque.

Seymour Cray, chairman and genius, Cray
Computer Corporation.

Officials stressed that there was no risk of a nuclear explosion. It was Hecker and his two fellow lab directors who brought the safety hazard to the Pentagon's attention. The warheads were shelved until improvements were made.

There's another safety hazard at Los Alamos—the environment. The provider of jobs and income here, the sole reason the town exists, is also a major polluter. And when Los Alamos pollutes, it doesn't just spill sludge or spew ash. It dumps plutonium down canyons and into streams and rivers. When Los Alamos announces plans to build a new waste incinerator, the debate turns into how much radioactive debris is going to get into the atmosphere, and how much is too much.

Like other weapons labs in the DOE system, Los Alamos is undertaking a massive cleanup following acknowledgment under Energy Secretary James Watkins that the labs are among the nation's worst polluters. Los Alamos ranks second on some DOE hit lists, behind the Rocky Flats plutonium processing plant in Denver, three hundred miles up the Nuclear Highway. Since its creation, Los Alamos has polluted groundwater under the mesa and spilled hazardous waste into the Rio Grande just below the Otowi Bridge. It is 'fessing up only now.

The problems date back to the beginning. With a war on and a race to be first with the bomb, safety precautions and pollution control were not major considerations in Manhattan Project planning. "They took some shortcuts we couldn't take today," said Hecker. "Now we've got to clean that up." What exactly did they do with the dangerous wastes? "They were dumping raw liquid radioactive waste into the canyons," Wayne Hansen says rather matter-of-factly. Hansen is the Los Alamos scientist in charge of environmental compliance. He has just five employees but 608 sites waiting for "remediation"; they date back to the Manhattan Project. The waste, plutonium and other stuff, could just sit there for centuries, or it could get ingested, cause cancer, and kill. It's not your average industrial chemical spill. Until recently, there have been no studies of health problems from the Los Alamos pollution and no widespread evidence of ailments. But in the summer of 1991, a local physician revealed that he had counted at least eight deaths in Los Alamos from malignant brain tumors in the previous three years. That was more than three times the national rate. Community concern prompted the DOE to launch an epidemiological study of all cancers in Los Alamos.

One of those canyons where the radioactive wastes were dumped like stale bread thrown out for birds was Pajarito, where Peggy Pond Church played as a girl. Pajarito Canyon was also the place where Louis Slotin was killed. Peggy Pond Church was never able to go back inside the fences and recover her childhood treasures. Even today, Pajarito is a high-security area with a guard tower, fences, monitors, and Geiger-counter-equipped gates. At its mouth is Los Alamos's waste dump. And down at the bottom, blooming purple asters and a peaceful DEER XING sign clash with the tangle of barbed wire, NO TRESPASSING warnings, and DANGER. EXPLOSIVES. KEEP OUT.

For a time, DOE fought the nation's environmental laws, claiming that atomic weapons facilities were exempt. But in 1984, a federal court ruled against the government, and DOE found itself, well, "behind." Hansen says Los Alamos and the other labs were more behind on paper compliance at that point than in actual dumping. Every piece of waste has to be documented, and Los Alamos had to create a paper trail. It's still trying to catch up. A 1987 DOE survey found improper disposal of hazardous wastes at Los Alamos, according to a report by the General Accounting Office. The survey also uncovered releases of hazardous material, toxic chemical leaks, and "off-site releases of radioactive contaminants into canyons where they polluted soil and sediments."

The lab wanted to use a new incinerator for hazardous and radioactive waste in 1990, claiming it wasn't subject to regulation by New Mexico. The courts disagreed and decreed that a state permit was required. Hansen says pollution control equipment will cleanse the emissions so well that no hazardous or radioactive waste will be detectable. That doesn't mean they won't be there. "I can say I can't detect, but I can't say it will be zero," Hansen said. The incinerator has drawn protests not only from the antinuke contingent in Santa Fe but also from more conservative Los Alamos residents and neighbors. And there also has been considerable resistance to a Los Alamos proposal for a new plutonium process facility. The lab says it is needed for the continuation of scientific experimentation. The activists charge it is little more than a backup bomb-part manufacturing plant should Rocky Flats be declared hopelessly polluted and shut down by Colorado. Then the manufacture of the "plutonium triggers"— the euphemism was created by some public relations whiz (they are really Fat Man–type plutonium implosion bombs)— could continue at Los Alamos, and the nation's nuclear arsenal would not be at risk.

In the old days, such a proposal might have been welcomed as offering more jobs and more job security. Or maybe in the old days somebody would have just gone ahead and ordered the plant built, labeled it "Tech Area 92," and nothing more than rumors would have risen up over it. But in these days of triple-layer oversight, the DOE is out in the open and there's not much trust. Good fences, no matter how much barbed wire they have, don't keep radioactive wastes out of the environment, out of the groundwater, out of the air. Good fences don't always make good neighbors.

John Bartlit has learned that lesson from an interesting

perspective. Bartlit's had a long career as a chemical engineer at Los Alamos, working on everything from cryogenics to the handling of nuclear fusion fuels—tritium and deuterium. And he's had a long career as chairman of New Mexico Citizens for Clean Air and Water, the group of environmental activists Fermor Church was involved with.

Environmental activists inside Los Alamos? Most of the board members of New Mexico Citizens for Clean Air and Water are Los Alamos scientists. They run one of the most effective environmental groups in the country because of their scientific expertise—they can outdo just about any expert offered up by a polluter who tangles with them at regulatory hearings. They don't tie themselves to trees; they just match graphs and charts with the other side. For fifteen years they battled to clean up a coal-burning electrical plant in the Four Corners area—and won.

Bartlit has been chairman since 1971 and doesn't see a conflict between his civic activism and his job. Like many who work inside the fence, Bartlit finds concern among his colleagues for protecting the environment as well as the peace. But at meetings of conservationists, which often include antinuke activists, participants are surprised to find out where Bartlit and his friends are employed. "There are certainly some environmental people who dislike the work at the lab intensely," he said. "But others say, 'Well, he got the Four Corners plant cleaned up.'

"I like to think I've had some impact demonstrating to antinuclear people that there are better ways to attack the problems, with technical information and perseverance. That's how antinukes can be more effective than holding skeletons and screaming 'Plutonium Kills!' "

Bartlit and his fellow environmentalists are a symbol of Los Alamos's dichotomies. The group's Achilles' heel is the pollution from Los Alamos itself, an issue the scientists have largely ignored, leaving it to the "screamers." Los Alamos management has never told him, or other members, to back off or tone down. The lab even honored Bartlit and three others on Earth Day for their volunteer work. But, he says, "It would be somewhat hard to beat on the lab. That's the way the world is."

To Bartlit and the others, reality wins out over ideals. It's easy to rationalize: there's only so much environmentalists can do. They've been effective by carefully picking their targets and sticking with them until they win. They've stuck to basic air and water issues, and there are lots of other environmental problems they haven't been able to get to. Carping about the lab would be complicated and perhaps unproductive.

Los Alamos will always be the center of the nuclear weapons creation business—that is the town's role in life. As long as America has nuclear weapons, it will have Los Alamos. The mesa will always serve as a reminder of good, of evil, and of the potential that science has for changing the world one way or the other. Los Alamos is a monument to the conflict between science and society. Is the town a symbol of peace? Of war? Will its work save the world? Or destroy it? To millions, Los Alamos is a symbol of the greatest tragedy of our age. Millions more believe it represents one of man's greatest achievements.

That conflict will probably have a half-life longer than plutonium. Perhaps Los Alamos will too.

6

PIKES PEAK OR BUST

*Akin to, and largely responsible for the sweeping changes in
our military-industrial posture, has been the technological
revolution. . . . In this revolution, research has become
critical; it also becomes more formalized, complex, and
costly. . . . Today, the solitary inventor, tinkering in his shop,
has been overshadowed by task forces of scientists in laboratories and testing fields.*
    PRESIDENT EISENHOWER *in his farewell address
    to the nation, 17 January 1961*

The project's eccentric leader works with a small, devoted cadre of loyalists who believe totally in his vision, even
though they cannot see the same distant goal. He constantly
pushes his team harder, faster, but never as hard or as fast
as he pushes himself. He has always stayed so far ahead of
the pack that infidels inevitably—and prematurely—predict
disaster while still holding out slim hopes for his success.
Like the stunts of exhibitionist Evel Knievel, he dares to go
where no man has ever gone, as deliciously horrified watch-
ers line up to cheer his failure. He's like the first—the only—
man at the gaming table, always going for broke against the
house.

A physically unimposing fellow with a dated look about
him, he could be the father of Beaver Cleaver's best friend.
As he's grown older in the glow of repeated successes, this
devoted fan of *Star Trek* has evolved into the sort of scientist

about whom others tell stories: by the age of ten he'd built a telegraph machine that would translate punched paper tape into Morse code; during high school he substituted when the physics teacher was sick; his children were not allowed to talk during long car trips because Daddy was thinking; for many years he built a new sailboat every winter, then inexplicably torched it in the fall when the sailing season was over (a daughter remembers him doing that only once, but the myth grew anyway). The man who increasingly shunned publicity as his fame grew has, in his sixth decade, walled himself off from all but his closest working companions and inner family circle.

If the clock could be wound backward, the description would loosely fit J. Robert Oppenheimer, headmaster of the Manhattan Project's class of geniuses. Like Oppenheimer in the 1940s, Seymour Cray in the 1990s works mostly in his head, at all hours of the day and night, in an atmosphere of tension and anticipation, with a dedicated team to follow through on his hunches and his revolutionary breakthroughs. What Oppenheimer was to the atomic bomb, Seymour Cray is to supercomputers. Since 1960, this one man has invented five major computers, each of which was the fastest machine of its day.

Now, alongside Interstate 25 on the affluent southern fringe of Colorado Springs, Seymour Cray, at sixty-five years of age, is trying to invent a sixth wonder box. His frenzied race to beat his international competitors is taking place three hundred miles up the Nuclear Highway from Los Alamos in the shadow of Cheyenne Mountain, where the North American Aerospace Defense Command (NORAD) is buried deep in the granite heart of that graceful peak. Just three miles north of Cray headquarters is the United States Space Command (SPACECOM) at Peterson Air Force Base, and fifteen miles east, two Cray-2s already spew forth information in a continuous blizzard of calculations for the Strategic Defense Initiative's experimental brain at Falcon Air Force Base.

If he can pull it off, the Cray-3 will be a mathematical wizard crammed full of tiny microchips capable of 16 billion—*billion!*—calculations per second. Some 1,024 of these teeny slivers will be on each of 208 4-inch-by-4-inch modules, which make up the computer's heart. Innocuous as a sleek, museum-quality coffee table, the Cray-3 will be octagonal, with a 32-inch diameter.

So far, like Oppenheimer, Seymour Cray has just one taker for his team's invention—Uncle Sam. The price tag is $42 million.

Why push the edge of the scientific envelope further into the unknown? Oppenheimer was asked the same question during hearings before the Atomic Energy Commission in 1954. Why, when the uranium gun bomb and the plutonium implosion bomb had been so successful against Hiroshima and Nagasaki, did the world need a hydrogen bomb—the so-called Super?

"The program in 1951," replied Oppenheimer, "was technically so sweet that you could not argue about that. The issues became purely the military, the political, and the human problem[s] of what you were going to do about it [the thermonuclear device] once you had it."

Technically so sweet. That, to a scientist, is romance. Oppenheimer, in his time, understood the legacy of all who had gone before him. He wrote in a series of 1953 lectures:

"A great discovery is a thing of beauty; and our faith—our quiet, binding faith—is that knowledge is good and good in itself. It is also an instrument. It is an instrument for our successors, who will use it to probe elsewhere and more deeply. It is an instrument for technology, for the practical arts, and for man's affairs."

Colorado Springs has always attracted dreamers as well as

126

schemers and scoundrels. If ever there was a dreamer, it is Seymour Cray, surely Eisenhower's "solitary inventor, tinkering in his shop." But ironically, the selection of Colorado Springs—one of Eisenhower's favorite places—as the home for Cray's new company, Cray Computer Corporation, was not based on the town's historic sweetheart relationship with the United States military or its patriotic populace. Rather, some of its most skilled technical workers were conveniently being laid off from IBM and Data General at the exact time Cray and his scouts were looking for a new home in early 1988.

"The town's military connection was not even a thought in our minds," said Neil Davenport, president of Cray Computer Corporation and Cray's Sancho Panza. "We believed it would be a good quality workplace with a skilled mechanical and electrical work force. Even its beauty was secondary, although we're glad it is a friendly, attractive place with low traffic."

Its skyline dominated by the 400-square-mile massif of Pikes Peak, which rises to 14,145 feet above sea level, Colorado Springs has always attracted opportunists seeking fortunes amid its crystalline air, invigorating winds, and nearly year-round sunshine.

Today, it is a mecca for everything from rich evangelical nonprofit companies to fledgling high-tech start-up firms whose yuppie CEOs put quality of life on an equal footing with making money, something unheard of in Oppenheimer's time (which was why his decision to execute the Manhattan Project in a beautiful place was so unusual to his Pentagon overseers). Because of its strategic location on I-25, the West's main north-south corridor, as well as its proximity to Denver's vast metropolitan area and its own enviable natural attributes, Colorado Springs's population has burgeoned from a mere 45,000 residents in 1950 to nearly 400,000 in 1990.

127

Dozens of man-made attractions compete with Mother Nature's blessings for the amusement and entertainment of locals and visitors alike. The attractions in what was once a dusty outpost on the frontier are as varied as the American Numismatics Museum, the ProRodeo Hall of Champions, the Figure Skating Hall of Fame, and Cameron's Doll and Carriage Museum.

These days, Colorado Springs is a company town. Half the work force is dependent on government spending. The thirty-employee Federal Electric Corporation, which has a contract with the Air Force to operate Arctic radar installations that warn of approaching aircraft or missiles, is typical of the smaller Springs companies. They are the Lilliputians to the government's Gulliver, nibbling off the massive multibillion defense budget and rising or falling with its cutbacks and buildups.

About twelve thousand civilians work in aerospace and defense-related companies in El Paso County. Combined with the thousands at the military installations, both civilian and in uniform, roughly 58 percent of the area's economy is based on Uncle Sam's largess. It is a position Colorado Springs's early arrivals would have envied.

The town's first grandiose dreamer was its founder, who rode in—straight of saddle, loose of rein, long of stirrup—on a fancy horse in 1871. He was, prophetically, a military man. General William Jackson Palmer was a Civil War cavalry hero who organized the Fifteenth Pennsylvania Volunteer Cavalry and finished the war chasing Confederate president Jefferson Davis all the way to Georgia. After that burst of excitement, returning to Philadelphia seemed boring, so he traveled throughout the West, looking for railroad routes. When his bosses back East ignored his advice, he decided to build his own narrow-gauge line from Denver to Mexico. He never quite finished it, but the Denver and Rio Grande Railroad did make it to New Mexico before Palmer ran out of money.

His lasting legacy, besides carving out a scenic railroad bed which later became the basis for highways in the San Juan Mountains, was Colorado Springs. Having fallen in love with a genteel maiden from Long Island, Palmer decided a rough-edged frontier town composed mostly of saloons and boardinghouses wasn't good enough for his lady, whose Christian name happened to be Queen. Palmer set out to create a cultivated, attractive, even snooty society that would "take the waters" of the nearby hot sulfur springs, plant lavish gardens, throw distinguished parties, and, by its high-priced real estate, exclude unworthies.

Of course, Palmer and his old-boy network of friends, through a series of his own subsidiaries, would control the real estate that couldn't be given away at $1.25 an acre before he started his crusade to convince investors that he'd found the Garden of Eden. Strangely enough, despite numerous pitfalls, gold strikes, worldwide depressions, a war or two, the permanent departure of his beloved Queen for the more manicured gardens of England, and the vagaries of his settlers, Palmer succeeded in conjuring his paradise from the prairie. By the time he died, in 1909, as the result of a paralyzing fall from a horse, Colorado Springs was teeming with parks, hotels, colleges, man-made lakes, wide boulevards for elaborate carriages and those noisy contraptions known as steamers, polo matches at Sunday garden parties, and tourists from all over the world, who came to "take the cure" and recover from tuberculosis or just sit in the sun and relax. Palmer had even built himself a castle called Glen Eyrie, and he lived near a wilderness preserve dubbed by a crony as the "Garden of the Gods."

His dreams, coupled with a lot of good luck and the national westward migration of a restless populace, had turned

Colorado Springs into what many well-to-do immigrants called "Little London," despite the unfortunate label pinned on it by a cheeky Colorado Springs *Gazette* reporter, who called it "a sunny place for shady people."

It was this kind of vision that inspired many who followed Palmer, including another Philadelphian, Spencer Penrose, who dared to gouge a highway to the top of Pikes Peak, build the sumptuous pink palace known in fashionable circles around the world as The Broadmoor, and ride his pet llama bareback down Colorado Springs's main street to protest Prohibition.

Palmer's decision to create his own town and thus make his fortune off the barren land it would sit on was prophetic; so was the U.S. government's decision in 1873 to build the Army Signal Corps's second-largest station atop Pikes Peak. Thus the two primary sources of money for local residents for the next century were established at the outset: land speculation and military spending.

After the flamboyant Penrose died in 1939, his longtime business partner, Charles L. Tutt, and other civic-minded town fathers decided to descend on Washington for help in yanking their town out of the Great Depression. Adolf Hitler and Emperor Hirohito unwittingly aided their cause. In 1942, the Army opened Camp Carson, now Fort Carson, a sprawling infantry base that anchors the south side of the city. Like the proverbial domino effect military leaders are so fond of invoking, Camp Carson begat Peterson Army Air Corps field in 1948, which begat Ent Air Force Base soon thereafter and, finally, the cherry on top of the soda—the North American Air Defense Command and Combat Operations Center buried in Cheyenne Mountain.

Meanwhile, a serendipitous relationship between a famous general and a Colorado educator was setting the stage for a coup of major proportions by civic boosters. Dwight D. Eisenhower, then president of Columbia University in New York

City, and Robert L. Stearns, president of the University of Colorado, were appointed cochairmen of a board of civilian and military educators charged with selecting a site for the $200 million Air Force Academy. Also on the board was Colonel Charles A. Lindbergh.

Eisenhower, whose wife, Mamie, was from Denver, liked to play golf in the Mile High City. In fact, he liked to play golf just about anywhere, but especially in Colorado, where the higher altitude gave the little white ball greater lift and longer distance. When he had to resign from the selection committee because he'd been elected President, he didn't forget his old colleague Bob Stearns or the many friends and supporters he had in the Columbine State.

On April 1, 1954, Eisenhower signed the bill establishing the Air Force Academy in Colorado Springs. With a flourish of a pen, he created the showpiece for an entire military reservation along the Nuclear Highway, one that continues to grow and multiply despite all attempts by Congress to rein it in.

If Eisenhower gave a mighty boost to Colorado Springs, Ronald Reagan sent it into orbit. Reagan's defense buildup was the blastoff everyone had been waiting for to give the town its economic torque.

No sooner had Reagan been inaugurated than Colorado Springs was awarded the Consolidated Space Operations Center (CSOC), which would merge all the communications equipment for all military space shuttle flights and satellites. Although the military space shuttle program eventually was shelved in favor of NASA's shuttle, that crucial decision pretty much established Colorado Springs as the Star Wars capital of America. Soon a cow pasture fifteen miles east of town was transformed into a sprawling military complex housing ten separate facets of Air Force space operations. Elaborate precautions, including a required retina scan to identify every

131

person authorized to enter, and a personal identification number, were part of the security net thrown around Falcon Air Force Base.

By 1986, cheerleaders for the Colorado Springs Chamber of Commerce and Economic Development Council were flying around America trying to lure space-oriented and high-tech companies into relocating at the foot of Pikes Peak.

"The economic magnitude of expanded military [research and development] in Colorado Springs is not yet quantifiable," crowed one of the mass-circulated booster publications of the time. "However, the potential exists that because of CSOC and SPACECOM, Colorado Springs could become the nation's headquarters for military space policy and procurement. Some observers also believe that Colorado Springs could easily develop into the nation's aerospace/software think tank."

The message was clear: get on the bandwagon and come get your piece of the action before it's too late and you're left out.

Besides the small start-ups, even major players heard the clarion call for a place so obviously touched by the Pentagon's magic money wand.

Digital Equipment, Honeywell, TRW Electronics, Rolm/ IBM, Raytheon, Kaman Sciences, Hughes Aircraft, Hewlett-Packard, and dozens of lesser lights in the electronics and military hardware field either opened new offices or expanded old ones in the wake of Reagan's military buildup. By 1987, at least fifty-seven companies in Colorado Springs had a piece of the Star Wars action.

Advertisements paid for by Colorado Springs companies and/or subsidiaries littered the pages of technical journals such as *Aviation Week and Space Technology*. Their products spoke to a very specific market, such as the one United Technologies' Microelectronics Center targeted, in its own technological gobbledygook: "Our UTE-R, with 20K or 50K usable gates, is guaranteed functional up to 10 rads total dose. And like all UTMC rad-hard circuits, the UTE-R is backed by Rad-Spec, your guarantee that we deliver DOD-Specified rad-hard levels—from kilo-rad tactical to mega-rad strategic." In other words, they claim their electronics can survive the radioactive environment of a nuclear battle.

The crest of the wave came with the announcement that a big chunk of the Strategic Defense Initiative's National Test Bed (NTB) would also be located at Falcon AFB. The test bed was created to simulate proposed United States defenses against an incoming intercontinental ballistic missile attack. Its job was to play large-scale "war games" to test command and control capabilities. At Falcon, the Cray-2 computers, as well as an IBM 3090-200 series supercomputer, are critical elements in the war games. They are linked to another supercomputer at Los Alamos. The computer system is supposed to simulate any known airborne threat with enough sophistication to determine individual warheads.

The NTB is also testing Star Wars gadgets such as laser beam weapons. Shuttle astronauts who eventually will participate in Starlab—point-tracking a U.S.-launched test ICBM with a laser—also train on the NTB simulators.

In essence, the NTB is the brains of Star Wars, and that makes Colorado Springs SDI's headquarters. The begats were still begatting.

And it wasn't just Colorado Springs that was reaping the benefits of the state's historic military connection and powerful political clout with a Republican administration. The entire I-25 corridor from Pueblo north to Cheyenne, Wyoming, was prospering. In the first seven years of Reagan's tenure, federal spending in Colorado rose 64 percent. Defense expenditures represented more than one third of the $12.3 billion the federal government spent in Colorado in 1987.

"We are a high-tech oasis," Democratic representative David Skaggs testified before the House subcommittee on science, research, and technology in 1988 when it was scouring the nation to find a site for the Superconducting Super Collider atom smasher, which eventually went to a rural area south of Dallas. "We have in this state over 1,000 high-tech companies that together gross more than $10 billion a year and employ tens of thousands of people. . . . Technology in Colorado is a bread-and-butter issue because technology means jobs."

Among the federal research facilities in the state are the National Bureau of Standards, the National Center for Atmospheric Research, the National Oceanic and Atmospheric Administration, and the Solar Energy Research Institute.

The state also hosts the contractors who build the two rockets capable of launching payloads into space. The Titan IV, built by Martin Marietta Corporation, rolls off the assembly line just north of Colorado Springs on the southern border of Denver; the Delta 181 rocket, a product of McDonnell Douglas Corporation, is assembled in Pueblo, the former steel mill town just forty miles south of Colorado Springs. The United States's only other means of launching payloads into space is NASA's trouble-plagued space shuttle system, which hit its low ebb after the Challenger exploded in 1986. That disaster plunged the whole space program into a period of institutional angst and reexamination, causing military naysayers who had consistently lobbied for a military launch vehicle to renew their hue and cry.

Seizing the opportunity, Martin Marietta and McDonnell Douglas teamed up to win a $97.8 million Air Force contract to work together on the government's next-generation rocket. A team headed by a NASA veteran will unite Air Force, NASA, and SDI forces to create a launch vehicle that can carry up to 160,000 pounds into earth's lower orbit at a cost of $300 per pound, a significant price reduction over the current $5,000 to $10,000 per pound.

Martin Marietta operates out of a huge facility employing fifteen thousand workers. The company's Astronautics Group continues to snag billions of dollars in contracts for their missiles while developing more delicate and sophisticated space hardware for SDI. They were the successful bidders to construct the National Test Bed at Falcon, a $508 million contract. Meanwhile, rolling out of the company's "clean room" was the fragile deep-space craft Magellan, which went on a fifteen-month voyage to Venus to map the planet's surface for NASA. The company also got the contract to build the rocket for the first U.S. spacecraft to Mars, which is supposed to orbit the planet thirteen times a day for two years. It is scheduled to be launched in 1992.

McDonnell Douglas's operation at Pueblo is much more modest. Its 62,000-square-foot facility employs fewer than one hundred people and was built by the Pueblo Economic Development Corporation as the anchoring carrot in hopes of attracting more high-tech spin-off companies to a town hard hit by the dwindling production of its steel mill. Pueblans' gritty can-do spirit even got the attention of George Bush, who went to the town in 1986 and ate lunch with hundreds of townsfolk. Said Bush at the time: "If you ever need to get your spirit refurbished, get out of Washington and see where the action is. My recommendation to those with whom I serve is to go to Pueblo [and] watch what's happening."

In 1988, Pueblo's reputation as a "come-back city" climaxed with its selection by a panel of professors as the number 1 place to live in the United States. The ranking was for quality of life among 253 American counties, and the winner was picked based on a complicated formula involving climate and urban and environmental conditions. Pueblo, south of Denver and farther out on the plains, had much cleaner air.

In fact, Colorado placed five counties in the top fifteen slots—and all of them paralleled the I-25 corridor but were not caught in Denver's bowl-shaped pollution trap.

Up and down the Nuclear Highway, Uncle Sam's business was booming throughout most of the 1980s. In 1988, the Colorado Office of Economic Development estimate of defense spending accounted for at least 17 percent of personal income in the state. That same year, Colorado ranked eighth nationally among states for per capita federal procurement spending—about $1,200 for every man, woman, and child.

Then the bottom fell out. The national debt soared, we made peace with the Soviet Union because they were going broke building weapons instead of baking bread, the Berlin Wall practically fell down through the sheer will of people on both its sides, and the U.S. savings and loan system went bankrupt. All those factors colliding at the same time brought the supersonic growth of Colorado Springs to an abrupt halt, and the high-tech and real estate speculation shakedown began.

Major companies laid off hundreds of workers, real estate prices plummeted, and land speculators, always the other leg of Colorado Springs's expansion ladder, declared bankruptcy, their S&Ls a smoldering pile of rubble too.

No one bombed in a bigger way than Frank Aries, a multimillionaire who arrived on the scene in 1985 aiming to make a killing off the boom. Aries became a metaphor for what happened to Colorado Springs in the last half of the decade as the dreamers were forced to give ground to reality.

A Chicago-born entrepreneur, Aries accumulated a fortune developing a gargantuan chunk of Tucson, Arizona, which he had bought from Howard Hughes. Then he turned his sights on Colorado.

Convinced the Star Wars bonanza was just the beginning of a spectacular era of growth for El Paso County, Aries looked around for a tract to buy and exploit, adhering to the best traditions of Palmer and Penrose before him. There was only one direction to look. Pikes Peak and its Rocky Mountain barrier blocked any expansion of the city in a westerly direction. The Air Force Academy's vast reservation to the north stopped growth there, and Fort Carson did the same thing to the town's southern boundary. That left the eastern prairie.

Within a year, Aries had acquired 29,000 acres of land, most of it heavily mortgaged but under his control. The property included the historic 20,438-acre Banning-Lewis ranch, 4,400 acres of a cattle ranch previously owned by the Mobil Corporation, and an additional 4,000 acres that included a foreign trade zone. His acquisitions were contiguous, bracketed on the west by Peterson Air Force Base and the local Colorado Springs airport, which share the same runways, and not far from Falcon Air Force Base to the east. The pristine landscape, roadless and nearly treeless, bordered the city limits for 14 miles and comprised 90 percent of the land on Colorado Springs's eastern edge. The purchase price totaled about $225 million for 38 square miles.

In 1986, *The New York Times,* in an article headlined "Safe Bets on the Future," hailed Aries's business sense. Said the *Times*: "Frank Aries has developed the uncanny knack of buying up huge tracts of land around growing metropolises at just the right time. This time he may have struck it particularly big."

Aries and his clean-cut cadre of executives who'd been enticed from the megasprawl of southern California went to work doing lunch with everybody of any note in Colorado Springs, trying to woo city fathers into annexing his property. That would mean taxpayers would have to provide utilities—including precious western water, of which there is too little for too many—to his development. Asked at the time what he would do if the city denied him annexation and he was forced to siphon water out of the Arkansas River via an expensive pipeline system, Aries claimed it was "just a technicality."

Within weeks, he had acquired posh offices on the top floor of Colorado Springs's tallest building. Contracts were let all around town for elaborate charts, graphs, mock-ups, and corporate reports. Investors throughout the country were invited to inspect the property and hear the pitch. His dreams were just like Palmer's dreams, excepting perhaps the element of exclusivity and conservative taste the old pioneer had demanded. Aries had his draftsmen draw up a thirty-year plan that included 74,000 housing units, a vast web of roads, more than a dozen parks, and numerous commercial zones to accommodate "clean" companies that would naturally want to relocate in what he was proclaiming as a prestigious area. The Banning-Lewis promoters left no marketing gimmick unused. There were even gilt lapel pins of a well-horned ram (the astrological symbol for Aries) and a complimentary video available for take-home viewing if the inquiry was from a potentially hot prospect. Less than three years after his arrival, Aries had a full-time Colorado Springs staff of thirty-five. But not a single bulldozer had scraped one foot of road, not a single shovel had dug one inch of sewer line, not a single streetlight had been installed.

All of the hype was predicated on the military buildup that had sent Colorado Springs's growth rate soaring at 4 percent a year in the early 1980s. Frank Aries's vision was still just drawings on a lot of paper.

Hans Pike Oliver, a veteran of the Irvine Company, which pioneered the planned-unit development concept in southern California, said in 1988 that he'd joined up with Aries in Colorado Springs to escape the congestion of Los Angeles and because he was "tired of terminal sophistication. Besides, I couldn't resist the opportunity to work on a 38-square-mile blank sheet of paper. We have a significant opportunity to enhance land values by getting in on the ground floor. Colorado Springs is really taking off. We believe the simplest solution for this project is to be part of the city of Colorado Springs, but we are big enough to pursue this on our own. As the new kid on the block we don't want to say we can play with our own marbles—but we can.''

As an inducement to attract other showcase businesses and facilities, one of the first things Aries did was donate land for a U.S. Olympic Committee Hall of Fame and a museum site for the U.S. Space Foundation, a nonprofit organization dedicated to promoting further national involvement in space exploration. That won him instant friends in high places within the social and economic superstrata of the city.

In 1988, the city council finally gave Aries's annexation the green light, thus absorbing into the city limits the largest single parcel in the city's history and nearly doubling Colorado Springs's size overnight.

But then Aries's fabled luck ran out. Phoenix-based Western Savings and Loan Association, a high-flying, risk-taking, money-squandering S&L and Aries's rubber-stamp backer in the vast project, went under like so many other thrifts in the Southwest. Western held a $225 million mortgage on the property. The Banning-Lewis ranch was taken over by the Resolution Trust Corporation, the agency created by Congress to dispose of assets of failed thrifts. At the same time, the national economy was slowing, Gorbachev was touting perestroika, and the defense budget was shrinking.

In the last week of August 1989, Frank Aries bought a ninety-eight-foot yacht, took a spin in his Rolls-Royce, and looked at property to buy in Houston. That same week, in default on his mortgage, Aries gave the keys to his Colorado Springs empire back to the brain-dead thrift, and thus to the RTC. Actually, the American taxpayers owned it. Friends

139

said the fifty-five-year-old, three-hundred-pound entrepreneur wasn't depressed by the loss. They also said they don't know where he went, or what dreams he's cooking up now.

"I think Frank's on a boat someplace," said Rocky Scott, director of the Greater Colorado Springs Economic Development Council.

By the time the project went bust, not a single building had been built. The Banning-Lewis Ranch was still a vast tract of plains, waiting for its future. It became one of the biggest items in the ignoble portfolio of RTC properties, one of the biggest white elephants of the whole S&L debacle. Still, friends defended Aries's dreams.

"He became a victim of circumstances beyond his control," his Colorado Springs friend and fellow developer Steve Schuck said at the time. "It's an unfortunate tragedy."

The mayor agreed. "I believe he [Aries] kept his word," said Mayor Bob Isaac in a newspaper interview. "It was just in this case there wasn't the type of growth to support that kind of development . . . everybody thought we were going into a boom period."

In July 1990, the RTC hired a Los Angeles marketing company to try to get rid of the Banning-Lewis ranch and the rest of Aries's defaulted property, targeting Japanese and European buyers. In 1991, American taxpayers were still paying the marketing company $39,500 a month to unload it. Meanwhile, Pike Oliver, the smooth-talking vice president of Aries's Colorado operation, had left town, and it was rumored he had returned once again to California and its terminal sophistication. Like many of the local high-flying developers caught in the S&L squeeze, he vanished from the scene without a ripple.

As might have been expected by its history, Colorado Springs became a hotbed for S&L woes. Three of the town's six S&Ls were taken over by regulators in 1990. The federal

140

government ended up with thousands of homes, office buildings, and undeveloped acres nobody wanted, ironically making it the newest and biggest land speculator on the Colorado Springs scene.

Schuck's and Isaac's reaction to Aries's departure was typical of the loyalty shown to wheeler-dealers who arrive with grandiose ideas they swear will help Colorado Springs grow. Even if they fail, a latent affection seems to linger on, on their behalf. That is because the core of such a patriotic, deeply conservative community is interconnected, tight-knit, and professionally incestuous.

Typically, a career military veteran who chooses to retire in the Springs is almost automatically guaranteed some kind of comfortable job with a real estate or development company when he trades in his uniform for civvies. Estimates vary slightly because some men keep a lower profile than others, but several city fathers guess there are at least eight four-star Army and Air Force generals, or their Navy equivalents, retired and residing in El Paso County.

Jim Hill is a prominent example. A World War II fighter ace who flew 127 combat missions in a P-47 Thunderbolt against the Nazis, he received the Silver Star and a Croix de Guerre, and his career in the Air Force took off like a supersonic jet, all the way to commander in chief of NORAD. He retired in 1980 and was immediately hired as head of the Colorado Springs Chamber of Commerce. He later left that job to run the Olive Company, a real estate development firm. In his postmilitary life, he is typical of his peers in the Springs.

Even though Jim Irwin retired as a colonel and not a general, he has a leg up on just about every military veteran in the whole state—he was *astronaut* James B. Irwin, who flew Apollo 15 to the moon in the summer of 1971. A heart attack forced him to retire early, but a strict regimen of exercise and diet, combined with a religious born-again philosophy, led Irwin on a new path when he settled in Colorado Springs.

Today, his High Flight nonprofit ministry, founded in 1985, takes him all over the world to preach about his lunar experiences and implore his audiences to believe that "Man's flight through life is sustained by the power of His knowledge." He has led several expeditions to Turkey's Mount Ararat to look for evidence that Noah's Ark disintegrated over the ages on the side of the mountain. So far he hasn't found a trace of the biblical boat, but it's not for lack of trying.

"I have walked on the surface of the moon and ventured as deep into space as any man, yet my highest flight—my greatest adventure—has been to know Jesus Christ as my personal Savior and Lord," preaches Irwin. He's also led pilgrims to China and Europe on tours financed by the faithful, and his office does a brisk business selling books written by Irwin and his wife.

Like fellow astronaut and car dealer Frank Borman, just five hundred miles down I-25 in Las Cruces, New Mexico, Jim Irwin has found his true calling alongside the Nuclear Highway.

Newman McAllister has been a lifelong Republican and a successful lawyer in Colorado Springs for two decades. But unlike most of his fellow attorneys in town, he has had some rather unorthodox clients in recent years. His decision to represent peace protesters arrested for trespassing on local military installations has brought him notoriety and ostracism by some of his old buddies.

"The military mind-set here is very pervasive," said McAllister, a Star Wars opponent who, because of his personal prestige, professional reputation, civic service, and conservative life-style, still manages to straddle the gap between peaceniks in sandals and jeans and the establishment crowd in three-piece suits and uniforms. McAllister is about the only attorney in town who consistently has represented peace activists.

"So many people are dependent for their jobs on the military—the whole economy and much of the power here is tied into it—that most people you ask would say SDI is progress. I think there's a substantial minority of people here who disagree with SDI, but you feel like you're swatting at the breeze when you try to convince pro-SDI people otherwise."

McAllister said his outlook on the peace movement was reshaped when two nuns were arrested at Falcon AFB in the mid-1980s because they were kneeling against the fence, praying and planting wheat seeds, the symbol of life. Although later convicted, the nuns did not go to jail but were fined and warned not to do it again.

"I defended them, and we had an opportunity to exchange views. We lost the case, but they gained a pro bono counselor. I am part of the establishment, and I am always reminded of that when I represent my clients. I don't feel like I have to renounce my wealth and take a vow of poverty to be in favor of peace. But I have always believed in free speech. I haven't really been surprised at my changing attitude; I just wonder why it took me so long to figure all this out."

The three consistent aphrodisiacs offered by Colorado Springs throughout its history have been style, splendor, and snob appeal. From the days of Palmer and his Glen Eyrie, to the heyday of The Broadmoor and its entourage of presidential lackies during the Eisenhower years, to the present, the landscape in the shadow of Pikes Peak has been a Circe to true believers.

Seymour Cray ought to feel right at home in the company

of such ghosts and their monuments. But he does not cut the social swath that his flamboyant predecessors did, nor does he sit on civic boards or "do good works." Ever since he came to town he's been a demon for work, and except for a rumored few games of tennis every week, he doesn't venture much past the carefully groomed 60-acre site of the 127,000-square-foot building Cray Computer, bought from another high-tech firm that folded its Colorado Springs tent in the shakeout.

Like so many before him, Cray's professional reputation and future success depend on what happens to him in Colorado Springs. When he decided to spin off from Cray Research Incorporated, the Minneapolis company he founded in 1972 with a handful of friends and associates who followed him from Control Data Corporation, the corporate world was astounded. After all, Seymour Cray *was* Cray Research: the man who started it, the genius who invented its only products. But Cray reportedly chafed at the bureaucracy in a burgeoning company that had started lean and had cornered 65 percent of the world's market for supercomputers costing between $5 million and $25 million. When he left Cray Research, it was valued at $785 million.

The divorce was amicable: in fact, Wall Street was astonished that the parent company was transferring $50 million in equipment and $100 million in operating money over two years to Seymour's new project. In financing the start-up costs of its instant rival, Cray Research said it was doing so because it believed competition was essential to permit the United States to continue its leadership role in the supercomputer industry. All government contracts require at least two bids, so henceforth, Seymour Cray's two corporate offspring would vigorously compete against each other.

Cray's latest gamble rides on replacing the traditional computer chips made of silicon with faster but more unstable and fragile ones composed of gallium arsenide. Because of the incredible compactness of the chips, Cray had to design robots and program them to handle millions of computer parts thinner than a human hair. A Cray-3's circuits will be so fast there are no instruments yet invented that can test them.

But like so many geniuses who have dragged a disbelieving mankind into the next realm of progress, Cray was not discouraged by the overwhelming technical challenges or the soaring costs of his tinkering.

With only the one order so far for his latest wonder box, he has plunged on into the scientific netherworld, piling up millions in debt. In 1989, Cray's fledgling company lost $42.6 million; a year later, it lost another $46.4 million.

But the dream of working with Seymour Cray is still a powerful lure for true believers. Neil Davenport, the detail man who runs Cray's daily operations, said that when the announcement was made that Cray was moving to Colorado to try and achieve his latest goal, "we got 10,000 résumés submitted to us in 18 months for only 270 jobs. We are right on the leading edge of science, and when you are in that position you need patience and courage. We have peaks and troughs of activity. It is not a constant regular environment, nor is it an environment for someone who likes regular habits. We're only spending money, not earning it. We are taking the difficult route to the new technology. It is not an easy ride, and it is not a journey the fainthearted would enjoy."

But the payoff for Cray is that if the Cray-3 is successful, there will be an influx of orders from governments and big companies that can afford them. The start-up money could be recouped in no time. Which would let Seymour Cray do what he says he *really* wants to do: build a Cray-4, and make *it* the fastest and most powerful computer system in the world.

After all, he is still the same Seymour Cray who, as a young engineer, was asked to write a five-year plan for the infant Control Data Corporation. The results came back to CDC's president in two sentences: "Five year goal: Build the biggest computer in the world. One year goal: Achieve one-fifth of the above."

7

THE GENERAL
IN THE MOUNTAIN

And when at some future date the high court of history sits in judgment on each of us, recording whether in our brief span of service we fulfilled our responsibilities to the state, our success or failure, in whatever office we hold, will be measured by the answers to four questions: First, were we truly men of courage. . . . Second, were we truly men of judgment. . . . Third, were we truly men of integrity. . . . Finally, were we truly men of dedication?

JOHN FITZGERALD KENNEDY, *speech to the Massachusetts Legislature, January 9, 1961*

As it snakes its way through Colorado Springs, following the labyrinth of the old riverbed, which is nearly devoid of water but choked with the splintered Styrofoam, crushed pop cans, and discarded paper of the only species that fouls its own nest, Interstate 25 is like a poorly engineered Main Street where everybody drives too fast but gets everywhere too late.

Instead of stretching out, lean and straight, down the prairie side of the Rocky Mountains, where Pikes Peak dominates the sky and dwarfs hills that would be pointed to with pride in such flatlander country as Kansas and the Dakotas, I-25 looks like a first-year draftsman's failed final exam. It twists and turns with heart-stopping grades as it squeaks past the inevitable flotsam of modern life: a three-bay McDonald's on the left, a Holiday Inn with hot tubs on the right, the central business district off to the east somewhere, behind Lady Bird's landscaping run amok.

Like so much of Colorado Springs's history, I-25 is anchored at each end of the city by military installations. Bracketed on the north by the shining spires of the Air Force Academy chapel and the Falcons' football stadium, it has a matching milepost to the south, obliquely identified in a road sign as Cheyenne Mountain Air Force Station—which is known to the locals as the Mountain.

The Air Force Academy was the pride of the Eisenhower administration and the major chamber of commerce coup that launched this backwater poor relation of Denver into its golden age of military boosterism. A stunning departure from the Long Gray Line's ivy-covered old brick and the midshipmen's whitewash, the Academy is all chrome and glass, exposed beams and Tinkertoy ceilings. Born in a new generation's quest for the wild blue yonder, the Academy—created by congressional act in 1954—epitomized the spirit of the High Frontier when it graduated its first class in 1959. Carved in granite on a soaring wall is a verse from Sam Walter Foss's poem "The Coming American":

> *Bring me men to match my mountains,*
> *Bring me men to match my plains,*
> *Men with empires in their purpose*
> *And new eras in their brains.*

Like West Point and Annapolis, the Academy is where the best of the bold begin, in all innocence, to become warriors. They all will tell you they do it for exalted and noble reasons: they want the finest education the American taxpayer can buy; they want specialty skills they can't learn on the "outside," at Harvard, or MIT, or the University of Idaho; they want the discipline, the athletic glory, a free ride that

148

could end up in the driver's seat of a nuclear submarine, an Abrams tank, a B-1 bomber.

But scrape away the rhetoric, all the "correct" replies, and what the listener hears, in the undertow of a young soul, is a drumbeat straight from the Mesopotamia riverbed, from the French caves at Lascaux where the first artist drew a bison with an arrowhead through its heart:

> *I want to be a warrior . . .*
> *I want to be a warrior . . .*
> *I want to be a warrior . . .*

If the Academy is the beginning for the pure of heart and clean of hand who seek to learn the theory of war, then the Mountain is the place where battle-scarred veterans sit and wait for the real thing to begin.

The Mountain. The mere audacity of it convinced the macho crowd in the Congress of the 1960s to push through enough funding—$142.4 million back when gold was $35 an ounce—to get the job done. The generals' proposal was simple: take a 100-million-year-old granite mountain 7,200 feet above sea level in the middle of nowhere, hollow it out with revolutionary tunneling techniques, move 693,000 tons of rock (dump it over the side and make a parking lot—gotta have a parking lot!), and create six connecting caverns.

Then, three years and a million pounds of explosives later, use 110,000 bolts in three miles of tunnels to install netting to keep the whole thing from falling in. Truck up 7,000 tons of steel. Build everything from a general's latrine to a command center linked to Alaska and Australia. Install six diesel engines, each hooked to a 1,750-kilowatt generator, to power the fifteen freestanding buildings that make up the 200,000-square-foot "Steel City" complex. Then put all the buildings on 1,380 shock absorbers weighing a thousand pounds apiece.

149

It gives them independent suspension, like the wheels on a car. Dig a six-million-gallon reservoir for drinking and industrial water siphoned from an underground spring, then invent a new ventilation system to supply nonradioactive air in case the Bomb goes off.

Finally, build a kitchen to feed five hundred workers a shift, set up an operating room, a dentist's office, a pharmacy, a barbershop, a gymnasium, and a store, and you have created the world's most secure, functional, and comfortable . . . cave.

It is inside that cave, with its government-issue beige-paint walls, its faint smell of mold and mildew, its plaques for airman of the month and best bowler of the year, that the North American Aerospace Defense Command and the United States Space Command eavesdrop on the world.

After a single B-29 dropped a single bomb on Hiroshima and precipitated the end of World War II, air defense of the United States found a powerful niche in the national budget. But as America's nuclear superiority continued to prevail, Congress whittled away at it, decommissioning a squadron here, closing a base there. Then the Soviet Union successfully exploded a nuclear bomb and launched Sputnik, the world's first satellite, in October of 1957. One of the responses was NORAD, a joint Canadian–United States command, also created in 1957. Back then, the *A* in NORAD stood for Air: in 1981, catching up with the times, it was changed to Aerospace.

NORAD's main job is to listen for the ignition of the engine that will start World War III. In 1989, more than 1,500 rockets were launched by two dozen nations. Each time one of them lifted off, the generals had to decide whether to warn the President of the United States that Armageddon was at hand. The top brass calculates it has four minutes—*four minutes*—to "evaluate and assess the validity of the incident" before advising the Commander in Chief that 275 million Americans are at risk of annihilation.

The Space Command keeps its unblinking electronic eyes on more than seven thousand objects beyond earth's atmosphere, floating in space. Some weigh a few ounces, others tons. There's a screwdriver inadvertently fallen from the space shuttle and a stray mitten dropped by an astronaut. There are also obsolete satellites and the Hubble telescope. Each alien gets a number in the space surveillance center's computerized data base. Example: 1982-033L, object number 13332, a garbage bag stuffed full of food wrappers and dirty clothes, launched from the Soviet space station Salyut 7, became a satellite for forty days and made more than six hundred orbits of earth before it burned up on atmospheric reentry on August 11, 1982.

Occasionally trackers indulge in frivolous pursuits. Every Christmas Eve, NORAD and the Space Command team up to broadcast bulletins on Santa Claus's progress by plotting the route of Rudolph and the gang.

That's a tension reliever, an A-team video game highly trained grownups play in their downtime. But no one inside the Mountain ever forgets the real reason they're there: they are waiting for a war nobody wants, the one that could end the world.

In the past decade, a series of defense secretaries have fought to upgrade the 1960s technology at Cheyenne Mountain and defend the early warning complex against critics who charge it is archaic, even dangerous, because it frequently breaks.

In 1979, a repairman accidentally inserted a test tape into Cheyenne Mountain's computer system. The error triggered a mad scramble to verify what the tape was telling the experts: that the Soviets were attacking. It didn't take long to discredit the computer data—the Air Force won't say how long but claims it was done by an elaborate system of checks and balances, which includes actually picking up the phone and talking to satellite monitoring crews strategically based around the globe. But by the time the mistake was discovered, fighter and bomber pilots were poised at the edge of runways, ready to take off with nuclear warheads on board.

The very next year, a faulty computer chip signaled another false attack. The Air Force claims it took less than two minutes to catch the error. But the fact that a mistake occurred fueled doubts about NORAD's highly touted redundancy and guaranteed fail-safe procedures.

Such screwups have led to a projected $1.6 billion upgrade at the Mountain. But modernization has not silenced opponents, who remain convinced the Cheyenne Mountain crowd is still capable of bungling on such a colossal scale that the United States could accidentally go to war because of flaws in the warning system. Daniel Ford, a former executive director of the Union of Concerned Scientists, argued in *The Button,* published by Simon and Schuster in 1985, that the President might be pressured to fire American ICBMs first because he was afraid he wouldn't be able to communicate with his pilots, submariners, and missileers by the time the Soviets actually launched their weapons.

Ford's recitation of horror stories—ringing phones that went unanswered, the malfunctioning chip, broken radars, ailing computers thirty years old—has less credence as NORAD undergoes its billion-dollar face-lift.

In a perfect scenario, sensors and computers inside the Mountain, which are married to sensors and computers under the sea, atop volcanoes, and in the sky, can warn of a missile attack or an assault from space in microseconds . . . but there is no way the United States can respond to stop the incoming death. The only thing we can do is shoot back, a last-act retaliation, the ultimate MADness—Mutually Assured Destruction. NORAD's role in the nation's defense system is to warn of an attack. Retaliation is the responsibility of other military commands.

If the attack comes, an alarm would go off inside the Missile Warning Center buried 1,700 feet below the summit. There are other command posts inside the Mountain: the Space Defense Operations Center, the Space Surveillance Center, and the Air Defense Operations Center. But it's where vigilant men and women wait for missiles to fire that there's sweat on uniforms and furrows in brows when the alarms go off.

The nerve center is a dimly lit auditorium, much like a movie theater where everybody's perpetually waiting for the feature to start. It is sleek with molded plastic, textured fabric, neutral colors, and consoles covered with buttons. Comfortable as a corporate boardroom, the center's chairs are deep and plush, especially designed for eight-hour shifts. Banks of phones are within easy reach of each of the dozen or so officers and enlisted personnel on duty. The phones look normal but come in several colors—including red.

The room is dominated by a huge screen designed to bring the whole world into close-up. Depending on its operator's commands, the screen will track space objects, illuminate NORAD checkpoints, follow the track of Soyuz, the Soviet space station—or do everything at once. Its instantaneous fine tuning makes it the ultimate big-screen TV.

Even though NORAD public relations experts doggedly tell every tour group the command center bears little resemblance to the Hollywood mock-up in the mid-1980s movie *War Games,* a cursory glance proves them wrong. It does come with bells and whistles, bright lights and neon lines.

When visitors without security clearances enter the room on tour—as they do at least once a day—the monitors and giant screen are declassified. But if a Soviet missile—for that matter, any foreign missile, mystery airplane, or unidentified submarine-launched projectile—was suddenly fired on a trajectory toward Kansas City, the room would instantly be cleared of all but the wizards.

A hostile-weapons launch is first evaluated by the one-star general who's always on duty inside the Mountain. He seldom leaves his chair, except to go to the bathroom in an adjoining room. He eats meals at his console. Mostly he stares at the screen. He is the first link in the warning chain. If he doesn't like what he sees, he picks up the direct line to the four-star general who is the commander in chief (CINC) of both NORAD and the U.S. Space Command. No matter where the CINC goes—to the Pentagon or to bed—the phone goes with him. It's his responsibility to warn the Pentagon and the President of an imminent threat to the United States.

The CINC makes the decision, day or night. One commander said that during a spate of middle-of-the-night phone calls initiated from the Mountain because of foreign missile launches, he found himself in, well, an uncomfortable position. Each time he answered the phone, he realized he was trying to decide what was more important at that instant— evaluating whether he had to alert the President to an attack, or whether he should first go pee.

In the event of war, the Mountain's pair of massive blast doors—three feet thick, twenty-five tons apiece—would hydraulically snap shut in forty-five seconds. Once closed, the first door is flush with the rock wall of the main tunnel, so that an atomic blast and its vaporizing heat would whoosh past the Steel City entrance and keep on going until it blew out of the south side of the mountain.

The second blast door, set fifty feet farther inside the Mountain, would entomb the men and women on duty. There would be no time for a last kiss, a whispered "I love you" to families still innocently going about their day in the suburbs and schools far below, where lives would end in a blinding flash less than half an hour after somebody halfway around the world pushed a button or turned a key.

Would the troops encased in the Mountain's four-and-a-half-acre bomb shelter survive? Probably, unless the enemy intercontinental ballistic missile (ICBM) scored a bull's-eye. As the attack progressed, four separate warning systems would tally the end of civilization on a scoreboard much like the one at Yankee Stadium: warheads already impacted (IMPD), warheads not yet impacted (NYI), time to go until next impact (TTG). It is the ultimate World Series: first strike and you're all out. The ball game is over.

For the warriors left alive behind the blast doors, and the handful of others burrowed deep in the earth under the Pentagon, the White House, the National Security Agency, or still flying around in the presidential command post or the Strategic Air Command's Looking Glass bomber, there would at last be time to think. Perhaps even to pray. Too little comfort, too late.

But in peacetime, there is comfort in routine. Any parent knows that babies, deprived of their regular cribs, their familiar blanket, their anticipated bottle at bedtime, become cranky and cross. So, too, do grown-up men and women.

That is why, 24 hours a day, 365 days a year, life inside the Mountain is predicated on routine. Even surprise alerts have a familiar pattern. Preparing for nuclear war is not a serendipitous enterprise. Three times a day, the Mountain greets a shift of experts who pass by guards with guns, stride through the open blast doors, and enter the command center's cocoon. Each expert is trained for a highly specific job involving monitoring the safety from attack of North America.

And all of them, as well as the radar operators at Shemya Air Force Base in the Aleutian Islands, and trackers on the coral specks of Kwajalein, Ascension, and Antigua, as well as remote listeners in Greenland, Turkey, and England, answer to the CINC. There are more than twenty thousand officers and enlisted personnel under the CINC. He reports directly to the secretary of defense. It has always been a "he" and will probably stay that way for years to come.

There have been nineteen NORAD commanders. The CINC has always been an American, since the U.S. has more, and bigger, military hardware than the Canadians. Conversely, the DCINC—deputy commander in chief—always hails from across the northern border. The Maple Leaf flies in tandem with the Stars and Stripes on the perfectly manicured lawn of the command building at Peterson Air Force Base, just east of Colorado Springs. Relations between the two forces, which are completely integrated at all levels, are almost always cordial and correct. But everyone knows who carries the biggest stick.

Unlike NORAD, which has long been an institutional tradition and during the 1962 Cuban missile crisis had more than a quarter-million troops under its shield, the U.S. Space Command is relatively new. It was designated a separate entity only on September 23, 1985. The first boss of both outfits was General Robert Herres, a movie-idol-handsome Naval Academy graduate who took over NORAD on July 30, 1984, and also assumed the mantle of U.S. SPACE COMM CINC upon its creation. At the pomp-and-circumstance ceremony marking Herres's ascendancy, the chairman of the Joint Chiefs of Staff, General John Vessey, Jr., said: "NORAD is the one command in the world where we can't go out and correct our failures. We have to be right the first time."

Herres, at fifty-one, was a young four-star general in a hurry. Eloquent and politically astute, the Denver native was the grandson of a German immigrant who started a laundry and dry cleaners. His father ran the family business until he went into real estate. His older brother, Will junior, was graduated from West Point in 1943, and Herres followed with his own diploma from Annapolis in 1954 but opted for a commission in the Air Force instead of a career in the Navy.

From then on, his credentials were as fast track as a warrior's could get: fighter pilot, bomber pilot, intelligence analyst, astronaut, electronics wizard, a master's degree in electrical engineering from the Air Force Institute of Technology, a master's degree in public administration from George Washington University, and a stint with honors at the Air Command and Staff College and the Industrial College of the Armed Forces.

When he turned over his commands to General John Louis "Pete" Piotrowski (pronounced Pa-trau-ski) on February 6, 1987, he collected the Defense Distinguished Service Medal, the country's highest peacetime military award, and went off to Washington to become vice chairman of the Joint Chiefs for about a year. Then, in the tradition of thousands before him, the young, athletic general retired to the Sunbelt and took a cushy, well-paying civilian job. In insurance.

As president of the property and casualty insurance division of the United Services Automobile Association, headquartered in San Antonio, Texas, Herres is forever assured of being called "sir." The big insurer is exclusively for active-duty military or military retirees and their dependents. San Antonio, like Colorado Springs, Orlando, San Diego, and a handful of other genteelly conservative, blatantly patriotic, relentlessly upscale communities, is a mecca for retired officers.

In such enclaves, the rigid military protocol that holds the active-duty services together at U.S. bases around the world is still all-pervasive. Herres, who came just one promotion short of the pinnacle of military life as chairman of the Joint Chiefs, is at the top of the social heap in San Antonio.

If Herres was as sleek as a Gucci loafer, Piotrowski is as unpretentious as an old boot. Both men's personalities were mirrored in their differing visions of their responsibilities as CINC.

"My predecessor—and I'm not being critical when I say this—he emphasized 'this is how you advise the President, this is what happens, this is what you do.' He didn't tell me—maybe he hadn't figured it out—the fact that your most important responsibility is not falsely going to war."

Piotrowski reflected on Herres's advice after he, too, had retired as commander in chief of NORAD and the Space Command. He said his predecessor "worried about reliable and unambiguous data." His own midnight reflections were different.

"It took me about six months to realize what's important, to question 'What's my real responsibility?'" said Piotrowski. "You have these stimuli, these quiet periods when you reflect on what's happened and what you need to do. I've always been a believer in something somebody told me long ago, that you have to make it happen, make it better, make it last.

"So you're sitting around trying to figure out how to make it better, how to make it happen. Making it last comes after that. You start thinking: What's really important? What am I trying to do here?

"In that reflectivity I had a blazing glimpse of the obvious: Pete, your job is not going to war. That's easy. Your job is not going *falsely* to war.

"The Soviets are launching all the time. We see missile launches two or three times a day. Every launch could be a decision, but the only time I need to enter into the decision process is if the missile appears to be a threat to North America or one of the overseas warning areas NORAD watches. And a lot of them do. I'd say two or three times a

THE GENERAL IN THE MOUNTAIN

week, and the reason they appear to be a threat is that the Soviets launch them on an azimuth, a compass angle. If the missile flew its theoretical limit it could reach North America. That means NORAD has to make an assessment.

"A woman once asked me, on one of the many tours we have, she said, 'General, how do you live with this enormous responsibility?' I'd never really thought about it. Well, the answer I gave her is one that it took me about thirty seconds to come up with. . . . In the Air Force I've learned to live with responsibility one day at a time. I've been given increasing responsibilities over time, and you never notice the fact that they're significantly greater than what you started out with. I guess challenge is a good word, but I never even considered it a challenge, but more a responsibility. A duty.

"It never struck me as being weighty or difficult or whatever. The most difficult part of a CINC's responsibility is not to go to war falsely. The difficult part would be, in the face of false stimuli, to convince the President this was NOT an attack and here's why. Or, in the event of a real attack, to convince the President: 'We're under attack and you have to make a decision!' . . . and to be able to do that succinctly and cogently in one or two minutes.

"Also, the responsibility is on me to get off the phone. I figured out that people who have difficult decisions to make generally procrastinate by asking for more information. Well, I couldn't afford to let the President ask for more information. I had to give it to him and shut up. And if he tried to get more information out of me, then I would have to tell him, in a nice way, 'This is what's happening, I told you all I know, and now you have to make a decision. Sir.'

"As I said, it took me six months in the job to figure out what it was."

Thoughtful words spoken by a fifty-six-year-old man who, four decades ago, couldn't afford to go to high school.

Today, after cresting at the highest level of his profession, Piotrowski is a civilian again, and I-25—America's Nuclear Highway—is his Main Street. A devoted family man with a severely retarded twenty-two-year-old son living at home, the general has retired with his wife, Sheila, in Colorado Springs. There he plans to build his dream house and settle down after twenty-nine transfers in thirty-eight years.

But after three decades of intense mental labor, his mind is far from idle. Colorado Springs has become a springboard for a burgeoning consulting business that often takes him behind the electronic barriers that protect the Lawrence Livermore National Laboratory, in the California desert sixty-five miles east of San Francisco. There, Piotrowski works on top-secret research with Manhattan Project legend Edward Teller and his brilliant protégé Lowell Wood.

A devoted advocate and contributing architect of the Strategic Defense Initiative's "Brilliant Pebbles" concept, Piotrowski was the military point man for the project before his retirement. Now he increasingly is in demand by SDI proponents trying to salvage Reagan's multibillion-dollar Star Wars in an era of perestroika and trillion-dollar deficits.

Theoretically, Brilliant Pebbles—originally called "Smart Rocks," before someone pointed out that it invoked an image of Stone Age and caveman warfare—would scatter a missile shield high in space and defend America against invading ICBMs by crashing into them.

The fleet of about five thousand independent, self-orbiting interceptors, each weighing one hundred pounds and costing about $1 million, would continually circle the earth, carrying their own computers. Each could detect the fiery exhaust of an ascending ICBM and fling itself into the path of the missile and destroy it. Sort of like a robot kamikaze. None of the "pebbles" would be armed with any kind of explosive.

Piotrowski and his cohorts are absolutely convinced Brilliant Pebbles is the surefire answer to defending America against a nuclear attack; critics say the technology will never be developed to make the concept succeed, and if by some incredible fluke it is, it will cost too much to deploy.

So who is Pete Piotrowski, the professional colleague of Teller, an adviser to presidents, veteran of years of congressional testimony and a thousand black-tie dinners? He is the quintessential Nuclear Highway Military Man, a role model for junior officers striving to succeed in the atomic age.

Supremely confident, Pete Piotrowski is the fearless fighter pilot at the controls of the nation's nuclear defense, Luke Skywalker ready to slay Darth Vader—but only if absolutely necessary. He is the thoughtful warrior, but a warrior nonetheless. As ordered, he will tell the President the missiles are coming. But unlike many of history's generals, he will not take any pleasure in the war.

A natural pilot, a genuine patriot, a political survivor, Piotrowski is surprisingly articulate and outspoken for someone who's spent his whole career following the chain of command. Unlike many soldiers who take the oath early and retire young, he has hobbies and extracurricular pursuits. He is an accomplished fly fisherman who can lay down a line between two high-summer willows and not disturb a leaf; a downhill skier who seeks out the most difficult black runs on any mountain; a precise carpenter who takes pleasure in remodeling his own house; a big-game hunter who doesn't brag about his trophies.

Piotrowski is Jack Armstrong, the All-American Boy, who grew up to be Horatio Alger, Self-Made Man. He even looks like Gary Cooper. Not the young Sergeant York Cooper but the older, wiser Cooper who stood in the street at high noon and faced down all the evil that men do, the Cooper of straight back, strong jaw, square gaze. Piotrowski's eyes, on a clear Colorado afternoon, match the blue of the sky. His head is

finely sculpted, the skin tight across his bones. His graying
blond hair, clipped short in military fashion, rebels with a
slight curl at the forehead. His manner is direct but always
courtly and attentive, like that of an older Ashley Wilkes come
to visit Tara with his grandchildren.

He is a man who has struggled to make his life happen,
who got nothing on a silver platter, or even a chipped plate.
His father, also named John, was a rough-edged petty officer
in the Navy in World War I, an orphan from Ford City,
Pennsylvania, who left as a teenager in search of adventure.
He got as far as China and a gunboat on the Yangtze River,
so it was natural that when the orphan child came home a
man, he still had itchy feet. Pete's father played the minor
league baseball circuit in the '20s and '30s, for such teams as
the Buffalo Bisons, a tough way to earn a living but a chance
to be footloose a little longer.

When John married Mary Hellstein, she was an educated
schoolteacher. It was time to settle down. First came daughter Marilyn, then Pete, on February 17, 1934, in the cradle
of the Depression.

"I was smart. I was a voracious reader. I read everything
in the house, everything I could get my hands on, a lot of
things three or four times. My mother taught me to read; she
was the educated one. My dad told me sea stories about places
he'd been, things he'd done, a lot about the world, romantic
things about the Mediterranean, the South Pacific. I'm sure
that's why I started out wanting to be a navy officer.

"We were poor. We didn't consider ourselves poor, just
middle class, but we were at the bottom scale of the middle
class. I went to a trade school—the Henry Ford Trade School;
they paid fifteen dollars every two weeks."

For three years, Piotrowski went to school one week, then
worked two weeks in the factory as an apprentice tool-and-
diemaker. There were no vacations, no time away. Like his

neighborhood friends, he figured a job at Ford Motor Company was his future at age eighteen.

"My problem was, I graduated when I was just seventeen, because I'd skipped the third grade. Ford offered to keep me in a semi-status for fifty dollars a week for another year, but I wanted to go to school. They wouldn't send me, so I quit and went to work in drafting shops. I started making enormous money. I was one of the most skilled draftsmen in Detroit and probably making four hundred dollars a week. I was a major in the Air Force before I earned as much money as I did back then as a kid doing free-lance drafting. Since I was still at home, I continued to contribute to the family."

The poor kid with the trade school diploma had a dream of a free college education on a military school scholarship. He had heard the faint first echo of the drumbeat: *warrior . . . warrior . . .*

"I applied for the Naval Academy but couldn't get an appointment. The Coast Guard Academy was competitive, and I was always an 'A' student. Grades were easy to come by, so I had no qualms about being accepted."

He was right. But a month before he was due to report, he got a letter telling him not to come: the Academy didn't think his trade school math courses were sufficiently difficult.

"What I really think happened, with the hindsight of years and years of experience, is that somebody was a late applicant, and the Academy said, 'Gee, here's this guy Piotrowski, he doesn't have any influence or family connections, we'll just bounce him off the bottom.' Which is probably the greatest thing that happened to me. I'm a fatalist, I believe in fate, and I think that just firmed my resolve to get a better education, which I knew I had to work my way through."

Pete Piotrowski came of age with the Korean War, so he shopped around, interviewing military recruiters as though he were buying a new car from an eager salesman.

"The Air Force was the most progressive, had the most to offer. I was technically oriented, and they could give me a better education. I was told I was the only person they'd ever seen that scored 100 percent on the enlistment exam. I signed up on September 2, 1952, for four years at $75 a month, plus room and board."

And so it began, the great personal odyssey of a skinny poor kid from Detroit who just wanted a good education and a chance to work hard. Later, he would tell another generation of enlisted men how he saw his first USO Doughnut Dollies when the train from Detroit to Texas rolled through anonymous stations at midnight on its inexorable journey south. And there was another memory, one that would forever influence his style of command.

"When I got off the train in Missouri, there were both colored and white bathrooms and water fountains. While Detroit wasn't exactly a model of integration, I went to school with all minorities, so that sight was sobering. What struck me—I never forgot it—was that the black kids on the train that I enlisted with were raucous and friendly and outgoing as long as we were in the North, but when they got off the train in Missouri, there wasn't any question in their minds, they had to drink from the colored people's water fountains. They just automatically did it. They knew that segregation existed and that they were going to be treated differently in the South. And although I'd come from the same environment, I didn't know. Until that trip, I didn't have the foggiest notion of what was going on. I made up my mind I never wanted that to happen to me again."

When the *Enola Gay* dropped Little Boy on Hiroshima, Pete Piotrowski was eleven years old. Seven years later, when he felt the urge to serve his country and help himself at the same time, he was still, like the nuclear era, an adolescent. Over the years, they grew up together, the Kid and the Bomb.

The first experimental thermonuclear device, code-named Mike, was developed at Los Alamos and shipped to the South Pacific. On November 1, 1952—just sixty days after Piotrowski was sworn into the Air Force—the tiny Marshall Islands atoll of Elugelab vanished in the vaporizing effects of the atomic equivalent of 10.4 million tons of TNT—a bomb blast nearly a thousand times more powerful than either of the weapons dropped on Japanese cities to end World War II.

The inauguration of the thermonuclear testing age unleashed shock waves that eventually rained down on thousands of people who would become afflicted by deadly fallout, in the Pacific and in the American West when the test sites were shifted to the Nevada desert. But in the aftermath of Mike's success there was nothing but jubilation at Los Alamos. America was definitely ahead in the Cold War.

Piotrowski was still in basic training, a lowly airman—serial number AF16426048—at Lackland Air Force Base in San Antonio when Elugelab burned in a three-mile-wide fireball. Because the test was top secret, he, like the rest of the world, was unaware that the free world had upped the ante.

He'd enlisted to become a draftsman, a skill he'd already perfected. With the institutional wisdom recognized by anyone who's ever served in the U.S. military, the Air Force told him he wasn't qualified because he was a tool-and-die draftsman, and what their designers drew were barracks and hangars. So they sent the kid who didn't know one end of a light bulb from another to electronics school. Fortunately, he was good at that too. Being good at things meant applying himself to the task until he got it right. It was an ethic he'd been taught since childhood.

"My father was a craftsman in his own right, even though he was on the police force. He took enormous personal pride in the way he dressed, he always wore his uniform impec-

165

cably, and when he did things around the house, they were a source of pride. So I grew up with a sense of 'Always do the best you can and be proud of what you do.' As I look back on my life, I think that's the reason for my success. I always wanted to produce more and wanted my work to be precise. I was very technically oriented and very idealistic."

The recruit with one stripe on his sleeve was learning how to fix radar when he hit on the idea of applying for cadet school. He was nineteen.

"My eyesight was very good, something like twenty-fifteen. So they said, 'What would you like to be?' and I said I'd like to be a pilot. They said, 'Great, we'll put you in for pilot training, and it will be about two years before you get accepted.' But then they said that if I wanted to be a navigator I could get in right away. It took me about half a second to figure out the difference between the $75 a month I was making as an airman and the $300-a-month officers' pay. Besides, officers dated all the pretty girls. I said, 'You just got yourself a navigator.'"

By the time he was commissioned, the Korean War had ended, but Piotrowski was a diligent student and was soon leapfrogging ahead of his instructors. At a time when a lot of GIs were coming home, his superiors decided to send him overseas. He got to Seoul in February of 1955 and flew B-26s as an electronics warfare officer. Although his unit was later assigned to an American air base outside Osaka, Japan, Piotrowski continued to fly missions over Korea, fingerprinting and occasionally jamming enemy radar. In those days, the enemy was Communist China and its North Korean ally. It was exciting, challenging work, but after a while even that became . . . well, routine.

Then along came Marlon Brando. And Red Buttons. And two months in a posh Kyoto hotel during the filming of the movie classic *Sayonara*.

"I was in it. I *am* in it. They didn't cut me out." Piotrowski recounts his cinematic debut—and farewell performance—with the glee of an ingenue accepting her first bouquet. The two months he spent as a "technical adviser" on the film were clearly a highlight, albeit a frivolous one, of his life.

"They were looking for a drunk in a bar scene. The role models back in Korea wouldn't fit the mold today. All my heroes were alcoholics, and I was, I guess, a good hard drinker even though I didn't like the stuff. But if you didn't drink, you were an outcast. So one day at what we call happy hour at the officers' club, I was lifting my roommate back onto the barstool when a fella came up and said, 'How'd you like to be in the movies?' I said something terrible to him, and he came back and said, 'No, I'm serious, we need a couple of drunks for a bar scene.' We said, 'We're your men!' Me and Vaughn Lancaster, who was an absolute reprobate, one of the guys I went through school with. We flew together, drank together, rode motorcycles together, played golf together."

Lancaster, who retired as a major in 1970 and now drives a school bus in Oklahoma City, can't stop himself from chuckling when he thinks back.

"We met when I was a staff sergeant and he was barely a corporal. For a while I was his boss, which gives me a kick now when I think about it. Then we went through cadets together—he got his commission before he was twenty-one, a rare event even in those days—and we got shipped overseas. How did we get in the movie? You might say we just sort of fell into it. We were footloose and fancy free and did what every bachelor did in those days. They were great times, and Pete was in the thick of it. 'Course, in the movie, I'm the one laid out on the couch."

Piotrowski remembers their sole "advisers" task as

"keeping the ribbons straight, the brass polished, and actors talking the right jargon. For ninety days we partied. Then I came home to be a pilot."

The drum began to beat with a steady cadence. *Warrior . . . Warrior.* To come up through the ranks and get commissioned is rare in the military, and Piotrowski realized he was beginning to step ahead, beyond the bar scenes with the boys. He graduated first in his class in the aviation cadet program at Harlingen Air Force Base, Texas, and became a second lieutenant in the U.S. Air Force in August 1954. When they pinned on his shiny new wings, he at last broke from his chrysalis to fly away and become a full-fledged warrior committed to a cause.

"I went home to visit my sweetheart and family and friends, people I'd admired, people I really had looked up to. And I discovered they were terribly shallow. Their interests were focused on the bowling alley and the neighborhood grocery store and boating on the lake. They didn't have the foggiest idea that was happening in the world. That's the first time I knew that people I was associated with in the Air Force were a cut above the rest in terms of commitment, dedication, and wanting to make a difference."

The twenty-three-year-old hotshot was soon flying fighters in the desert outside Phoenix. "It was wild, exciting, every man a tiger." And as an officer he got the prettiest girl. Sheila Dee Frederickson was a secretary, daughter of a crusty, entrepreneurial gas station owner who got his start selling apples in Wisconsin during the Depression and wound up in Arizona prospecting for uranium and mercury. The oldest of three children, Sheila was a spirited blonde with a tinkling laugh that came swift and often. Just when Piotrowski knew he'd fallen in love, he got transferred—across the sprawling suburbs to the other side of town. So night after night, he drove the hundred-mile round trip to go a-courtin'. With his new captain's bars on his shoulder, his fair lady on his arm, and a powerful jet engine in his hands, life was good.

And then a general came to see him.

"It was a little room, dark. The general said, 'I'm going to ask you three questions. If you answer the first correctly, I'll ask you the second one. If you answer the second one correctly, I'll ask you the third. Anything we say cannot leave this room.'

"The first question was, 'Are you willing to fly old, obsolete aircraft?' That was easy. I was already flying old, obsolete T-33s as well as F-86s. The second question was, 'Are you willing to fly combat?' That was easy too, 'cause that's what I'd raised my right hand to do in the first place. The third question was, 'If you're shot down and captured, are you willing to be disowned by your government?' It didn't take long to figure that one out, because I'd been in the service in the Korean War. I knew our POWs didn't come home because they were claimed by the government. It took action after the war to get them back. So I said, 'Yes, sir.' And the general said, 'Fine. Don't call us, we'll call you.'"

Piotrowski was ripe for the clarion call of the young, idealistic president who challenged him to look into his heart and "Ask not what your country can do for you; ask what you can do for your country." In April 1961, he called his fiancée and said, "I'm leaving. I'll see you sometime in the future." In May, at the start of training in the swamps of central Florida, Piotrowski learned he was to be one of seven officers in a new, forty-man top-secret unit nicknamed "Jungle Jim."

"Colonel Ben King was the commander. Marvelous man. He was like Patton, stood up on a stage to address us. We weren't told where we were going, but I well remember his initial words:

"'There are a lot of you here for a lot of reasons. Some of you because you think you're gonna get fame and glory, some of you because you think you're gonna get extra money, some of you because you're escaping other organizations and this is the only way out, and some of you because you want to make a contribution. All I'm promising you is long hours, hard work, and lots of it.'

"I thought I was gonna be a fighter pilot, but they needed an armaments and electronics officer. I went to see my superior and told him I really didn't know much about it. He reached in his desk and pulled out two books. One was about bombs, the other was about ammunition. He said, 'Everything you need to know is in these books.' I read them cover to cover ten times, and although I didn't realize it, I'd become the Air Force's foremost expert on ammunition and fuses."

Piotrowski's first assignment, on a Saturday afternoon, was to cannibalize nearly everything on the base to come up with bombs and guns for two antiquated airplanes his boss wanted to fly on Monday morning. He found a sergeant with a big toolbox and a lot of chutzpah, and together they raided everything from the ammunition dump to the marina at midnight, where they stole twenty-five-pound practice bombs that were holding down yachts. Then they conned a buddy into calling out false scores to the colonel as he flew their cobbled-together B-26 and T-28 on practice bombing runs.

"Nobody could see the bombs hit because the sand was wet and there was no smoke charge, so I was instantly a hero." For the first of many times to come.

During his mysterious training in the saw grass and stench of the Florida Everglades, the Bay of Pigs fiasco broke apart nearby on Cuban reefs. Piotrowski and his buddies thought they'd been slated to be part of that debacle, but their grueling conditioning continued. One day Colonel King met Piotrowski on the tarmac as he returned from a trip.

"He told me I was leaving the next day, and I was to meet

a fellow in Formosa [Taiwan]. I said, 'That's it?' and he said, 'Yes. And cover your tracks.'

"Meanwhile, I'd proposed to Sheila, and she'd just gotten to Fort Walton Beach. I took her to dinner, told her I was leaving but didn't know where I was going, I couldn't give her an address, and I didn't know when I'd be back. She told me that if we weren't married by Christmas, she wouldn't be around when I got back. That's how we left it, which wasn't very appealing to me, but I had to go.

"I dressed as a civilian, got a whole bunch of visas in Los Angeles, and flew commercial all around the Pacific on my own money for five or six days. I had no official orders, so I finally ended up in the officers' club in Taipei, sat down at the bar, ordered a drink, and waited. Then I saw a guy I knew and told him I was out of the Air Force, looking for work, and I'd heard a certain fella was hiring. He said, 'Oh, sure. He runs the CIA operation down in Tainan.' And that's how I found my contact, purely a stroke of luck." Security precautions prevented his superiors from giving him any more information.

When he hooked up with the CIA on Taiwan, which operated under the cover name Air Asia, Piotrowski's job was to redesign B-26s and T-28s left over from World War II and Korea to carry bombs for yet another war. The planes were flown from the U.S. to the Philippines, where their markings were changed and they were modified for low-level bombing and strafing missions. Then they were flown on to Saigon. Eventually the CIA ran its own airline—Air America—throughout Indochina during the war.

Which is how Piotrowski became one of the first Americans to fight in Vietnam. He was flying combat missions with the First Air Commando Wing in January of 1962, a full three years before the U.S. Marines stormed ashore at Da Nang and American troops officially entered the conflict between the Communist North Vietnamese and the Republic of South Vietnam.

"The CIA protected me from everything. My money was being deposited in a checking account back in the States. People would get on my back and I'd tell my CIA contact and suddenly they'd be nice to me. I married Sheila over the telephone and it only cost me twenty-five dollars.

"We were dropping bombs on the Vietcong, flying out of Vietnamese fighter bases all over the country, sleeping on the ground in tents until the buildup started. My bio says I flew 110 missions, but it was a lot more than that. Because it was a covert operation, there were no decorations, no medals, and no official combat. We wore Australian bush hats and were the Air Force's equivalent of the Army's Green Berets. There were six B-26s, eight T-28s, four C-47s, about 100 officers and a few more than 250 enlisted men."

Jungle Jim's official code name was Farm Gate, a spin-off from the World War II expression "he bought the farm" to explain that a fellow aviator had died in a crash.

There was always a Vietnamese pilot or observer in the back seat so the Kennedy administration could disavow any combat role in case the old planes crashed or were shot down, a frequent event. The standard line was that the Americans were merely "conducting training in a combat environment." Since the handful of foreign and American journalists assigned to Saigon, the sleepy backwater "Paris of the Pacific," were not allowed onto Bien Hoa or other Vietnamese bases, Piotrowski's and his buddies' increasing involvement went nearly undetected.

After six months he was ordered back to Florida to help orchestrate the buildup from behind a desk, but his reunion with Sheila in a tiny apartment was brief. He returned to Vietnam the following February for another six-month tour, to show the U.S. generals, now proliferating like mushrooms in Saigon, some fancy new weaponry to throw against a determined Charlie in black pajamas who was inventing a new style of warfare—and winning.

Piotrowski's historical footnote was assured by his fraternal connection with Jungle Jim. He got lucky, he got there first, and he didn't get killed or screw up. His superiors, quick to realize his potential as well as his patriotism, put him on a fast track. First they sent him to college—he got a bachelor of science degree at the University of Nebraska–Omaha—and then they sent him to the Air Force's "top gun" school.

"That's the Valhalla of fighter pilots. What happened there was the turning point in my career. I got there late and had two days of classes for a ten-day course. When I took the exam I scored one hundred. They accused me of cheating. I was incensed, enraged! I told them they thought I was stupid because I'd come from Air Commandos, but they'd ignored the fact that not only did I fly aircraft with similar equipment, but I also took the maintenance courses so I'd be as smart as the sergeant that worked for me. So they asked me a lot of questions, and I answered them on the spot. They decided that I hadn't cheated. But that incident changed my life. I decided that because of their accusation I would ace all the courses. I even went down to the hobby shop at night and built training aids that were better than the ones they had. I became the second man to graduate from the Air Force's Fighter Weapons School with a perfect score."

His flawless record catapulted him to Nellis Air Force Base, outside Las Vegas, to teach generals about weapons. He wound up an F-4 instructor pilot and chief of academics. But he was also in charge of testing a nuclear weapon—the Walleye—that potentially could be used against the North Vietnamese. The parallel roads of the Kid and the Bomb had finally intersected. For Piotrowski, there was no ambivalence about the value of splitting atoms to wage war.

"What I learned over time is that when you fight a war, you send in an overwhelming force and fight savagely at the outset. You save lives by fighting a short war and forcing the other side to quit. You don't have to use the atomic bomb, but when we did use it, it was humane in the long run. . . . Three hundred thousand to a million people, both Americans and Japanese, would have died if there had been an invasion of Japan."

Without arming it with its nuclear warhead, Piotrowski tested the Walleye missile on combat missions against the North Vietnamese along the Chinese border near Kunming, the same city that had been home to a renegade bunch of American pilots calling themselves "Flying Tigers" during World War II.

"I decided that most people don't know anything about the laws of probability and what it takes for a determined force to destroy a target. So I set out to find out. I discovered it didn't matter if you dropped six bombs at once or six bombs one at a time; you had the same probability of hitting something. Which means you don't have to buy six times as many bombs as you need, which the Department of Defense was doing."

Piotrowski calculated a mathematical equation he thought would knock out five consecutive enemy bridges in a single bombing run.

"It was a mission I'll never forget because of the stupidity of it. They sent us against a railroad that was five miles from the Chinese border. We had to fly at noon because the Walleye was an electro-optic bomb that looked at black-white contrast. In other words, we had to have sunlight and shadows on the target. We were ordered to fly up and back by an identical route. I figured if we got there we'd be lucky, but if we came home the same way they'd be waiting. Besides, we'd be out of gas and wouldn't be able to fight. Which meant that if we did fight, we'd wind up bailing out. I argued, but this lieutenant colonel sitting safe back in Saigon wouldn't budge. We had to do it his way."

So the warrior climbed into his cockpit and took off. Three companion F-4s were in the formation when it roared away from Da Nang in August 1967. Their luck held; they hit the bridges, then got jumped by MiGs north of Hanoi, escaped, and made it home six hours later. That night, Piotrowski found out that the "milk run" mission he'd been slated to fly with his old buddy and former student Chuck "Tippy" Tyler before he'd been reassigned to the "suicide run" had ended in disaster. Tyler was shot down and taken prisoner. He wasn't released until 1973, six years later.

"Fate intervened. It was one of those events you have no control over. I never tried to influence my career. The only thing I ever did was say, 'Yes, sir.'

"Most people believe it's the other guy that's gonna get it. If you put twenty people in a room and say fifteen of them aren't coming back, you look around and say, 'Gee, I feel sorry for those other bastards.' The only difference between me and most others in combat was that I never drank. I started out being an alcoholic in Korea, but by the time I got to Air Commandos I'd learned enough about combat to know that you needed all the advantages you could get.

"I never considered myself the best of anything. I always figured there was somebody better, so I had to work harder. Before a mission I was always sober and I always tried to get a good night's sleep.

"And of course, I'm not an excitable person."

Piotrowski's stateside reward was more schooling, this time at the Armed Forces Staff College. As a young captain, he had modest ambitions. But he was being groomed for bigger things.

"I still hadn't grasped the idea that I was going to be a

senior commander. I knew I was a good pilot—I'd survived!—I knew I had a good mind, that I scored well on tests, but I didn't figure I was special or unique or would be chosen for a responsible position. I believed in fate and luck. My goal was to make lieutenant colonel before I retired.''

Like a professional golfer who has a good round, the soldier dispassionately looked at himself and tallied up the positive and negative. He thought it came out about even. Others did not.

"Leaders are created, not born," said General W. L. Creech, Piotrowski's commander for nearly seven years of his career, and a major mentor. "Pete was always above the crowd. . . . He always had excellent insight into human nature, he understood that a leader creates more leaders, and he was always working the country's problems and the Air Force's problems before his own problems. And having been an enlisted man, he never forgot that commitment comes from the bottom up. He could always relate to the bottom of the pile.''

Creech, who retired as a four-star general in 1974, now lives near Las Vegas and has an international management consulting business. Like Piotrowski, he rose through the enlisted ranks. Less than 3 percent of the Air Force's generals achieve success by that route.

"There's not a strong leisure ethic in Pete Piotrowski," said Creech. "It's not a Mother Teresa sacrifice for him to decide whether to go fly fishing or go to work. Work is what he loves to do. To him, Saturday and Sunday is that unpleasant interlude between Friday, when people leave work, and Monday, when they come back to work.

"Pete's success isn't because of fate or karma. It's because of his talent and dedication. He's not unique; there are others like him. But the Air Force—the country—needs more of him. He's the epitome of the breed.''

176

When Piotrowski came home from Vietnam the third time, it was 1967. What followed was a whirlwind, even in the dry litany of an official biography:

A stint at the Pentagon;

Royal Air Force College of Air Warfare in England;

Bitburg Air Force Base, West Germany, as assistant, then deputy commander for operations, 36th Tactical Fighter Wing;

Commander, 40th Tactical Group, Aviano AFB, Italy, his first assignment from Creech and General Davy Jones, who eventually would become chairman of the Joint Chiefs and another Piotrowski cheerleader;

Commander, 552nd Airborne Warning and Control (AWACS) Wing, Tinker AFB, Oklahoma;

Deputy Commander, Tactical Air Command, Peterson AFB, Colorado;

Deputy Chief of Staff, then later vice commander, Tactical Air Command, Langley AFB, Virginia;

Commander, 9th Air Force, Shaw AFB, South Carolina;

Vice Chief of Staff, United States Air Force, Pentagon.

Finally, on February 6, 1987, Piotrowski became commander in chief of NORAD and the U.S. Space Command.

Twenty years. He and Sheila had produced three children, lived in nearly a hundred houses, apartments, or cramped rooms, and pinched pennies to make do on a soldier's pay, which never stretched far enough. When he finally made CINC, he annually grossed just $78,000, had an entertainment allowance of less than $2,000, and lost his $400-a-month flight pay.

The man who would be responsible for telling the President of the United States that World War III had started, who oversaw nearly 20,000 employees and a $900 million yearly budget and supervised assets totaling $10 billion, earned less than a second-year stockbroker or a junior partner in a mediocre law firm.

"It isn't the pay or the perks that keep you driving forward, striving for excellence," said General Creech. "With the best of the best, it never is."

Hal Frederickson, who owns a forty-five-pump gas station in Mesa, Arizona, is Piotrowski's brother-in-law and best friend. His favorite memory of Pete centers on a rugged mountain range in British Columbia in 1967, when the two of them were slogging through the wilderness, hunting mountain goats.

"We kept climbing and kept climbing, up over these ridges where there was barely room for your foot. I kept thinking we should turn back, it was really dangerous, but we kept pressing on. Finally, I suggested we go back. The guide turned around and said to us, 'Once you get up here on top of the mountain, you never turn back.' We kept going. When I think of that experience I think of the way Pete's lived his whole life. He keeps moving forward; he never turns back."

Piotrowski's whole professional life prepared him to assume command of NORAD and the Space Command. He was ready for the responsibility, and he welcomed it.

"I have given a lot of thought to space, to warfare, to nuclear weapons, to the quest for peace," he said after he put away his uniform and reentered private life after thirty-five years in the Air Force.

"It's hard to envision a situation where we would be willing to use nuclear weapons, absent all-out war with the Soviet Union. Not against Cuba. Not in Vietnam. It would be hard to advocate the use of nuclear weapons when the national security of the United States is not at risk. My biggest concern has always been Third World nations possessing weapons of mass destruction.

178

"I can't see any provocation, short of severe military defeat at the hands of the United States and her allies, which would prompt the Soviets to wage nuclear war. The reason is that it would invite their own destruction."

But the general had long believed that President Jimmy Carter's cancellation of the B-1 bomber and curtailment of other military programs prompted the Russians to begin modernizing their weaponry.

"They did not accept that the American President was building down military forces as opposed to building them up and setting an example he hoped they would follow. Instead, they just laughed all the way to the arms factory. If you look back at the late '70s and early '80s, the national security lexicon changed so that we no longer talked about mutual deterrence, which had prevailed for four decades. Instead, we talked about parity, sufficiency, equivalency. And all those words meant was nuclear inferiority. We were—we are—really behind. And as Winston Churchill said, 'I'm not going to take sides against arithmetic.'"

In the euphoric early days of Mikhail Gorbachev's perestroika, a Russian delegation was invited to the United States by Wisconsin's Democratic representative Les Aspin, the chairman of the House Armed Services Committee. One of its stops was Colorado Springs, and Piotrowski was the host.

"I had to switch on my 'Big Picture' mind and say, 'OK, Piotrowski, what is it that this nation would like to show the Russians?' I kept it simple and came up with two points that would address their paranoia.

"First, I wanted them to know that nobody in the world can launch a ballistic missile or a weapon in space without us knowing about it—knowing what it is, where it's going, where it came from. Second, I wanted to convince them the United States would never go to war falsely, because we have built so much redundancy and reliability into our ballistic

179

missile warning system that we will recognize peaceful activity for what it is and we will instantly recognize warlike activity for what it is.

"There is absolutely no chance that one of our missiles or bombers will ever, ever be launched mistakenly. Procedures exist today to guarantee that a missile can't squirt out of one of our silos and head toward the Soviet Union by accident.

"In other words, I showed the Russians they can never surprise us, and they can expect retaliation as an absolute certainty. I wanted them to understand that if the President orders us to retaliate against their first strike, they could be assured that all our systems will work and we will destroy them."

Among the delegation was a four-star Soviet general, a highly decorated helicopter pilot who fought in Afghanistan, and a member of the Supreme Soviet, the U.S.S.R.'s governing body.

"As I anticipated, one of them asked me, 'Where is the red button that you push to launch missiles?' I explained that we don't have a red button in Cheyenne Mountain. We don't have any buttons. I explained that my sole function was to warn and that in the United States the warning function had very wisely been separated from the retaliation function. That only the President could give the order to retaliate.

"The Russians said that in their country several people could push their red button."

In his last command, Piotrowski became a space warrior arguing for militarization of the stars. He walked hundreds of miles in the halls of Congress, lobbying on behalf of the Strategic Defense Initiative, because he earnestly believed then—and if anything, he even more passionately believes now—that a protective shield against incoming nuclear weapons is the only way to prevent an enemy from attacking the United States.

When he took off the uniform and put away the silver braid, Pete Piotrowski did not tuck his oath of "duty, honor, country" into a cedar chest along with the trappings of his former life. From a small den in a modest home near the Garden of the Gods rock formation in Colorado Springs, he soldiers on, writing research papers, reading voluminous scientific reports until 3:00 A.M., fine-tuning speeches he'll give to Fortune 500 executives curious about Star Wars.

All those years that he was commander of this, commander of that, Piotrowski kept an old pair of pants, a work shirt, and his fly-fishing vest in his CINC closet. They were more talisman than necessity, because there were so few times he could play hooky from his Cold War responsibilities.

But Piotrowski lived long enough to see Russians in his war room, have a piece of the Berlin Wall as a souvenir on his desk, and get the old fishing clothes out of the closet with so much frequency that his patient wife finally complained.

If it is true that old soldiers never die, Piotrowski contradicts the notion that they fade away. He hopes to be around for Brilliant Pebbles, for what he truly believes will be the beginning of a final peace.

8

MISTAKES

*In the laboratory we've got 18- and 19-year-old boys, you
know, 20 and 21. And they didn't have schooling, so they don't
understand what radiation is. And they were in there from 10
till 8 . . . in that air room, and the sample will verify that it
was "hot" in that room.*

    KAREN SILKWOOD, *1974*

Jan Pilcher was sleeping the heavy sleep of childhood when
her eyelids lit up. Sitting up in bed at her grandparents' house
far, far out in the empty desert of Utah on a summer night
in 1955, she saw the sky aglow at midnight. She didn't know
that the sun had risen twice that day because the government
had detonated a twenty-eight-kiloton bomb in an aboveground nuclear test code-named "Zucchini."

"The ground shook, the bed shook, and everybody ran
outside to see what they could see. But of course there was
nothing, just the loud explosion and then the sky lighting up.
The people in Cedar City and St. George, which were the big
towns, would stand on the hilltops as the sky would turn
pink, but they didn't know what it was, either. The government was just starting atmospheric atomic testing, and people didn't know. Of course, they were all getting radiated."

Jan Pilcher was forty-two years old as she talked about

remembering the nuclear weapons test near a town that isn't there anymore. She held her infant daughter, Lila, in her arms as she spoke and occasionally gazed out at the brilliant sunshine, marveling at the beauty of a Denver autumn day. With her long blond hair, carefully applied makeup, and fashionable clothes, she could have been any upper-middle-class matron, reminiscing about an innocuous event from her past.

But Jan Vittum Pilcher has never taken anything lightly in her adult life. After she became a Quaker during her college years, she went to Vietnam on a tourist visa to see for herself what the war was all about. She traveled to Guatemala at the height of the death squad murders to verify with her own eyes, ask questions with her own astute mind. Never content with other people's answers, the lady has never, ever felt that she doth protest too much.

Which is why she was one of the founders of Citizens Against Rocky Flats Contamination, why she got involved in protests against the nuclear weapons plant back in the 1970s, when the number of opponents of the factory could practically all fit on her couch.

"I grew up in Denver in the fifties, when they had civil defense drills and they would run us all down into the school basement or make us hide under our desks. I had a sixth-grade teacher who said if we ever heard a loud explosion or saw a bright flash, we should immediately get under our desks. He used to take out this real big ruler and slap it on the desk, which meant that everybody had to instantly throw their pencils out of their hands and take the duck-and-cover position," she said.

"Those were the days when officials told us they were going to evacuate the whole city in fifteen minutes flat. I used to wake up at night when I'd hear a loud noise and think World War III was coming. All of that fear had an enormous impact on this generation, but nobody talks about it. You would probably go crazy if you thought about what the nuclear age really means.''

But for almost two decades Jan Pilcher has done little else but focus on the nuclear age and what its horrific consequences could mean to her family, her neighbors, her community, and her entire world if a major accident occurred at Rocky Flats.

Just sixteen miles northwest of Denver, sprawling over the last plateau before the high plains become the soaring Rocky Mountains, Rocky Flats is where the government makes the plutonium triggers for all its atomic weapons. More than one million people live within a fifty-mile radius of the plant. They are nearly all downwind.

Like thousands of others in postwar America, Jan Pilcher's father settled in Denver because it held out promise of the American dream to all who worked hard, saved their money, and became good citizens. An Oklahoma transplant, he liked Denver's wide-open feeling, both physically and financially. It offered restless, ambitious ex-GIs a chance to get a fresh start in a clean place. Tract houses sprang up in clusters all around the old downtown core of the frontier town that didn't start coming into its own until after World War II. It was into one of those houses, on the northwest side of the city, that baby boomer Jan Vittum moved with her family in 1956, when her dad took five thousand dollars in borrowed money and opened a plumbing supply business.

"That was three years after Rocky Flats opened, but nobody talked about Rocky Flats. . . . My Brownie Scout leader was married to a man who worked at Rocky Flats, but I had no idea what it was, except that he had a big chart of atomic chemicals up on his wall in the basement, where we had all our Brownie meetings. When I was in the seventh grade, we moved to the east side of town, and the neighbors next door had an extensive bomb shelter in their basement.

The ventilation pipe that came out of it was the back of the basketball hoop. That's what I looked out on every morning when I got up, and every day I thought: Under that vent is the bomb shelter." It has since become a wine cellar.

In the mid-1970s, after a trip around the world and several diverse jobs, Jan found herself back in Denver, teaching school. Outraged by all the social problems she'd seen in her travels, she became active in the local Quaker community and discovered that the pacifists were organizing to try and stop weapons production. She decided it was time she found out exactly what went on at Rocky Flats.

Together with a small group of volunteers, she helped produce the first protest publication demanding the immediate closure of Rocky Flats. Printed on cheap paper, selling for a dollar, and numbering only twenty pages, *Local Hazard Global Threat* was published in August 1977 by the Rocky Flats Action Group. It was the first citizen salvo fired back at a military-industrial behemoth unused to opposition.

"Rocky Flats poses a threat to our health and safety," the pamphlet stated bluntly. "The daily use of hazardous radioactive substances at Rocky Flats Plant presents the entire Denver metropolitan area with the continuing possibility of a major catastrophic accident."

The pamphlet then called for the economically unthinkable: "Environmental hazards alone . . . demand that the Rocky Flats Plant cease nuclear weapons production and processing immediately." It was blasphemy in Denver, which viewed Rocky Flats as a stable economic golden nugget. It was also the start of a fifteen-year crusade for Pilcher. There would be shouts and threats and investigations and tears, not to mention all the protests, rallies, public hearings, and court cases. For years Jan became a fixture on the garden club and Rotary circuit, taking her message—that Rocky Flats was unsafe and a threat to everyone in Denver—to audiences that were hostile but nonetheless curious. She pored through thousands of documents and got together slide shows. Just about everywhere she went to address a public forum, Rocky Flats sent employees to rebut her arguments. All the while, she was putting in countless hours on a volunteer basis, with other Quakers donating what they could to pay for her telephone and gas.

"I didn't do civil disobedience, because I didn't think I'd be as effective behind bars. I didn't want to be tied up for years and years in litigation," she said. "I wanted to hit them on the facts."

Her supporters would grow to a handful, then hundreds, then thousands. Over time, public opinion would shift, and Jan Pilcher would finally draw some sense of satisfaction. She had made a difference.

But it may have been too late. By the time Jan and her couchful of cohorts were starting to wake up to problems at the plant, Rocky Flats had already experienced two decades of accidents, plutonium releases, and safety problems. The whole thing was literally a tragic mistake from the start.

In 1951, with the Korean War under way, the government began searching for a place to mass-produce nuclear weapons. It was a new concept, bringing Henry Ford's ways to the Bomb. Until then, the production of U.S. atomic and hydrogen bombs was handled by the scientists and technicians at Los Alamos. But as stockpiling increased, the military wanted an assembly line, and it wanted Los Alamos to concentrate on research and development.

The search was confined to the western United States, and proximity to Los Alamos was considered a plus. Rocky Flats seemed ideal because it was close to a small city, land was cheap, air-conditioning wasn't required, and at the time, it was "well-removed from any residential area," a government report said. Concerned about the dangers even then, the government wanted no population downwind of the plant, both because of the possibility of an accidental release of radioactivity and because some small amounts of plutonium would escape in the normal course of business. Since winds were from the south, radioactivity would be carried away from Denver, north over empty ranchland stretching to Wyoming and far beyond, government officials concluded.

They goofed. The government report used prevailing winds at Stapleton International Airport, which is just east of downtown Denver, farther from the mountains. As the Arapahos and the Utes had known for centuries, winds on the Rocky Flats shelf come through canyons just to the west and blow toward the east and southeast—back toward Denver. Sometimes wind speeds reach above one hundred miles an hour, and tons of dirt are swept off the mesa every year. Rocky Flats was jinxed from the start.

Unaware of what the future would bring, the *Denver Post* led the cheerleading on March 23, 1951: "There's Good News Today. U.S. to Build $45 Million A-Plant Near Denver," a headline said. The plant was constructed, and production began in 1953. The culture of secrecy that had been created with the Manhattan Project continued. Workers couldn't tell anyone what went on inside the plant, and most of Denver's inhabitants did not know what was really going on at the wondrous new employer. And another legacy of the fervor of the Manhattan Project carried over to Rocky Flats—worry about production first, safety second. It was not until 1955 that Denver had an inkling of what it had got itself into. The *Rocky Mountain News* disclosed for the first time that the facility used dangerous radioactive materials.

Not until 1957, the year when Jan Pilcher was having her Brownie troop meetings, did residents get a firsthand look at just how dangerous it all was. A fire ignited by plutonium spread rapidly through a plutonium processing building,

187

causing an explosion that rocked the building, blew out hundreds of ventilation filters, destroyed radiation monitors on smokestacks, and threw thick plumes of black smoke into the air. The smoke passed over Denver for twelve hours after the blaze. The government reassured a trusting public that little or no radiation had escaped, even though officials knew the stack monitors were destroyed. Six months later, a report kept secret at the time found more than eight thousand times the normal "background" level of radiation at a nearby ranch and two elementary schools. But nobody was told, and no cleanup was initiated. A later government report on the fire, also kept classified until recently, had an ominous unsigned margin note: "Anybody like to guess how much was released?"

To understand the dangers at the Rocky Flats plant is to understand a bit about plutonium and how nuclear bombs are made. Plutonium, one of the most toxic and deadly substances known to man, is a metal that can be machined into different shapes. It is eager to oxidize on contact with oxygen—in other words, it burns easily. The 1957 fire began with spontaneous ignition of plutonium. When it does burn, the fire creates plutonium oxide, which can break down into the tiniest of bits, even as small as one molecule. The bits are so minute that it's very difficult to screen them out and still let air, or smoke, pass through. You can't see it or feel it. Airborne plutonium is most dangerous since the human body has to ingest the radioactive metal, through breathing or even through an open cut, in order for it to be deadly. A lethal dose in the lungs is measured in billionths of a gram.

Rocky Flats, a complex of one hundred buildings and twenty-nine smokestacks, takes plutonium created at DOE weapons plant reactors and shapes it into disks akin to skinny hockey pucks. Working on an assembly line of sealed boxes with lead-lined gloves, workers machine and form the plutonium disks into softball-sized hollow balls that become the heart of nuclear weapons. The ten-pound balls are often called bomb "triggers," but they are really just Fat Man implosion bombs that generate tremendous heat—enough to set off the hydrogen components of the bomb. All the scraping and drilling and shaping that goes on at Rocky Flats produces plutonium shavings, which can easily ignite, and microscopic chips that can escape through smokestacks or become trapped in the plant's ventilation system. (Shavings can be recycled back into bombs.) Releases of radioactivity occur regularly. So do fires, large and small.

The 1957 fire roared out of control because the sealed boxes were constructed with highly flammable Plexiglas. But the plant stuck with its plastic glove boxes, which again contributed to a major disaster in 1969. Safety improvements such as better boxes recommended after the 1957 disaster had not been made. Officials from the Atomic Energy Commission, the forerunner of the Department of Energy, and Dow Chemical, then the plant's operator, blamed budget constraints.

On Mother's Day, 1969, a couple of plutonium briquettes stored in cans without lids ignited inside a plastic cabinet that was inside a Plexiglas glove box. A once-secret Atomic Energy Commission report, obtained recently from a DOE records warehouse, noted that the fire never would have gotten past the metal can if the plastic cabinet and glove box hadn't gone up like kindling.

Fire raced through the whole assembly line setup, which became a racecourse for flames. There was no automatic sprinkler system, because water is used on plutonium only as a last resort. Water can help plutonium go "critical"—it can help initiate the kind of spontaneous nuclear chain reaction that killed Louis Slotin at Los Alamos years ago. So firefighters at the plant attacked the blaze with carbon dioxide, but within ten minutes the fire chief resorted to water because the blaze was so wild.

The fire was the worst industrial accident in the country at the time, and it remains the worst accident in the history of U.S. weapons plants. Like the 1957 fire, it caused no immediate deaths, but it did cause $50 million in damage and shut down weapons production for six months. The AEC report noted that "the building was heavily contaminated with plutonium" and "Plutonium also was tracked out of Building 776 by the firefighters and was detectable on the ground around the building. There is no evidence that plutonium was carried beyond the plant boundaries."

Had the fire burned through the roof of the plant, hundreds of square miles would have suffered radiation exposure. As it was, a cloud carried smoke, probably radioactive, toward Denver. Plant officials issued the same assurances that all was A-OK. And the public, as in 1957, was unconcerned. The *Rocky Mountain News* carried four paragraphs on the fire on page 28, below the picture of the Pet of the Week.

Fires weren't the only problem at Rocky Flats over the years. In 1973, a large amount of radioactive tritium, which is a key component of hydrogen bombs, was released into a disposal pond. Tritium wound up in Walnut Creek, which runs through the 384-acre plant complex, and flowed into the Great Western Reservoir, contaminating the water supply for nearby Broomfield, a town of 27,000. Broomfield today has an alternate water supply, but the reservoir is still its primary source because the contamination is in very low levels.

Evidence quietly began mounting against the plant, but few were paying close attention. The Environmental Protection Agency produced a document in 1974 that said cattle in a pasture east of Rocky Flats had more plutonium contamination than cattle set out to graze on the Nevada Test Site, where hundreds of aboveground explosions occurred in the 1950s and 1960s. That same year, with nary a whisper of potential danger, the federal government purchased thousands of acres of contaminated land to the east and southeast—toward Denver—to keep it out of public use. The land was turned over to county and city governments—a huge park that, to this day, no one can use.

Then, in 1981, Dr. Carl Johnson set fire to the issue that Jan Pilcher and her cohorts had already set a-smoldering. Johnson, then Jefferson County health director, studied cancer rates in the area. He divided the county into parcels based on the amount of plutonium contamination found in the soil. What he found was that men in the most contaminated part of the Denver area did indeed have higher cancer rates—a 24 percent higher incidence of cancer than in the least contaminated section, which had little or no plutonium. For women in the most contaminated section, the cancer rate was 10 percent higher. For the first time, there was evidence that all the radioactive releases over the years and the black clouds from the major fires were having a health effect: it looked like Rocky Flats was indeed causing cancer in the population. Johnson said most of the excess cases, such as leukemia and cancers of the lymph, lung, thyroid, testes, and breast, paralleled those of Hiroshima and Nagasaki survivors. The common thread between Colorado and Japan: plutonium.

Johnson's conclusions were roundly discredited by plant operators and government officials, but he was ultimately vindicated in later years and hailed for speaking out when few local officials dared jeopardize the economy or their own careers by attacking Rocky Flats.

In 1985, the government again bought land around the plant, this time paying $9 million to settle a lawsuit from neighboring residents, who claimed the plant had ruined their property values. The case was sealed in court, but the *Washington*

Post obtained documents that cataloged some of the problems at Rocky Flats, including the facts that there had been hundreds of small fires throughout its history and that plant operators had known for years that radioactive materials were getting into the air and the groundwater.

By the late 1980s, a more complete picture of Rocky Flats was emerging. The complex, which had grown to nearly six thousand workers, was littered with contaminated holding ponds, waste dumps, and open-air incineration spots. And the radioactive waste, it turns out, came not only from Rocky Flats itself but also from numerous other defense and corporate sources, including hospitals and even the Coors beer company, headquartered in nearby Golden. Coors, which built its reputation on producing cold, pure spring-fed Rocky Mountain water beer, apparently did some secret defense research with radioactive waste in the early 1960s. (It's unclear what the beer-maker was up to at the time.) Coors had sent 253 of the 5,000 barrels stacked at the 903 Pad inside Rocky Flats. From inside the plant itself had come hundreds of 55-gallon drums filled with plutonium-contaminated oil. They were piled near the eastern fence, and they were leaking. Some 86 grams of plutonium were lost. Groundwater contamination by now was threatening the entire Denver area water supply.

On December 6, 1988, the Department of Energy, under intense national pressure to begin admitting to its weapons plant problems and start fixing them, as well as facing heightened investigations at Rocky Flats, ranked Rocky Flats as the worst environmental mess of the whole nationwide weapons complex: worse than the Hanford Reservation in the state of Washington, worse than Fernald in Ohio, or Los Alamos, or Sandia, or Pantex in Texas, where the final assembly of the bombs takes place. Rocky Flats won top billing, the DOE said, because toxic wastes are leaking into the groundwater and threatening public water supplies. The DOE recommended, in another report, that Rocky Flats eventually be phased out and the work of making plutonium triggers be transferred, probably to a plant in Idaho, but perhaps to Los Alamos too.

It was all a startling admission: until 1986, the DOE had maintained that there were no health threats at Rocky Flats. But all along, the DOE had been the fox guarding the henhouse, responsible for both plant production and plant safety.

Inside the plant, conditions did not appear to be much better. In 1987, an engineer died from burns. In 1988, one of the main processing buildings was ordered closed after an energy department safety inspector and two Rocky Flats workers inhaled radioactive particles in an unmarked room where contaminated equipment was being cleaned. (It may be years before health problems crop up, and even then they may not be traceable to the exposure they received that day. Such is the difficulty of proving the effects of Rocky Flats.) A General Accounting Office report cited a pervasive lax attitude toward safety inside the plant, including inaccurate radiation monitors and fire alarm systems so old that replacement parts are hard to get. Other studies found radiation detecting machines that didn't work, miscalibrated equipment, misplaced air monitors, sloppy record keeping, workers with torn protective clothing, or none, and contaminated parts that hadn't been changed. Machinery dated back to the '50s. A study of workers who handled beryllium, a strong, lightweight metal used in the plutonium bombs, found that a dozen of the first 391 tested had berylliosis, an often fatal lung disease. And then there was the matter of 62 pounds of plutonium that had accumulated in the air ducts of the plant—enough to make a half-dozen bombs. It seems the glove-box filters got clogged and a bypass line automatically opened, sending unfiltered plutonium-contaminated air into the ductwork. There was concern that the plutonium might be in sufficient concentration to "go critical" and expose workers to deadly radiation doses.

On June 6, 1989, another remarkable event in the remarkable history of Rocky Flats took place. Under the code name of "Operation Desert Glow," seventy-five agents from the FBI and the EPA raided the joint—one arm of the government in effect raiding another. The agents had been probing allegations of environmental crimes. The FBI said in an affidavit that it even had infrared aerial photographs that showed illegal waste incineration at night in a building previously ordered shut down for safety problems. A special grand jury was investigating Rocky Flats for criminal charges. Incredible.

That fall, Rocky Flats was shut down—temporarily. DOE Secretary James Watkins closed it for safety improvements, and at the end of the year he canceled Rockwell International's contract to run the plant and turned the task over to another longtime weapons contractor, EG&G Incorporated, of Wellesley, Massachusetts. Watkins vowed Rocky Flats wouldn't reopen until it was safe. But there were still other problems.

One of them was what to do with the radioactive wastes produced at Rocky Flats. In Idaho, where Rocky Flats had been sending drums of waste for years, Governor Cecil Andrus said the state would refuse to accept any more shipments—Idaho had about all of Rocky Flats' waste it wanted. A permanent depository that was supposed to be opened in 1988 in the ancient salt caverns of southern New Mexico was itself mired in its own safety questions. So more and more barrels stacked up at Rocky Flats, until Colorado Governor Roy Romer said, No more—the plant couldn't operate unless it had a way of moving waste.

The DOE has been juggling radioactive waste since the Manhattan Project. None has been permanently disposed of.

Someone once said the whole thing was like building a house and forgetting the toilets.

Weapons research and production yields four times as much waste as commercial nuclear power plants. The DOE has been constructing a permanent facility 2,150 feet underground near Carlsbad, New Mexico, east of White Sands. But the Waste Isolation Pilot Project (WIPP) is itself clouded by safety questions, the most basic of which is what happens to all this waste if water comes pouring into the caverns, making corrosive salt water that could eat through radioactive waste drums and cause spills, leaks, and all kinds of contamination. The WIPP site sits below an aquifer and on top of a huge reservoir of brine, which is under pressure. Critics say the $800 million WIPP can't meet EPA repository disposal standards. But the DOE, preaching concern about safety at its weapons plants while nevertheless pressing ahead with WIPP as fast as it can, is seeking an exemption from the rules. When it does open, WIPP will make I-25 an even more important route for trucking radioactive waste.

Already, the price tag for cleaning up the contamination of Rocky Flats has passed the $1 billion mark, and it keeps climbing. "We have one hell of a legacy to clean up," a top DOE official said. No doubt. Some scientists have suggested that it just be fenced off forever—a "National Sacrifice Zone." As the wind keeps blowing across the poisoned plateau, spreading the dirt and dust and toxics, some have described Rocky Flats as our own "creeping Chernobyl." Yet the suburbs of Denver continue to inch closer as the city grows out to butt heads with the plant. The decision now confronts the nation: Can bombs continue to be made here safely without killing workers and poisoning neighbors?

The story as yet has no end. But whatever the outcome, the decision will come too late to help Don Gabel. He was barely twenty-one, a young daddy with two kids and a pregnant wife, when he looked around for a steady, secure job and found it at Rocky Flats on October 12, 1970.

"We thought it was terrific because there was going to be wonderful benefits—health insurance, pension, retirement, everything—so we were all excited about it," remembered his widow, Kae. "He hired on as a janitor, but after six months they offered him a job as a process operator. That was working in the 'hot' areas, which would mean a whole ten cents an hour more pay. He would be processing plutonium."

To Don Gabel it was all a lark—the training, the orders not to talk about his new job, the occasional accidents when he had to put on an air mask.

"After a while it was mundane, everyday stuff. Periodically he wouldn't come home: I'd have dinner ready and get this phone call, and he'd tell me, 'I was exposed, and I have to be scrubbed until it's gone,'" said Kae. "This happened several times with his head, where they had to scrub his scalp with bleach. One day he called and he'd gotten an acid burn on his side, which had something to do with radioactivity. He came home with this big patch on his side and it was raw, where they had scrubbed him with a brush."

All the while Don Gabel was working with plutonium, he was being told by his supervisors that "as long as you respect it, you're fine," Kae said. "That was ingrained in them— you respect the materials you're working with, and you're safe. It means they've been brainwashed. It was like an everyday occurrence that the sirens would go off—the warnings—and they'd have to put their air supply on. It meant nothing to them. They were used to it. It happened all the time."

That was the mid-1970s, when the first protests at Rocky Flats were starting to be held at the front gate, when demonstrators first marched down highways and railroad tracks trying to disrupt workers' entry into the plant. Those were the days when Don and Kae Gabel resented all the protesters, people like Jan Pilcher, and thought they were trying to deprive the Gabels' children of food and shelter, paid for by Don's paycheck. The Gabels were firmly in the government's camp, vehemently opposed to the "fanatics."

"It's hard to explain how you get yourself into where you believe everything they [Rocky Flats officials] tell you," said Kae. "By the time you start having your doubts, you've worked there so long you're used to the pay, used to the benefits, you're trained only for that kind of work, and you can't go to another job and maintain the life-style you've gotten used to. So you start putting up blocks in your mind: 'Well, these things you hear are fanatical.' You can't let yourself believe it, because if you believe it you can't work there."

So Don and Kae Gabel and their children, Ron, Brenna, and Nathan, shoved away any doubts about the ethical and safety issues of living off Rocky Flats money and concentrated on creating a happy family life. Don loved his motorcycle, played weekends in a rock band, pampered his kids, and kept on getting his body scrubbed with bleach. But Kae's secret fears were growing every time she got a whiff of her husband's skin.

"When he came home from work he'd have a certain smell. Even though when he'd go to work he'd completely take off his clothes and put on the company's clothes . . . he'd come home and you'd smell it. He smelled like Rocky Flats. And that bothered me. I always worried he could bring any of it home. Maybe he never did on the outside, but on the inside, definitely. He was already contaminated. He was even taken out of the 'hot' building a couple of times because his body

197

[radiation] count was too high. They kept him until his body count went back down—you know, to 'safe' levels, those wonderful 'safe' levels.''

Kae recalled many times when Don and his cronies from the plant would sit around their new house in Arvada—just a half-dozen miles downwind of Rocky Flats in one of the nice, tidy subdivisions springing up all around the government reservation—and tell stories about their work.

"I can remember Don saying something about the glove boxes where they would mess with the stuff, and somehow or other the trigger part—the pellets?—actually fell out onto the floor with them, and it was no big deal. They were regularly supposed to bring in urine and feces samples. Sometimes they did, sometimes they didn't. Nobody got on their case about it. They just goofed around.

"I never really knew, until he was ill and after he died, how dangerous working out there was, because Don treated it so nonchalantly. I've heard secondhand from people who still work at Rocky Flats that the story they're told about Don Gabel now is that he was a sloppy worker and that's why he got himself in the predicament he did. If this was true, it was common. Nobody was there to enforce the rules. I'm just saying that if indeed he was a sloppy worker—and I'm not agreeing to that—then he responded the same way everybody else there did. He was not unique.''

In 1978, Gabel began to get moody and forgetful; his left arm and leg occasionally tingled; and he started taking lots of aspirin for frequent headaches. In eight years at the plant, he'd gone from janitor to working on the furnace that processed the plutonium and other radioactive materials. He told his wife the furnace's exhaust pipe was six inches away from his head as he stood for hours at a time in the same place. He told her it "wasn't a lead pipe, just a regular pipe.''

On March 29, 1979, the couple went to bed early because

Don wasn't feeling well. The memory of that evening brings a look of pain to Kae's face as she tells the story. "I woke up about eleven o'clock, and he was having a grand mal seizure. I flipped on the light and started screaming at him. His eyes were open, but he couldn't respond and I didn't get any recognition." After a few more seconds of screaming at her husband to wake up, wake up, "I could get recognition in his eyes, but he couldn't talk to me and he still didn't have control of his body. The shaking went down, but he couldn't move."

After several days in the hospital and a barrage of medical tests, the Gabels' family doctor finally told Kae her husband had a brain tumor and needed immediate surgery. Following the eight-hour procedure, the neurosurgeon told Kae they couldn't remove all the tumor and that conventional radiation and chemotherapy treatments would not prolong Don Gabel's life beyond two years. His family chose not to tell him he was terminally ill, because "it would have crushed him, he would have lost hope, his quality of life from that time on would have been hampered."

But there was one last chance for recovery. Their family doctor told them that at Los Alamos National Laboratory, scientists were conducting experimental treatments on some kinds of tumors, and they'd agreed to give Don "pion" treatments. Doctors explained to Kae that the treatments involved immobilizing Don in a body cast and then shooting an element through a half-mile-long atom smasher straight into his brain tumor.

"They told me Don would be awake the whole time and not feel a thing, but that it penetrates and hits the target, which is the tumor, explodes, and chips the tumor away."

Kae Gabel did not realize that Los Alamos was run by the Department of Energy, the overseer of Rocky Flats. She didn't know then that Los Alamos was the place where the atom was unleashed on the world, and that scientists there were continually trying to find out what kind of damage nuclear materials could do to mankind, were trying to find out if the same elements that could destroy the human race might help save it.

Los Alamos paid for everything. The whole Gabel family moved into a tiny apartment near the laboratory and received money for food and expenses. Kae and Don stayed three months. When they returned home, CAT scans showed the tumor slightly changed—but not enough. It was going to kill Don, and soon. That's when Kae became determined to find out why.

Meanwhile, Don's sick leave at Rocky Flats had run out and he'd started collecting Social Security disability benefits, retroactive to the time of his collapse.

"We still had bills to pay and food to buy, so when I got this money I put it into savings and used it when we needed it. Later on, when the retroactive Social Security money was all gone, I got a phone call from Rocky Flats telling me I owed them $1,300 because I'd gotten sick leave money from them and Social Security at the same time. That was the straw that broke the camel's back. A lady at church had given me Bruce DeBoskey's name months before and had suggested I call him. He was an attorney. Don and I had discussed it and discounted it because we were average nobodies. You're talking about fighting the government. But that day I called Bruce. That same day, the producers of the documentary *Dark Circle*, which was about Rocky Flats, called and asked if they could come over and talk to us. We said fine. That night, Bruce and his partner came and got Don's story and agreed to take the case. So this whole fight started because of Rocky Flats' greed."

By then Don was starting to fail. His body was swollen, his head was shaved, there was a plate in his skull over the area of the tumor, his speech was slurred, his thought processes were slowing down. The Gabels asked doctors what had caused the brain tumor: could it have been caused by where he worked?

"The only answer we ever got was, 'We don't know. I couldn't tell you that.' Nobody would come out and say yes," Kae said.

By the time Don and Kae Gabel filed a worker's compensation claim blaming Rocky Flats for his illness, most of his old buddies from the plant had stopped coming around. "They didn't want to face it. They wanted to think: It can't happen to me; it always happens to someone else."

DeBoskey pushed the case so Don could testify before he died. But there were snafus throughout the trial. Rockwell supplied the wrong blueprints of the room where Gabel had worked. The "hot" pipe located six inches above Gabel's head during his last months at the plant had been removed, cleaned, and dismantled before DeBoskey's independent expert could examine its radiation levels.

Rocky Flats steadfastly denied any allegations that evidence was tampered with or improperly handled. In its standard response to lawsuits involving ailing workers, Rockwell said: "We believe the evidence is not sufficient to show a causal relationship between radiation in the workplace and the type of claims in these cases. We still believe the low levels of radiation at Rocky Flats are not sufficiently high to cause cancer."

Testifying in the witness chair on June 27, 1980, Don haltingly described his job, which was to dissolve plutonium in acid and make it into the six-inch plutonium buttons—the "hockey pucks." The process involved firing the buttons into a furnace that first had to be purged with argon gas. To reach the valve that released the argon, Gabel had climbed on top of the furnace. He testified that in that position, his head was six inches from a bare metal pipe that was a ventilation duct from the furnace where the plutonium was being fired; he spent about 40 percent of his workday with his head half a foot from the pipe.

He also told the worker's compensation referee that he asked a supervisor if the radioactivity would be harmful to him, and the boss replied it was safe, "so long as you don't get your body close to it."

When Don Gabel died at Lutheran Medical Center, on September 6, 1980, the ultimate piece of evidence linking his cancer with his workplace vanished.

Kae had left the hospital briefly for the first time in weeks to watch Nathan play in a football game. When she returned, she was gently told that Don had died just a few minutes earlier.

"The whole family met in a room down the hall from where Don died, and then a nurse came in and told me I had a long-distance phone call. A man identified himself—and for the life of me, I wish I could remember the man's name, but I don't—as being from Los Alamos. Los Alamos had become like a small family and a support group, and I felt very secure and trusting of these people. I'm not a devious person. Even though I am going through this lawsuit, I want to believe that basically humanity is truthful and honest, especially these people. This man asked me if they could have Don's brain to test.

"I told them I was in agreement with that. I would make sure they got the brain, but I wanted it tested for plutonium, for any radioactive materials. I did say this. The person agreed, and I said I wanted a report in writing sent to me. They also agreed to that. And so I felt comfortable with it—stupid me. They picked the weakest moment in my life to do this to me, when I am not thinking clearly.

"Later, I would question how somebody hundreds of miles

away had known that Don had just died. My God, I'd just found out myself that my husband was dead! It must have been a setup at the hospital. The only thing I can think of is that when Don died, Los Alamos was immediately notified. It's another of those mysterious, never-to-be-answered questions."

Neither Kae and her attorney nor the worker's compensation referee ever found out what was in Don Gabel's brain. Kae never received that sincerely promised report from Los Alamos. Later, Department of Energy researchers told her that her husband's brain had been lost, and the only things left were fragments too small to test.

"I felt like I'd been raped. It's such a feeling of being used, you can't imagine it's happened to you, especially when you're talking about your husband's brain and about people I'd trusted. I had no idea they were so afraid of us," said Kae. "They've got to be so hardened, so cold-blooded, that it's beyond my realm of reality that anybody can do this. I don't know if, in my lifetime, I will ever know all the cover-ups they have done to us."

Rockwell sent flowers to Gabel's funeral and donated ten dollars to his memorial fund. One of his bosses told Kae after the funeral that if she ever needed a job, she should come look him up and he'd try to get her taken on at the plant. She was polite, but she swore in her heart that if it was the last job on earth, she'd find something else to do. Left at age twenty-nine with three children to raise on a meager government benefit and a twenty-thousand-dollar life insurance policy, Kae hid her fear of dogs, applied for a job with the Arvada police as the local animal control officer, and went to work nights to support her family.

Meanwhile, she and DeBoskey carried on their fight. British physician Alice Stewart—the first scientist to expose possible links between X-raying pregnant women and finding leukemia in children—provided critical testimony for Kae. Rocky Flats workers, testified Dr. Stewart, "are over three times as likely to die from brain tumors as other persons of the same age and sex. Mr. Gabel died from the effects of brain cancer, which, in my opinion, was probably caused by his exposure to plutonium and other sources of ionizing radiation while working at Rocky Flats." Dr. Stewart based her conclusions on her independent recalculations of Rocky Flats health studies conducted by the Department of Energy. Having made her own analysis of the raw DOE data at DeBoskey's request, she said that DOE studies had been incorrectly calculated.

Kae Gabel's case went on for eight years, and when a verdict was finally rendered, she was awarded fourteen thousand dollars by the State of Colorado for her dead husband's worker's compensation claim. A Division of Labor hearing officer ruled that Gabel's death was caused by on-the-job exposure to levels of radiation the government considers "safe," and the Colorado Court of Appeals ultimately let the ruling stand. Kae Gabel said DeBoskey was paid a third of the money for pleading the case, wages that amounted to less than the hourly rate paid to a high school baby-sitter.

"Bruce told me from the very beginning there was not much money involved," said Kae. "What we were seeking was causation. People think that you are vindictive and that you are out for money. But we weren't. I got what I went after: I got a judge to agree that 'Yes, your husband died from working with the materials he worked with.' We were out for justice. It's just in the last year that I feel that I've been getting my reward for perseverance, because the public is beginning to take notice of Rocky Flats."

After a brief, disastrous second marriage following Don's death, Kae dedicated herself to her kids and her job, living in the same house she'd shared with Don, in the same downwind neighborhood near Rocky Flats where they'd dreamed of growing old together.

Then, while visiting a friend in Casper, Wyoming, she met Joe Williams, a mechanic and welder, and married him on August 1, 1987—but the wedding took place only after Kae had explained to Joe that fighting Rocky Flats was a lifelong crusade for her and not just a battle that ended with a check.

"I'll never be done fighting Rocky Flats. My battle now is public awareness. I still want people to hear my story, relate to it, and see if it fits them. The only way we can get to Rocky Flats now is to prove that low-level radiation is indeed causing illnesses. Until people can see that that's a possibility, and can see other people fighting the government and giving them the courage to do it, too, I won't ever stop."

In 1991, nearly two decades after the first suits had been filed on behalf of ailing workers, Bruce DeBoskey said that in the ten cases he'd prosecuted so far, the government's total liability was only $400,000, but it had spent $2.3 million defending itself. That, he said, showed that Rocky Flats and the Department of Energy were very worried indeed about the precedent-setting cases such as the one fought—and won—by courageous, tenacious widows such as Kae Gabel Williams.

But even she hasn't moved away out of the shadow of Rocky Flats. Like thousands of others living close enough to the plant to see its eerie red glow in the sky during winter snowstorms, Kae is ambivalent about the threats versus the advantages of staying where she is. The decades have brought headlines and saturation awareness of many of the dangers associated with Rocky Flats. There are few people in Denver who don't know, who haven't made a choice. Some have taken a loss on property, uprooted their children from school, and moved as far away from the plant as they could afford to get. Others have convinced themselves that Arvada and

Boulder and Broomfield are just as safe as anyplace else in America. But even though they may not admit it, may never mention it to their spouse or their kids, somewhere in everybody's heart there's a little fear.

"I don't know if there's a safe place on earth," Kae said. "I feel it is too late for me to run from it. Whatever damage has been done is done."

Rocky Flats should never have been built where it is, because the wind direction should have been correctly measured and because it was inevitable that Denver and its suburbs would grow up and outward to surround the Flats in every direction. But closing it up leaves some six thousand workers unemployed and the U.S. nuclear arsenal in limbo. What hurts most is that secrecy prevailed, that innocent people died.

You can't see plutonium in the air and soil, you can't feel it, and you usually can't prove beyond a doubt that it was the cause of a deadly cancer. The government has hidden behind that fact—you can't prove it, so we think it's safe. How many releases and how much contamination and how many deaths will it take to prove it? As a nation, we spend millions on a hunch that we can make a better weapon or a faster missile. We shell out billions on a theory or a dream. We stretch the limits of science based only on educated guesses or intellectual curiosity. Yet at Rocky Flats, the standard has been different. You have to have proof. The onus is always on the victim.

As the nation tries to deal with the crisis in the weapons labs, new standards—safety, honesty, oversight—may finally evolve. Perhaps we will finally spend the money to do it all. Or we may conclude that it can't be done. We will make our pact with the devil and admit it—people are going to die because of this. Securing the peace always carries a high price. It's not all that different from a helicopter that crashes on a training mission: the soldiers on board knew the risks and lost the gamble. They died helping to keep the peace.

Beyond the Bomb, the true legacy of the Manhattan Project is secrecy. Maybe Jan Pilcher, Kae Gabel, and Rocky Flats itself will finally vanquish that evil.

9

HARVESTING MISSILES

When the Bomb split open the universe and revealed the prospect of the infinitely extraordinary, it also revealed . . . that each man is eternally and above all else responsible for his own soul.

JAMES AGEE, Time, *August 20, 1945*

It's human nature to take the path of least resistance, the shortcut from here to there. Why go up and down, over and across, when you can go straight through?

That is the logic of America's Nuclear Highway. I-25 has always been a thoroughfare because it has always been convenient. Line of sight down the 105th meridian tells the tale. To the west soar snow-crowned, nearly impenetrable peaks; to the east is "the hill," the gradually sloping prairie that rises from less than 1,000 feet above sea level at the Mississippi River to 5,280 feet at the Denver city limits.

Where those two geologic forces come together, there is a distinct demarcation of union. From the beginning of civilization, that natural corridor has been a path—often a warpath. Prehistoric mammoth hunters followed it to stalk their prey. Indians used it to move from summer encampment to winter quarters, their small dogs dragging tepees on lodge poles and wearing the first ruts into the decomposing granite ground.

The Spaniards, among the daring voyagers from the European continent to explore the territory, brought the modern horse. A few strays, escaping from the hobbles of conquistadores to the south, made their way along the Rio Grande into what is now Colorado and Wyoming. The barb—coffee-colored mounts with black stripes down their front legs and along their spine, offspring of the regal Arabians of the Sahara—probably followed the natural curve between the mountains and the plains like everyone else. The crease that had become a path was now a well-traveled trail. It was the easiest, if not the shortest, route, and like the prominent wrinkle in a hand, it became the lifeline.

Gradually, Paleo-Indian and archaic descendants took names: Comanche, Ute, Shoshone, Arapaho, Cheyenne, Apache, Navajo, Sioux, Crow. Astride their prized horses, surrounded by millions of buffalo and such bountiful numbers of elk, deer, antelope, bear, and moose that they could never consume them all, the Indians of the American West lived a hard life in harmony with their environment. There were frozen winters, blistering heat in high summer, no relief for the pain of childbirth, the loss of many infants, a strict social code that brooked no violation. But there was also a flowing rhythm to the days, the seasons, the years, the centuries. Life was ritualized, predictable, and self-perpetuating.

The horse revolutionized Indian society by making it more political, more structured, more warlike, and more mobile, but in the 1800s it also brought aliens to destroy it.

"Once we were happy in our own country and we were seldom hungry, for then the two-leggeds and four-leggeds lived together like relatives, and there was plenty for them and for us," remembered the Sioux holy man Black Elk much, much later. "But the Wasichus [white men] came, and they have made little islands for us and other islands for the four-leggeds, and always these islands are becoming smaller, for around them surges the gnawing flood of the Wasichu; and it is dirty with lies and greed."

To the Indians, the coming of white men soiled everything. To the majority of whites, Indians were filthy heathens to be subdued by force and corralled on reservations so civilized Christian folk could get on with their fresh start in a clean place, exploiting what they saw as limitless natural resources to be used solely for opportunity.

"These savage tribes are all waning and must finally become extinct, leaving their rich possessions to be occupied and developed by a more appreciative race," wrote Carl Abbott in 1850 in *Colorado: A History of the Centennial State.*

The Clovis point and Folsom arrowhead gave way to .50-caliber Sharps rifles slung over buffalo bounty hunters' saddles, a quantum leap on the Richter scale of killing. The cavalry imported the Remington repeating rifle and won every battle after Little Bighorn. The first machine gun, invented by Richard J. Gatling, was a forerunner of automated destruction. When it showed up along the western warpath to protect garrisons and safeguard settlers, Indian resistance was doomed.

It was the cavalry that was picking up the same worn-down route between the mountains and the plains. Unlike the rest of the country, where soldiers followed settlers, the military came first in the West, along with the pony express, the overland stage, and the iron horse. History doesn't tell us whether the country created the characters or the characters shaped the country, but the legends survive:

- Kit Carson, the solitary trapper who became the most famous army scout of all and miraculously survived to spend his last years as an Indian agent in New Mexico, a regular commuter along the warpath.

- West Point graduate John C. Frémont, who won his sobriquet "Pathfinder" by mapping much of the high-plains West, a success in the wilderness but a failure in the political maze of Washington.

- Zebulon Pike, who gained immortality by naming a Colorado mountain before anybody else.

All of them bedded down beside what is now the Nuclear Highway. They were among the first white men to use it to further their own ambitions, solitary voyagers who heard the siren's call of East Coast editorialists exhorting them to "Go West and grow up with the country."

Soon other adventurers were following in their tracks, and by 1850 what started as a trickle had swelled to a flood of humanity inching its way across the continent in bulging Conestogas, weary mules and oxen pulling toward the future at the rate of two miles an hour on a good day.

"Eastward I go only by force; but westward I go free," penned New England author and naturalist Henry David Thoreau at the time. ". . . I should not lay so much stress on this fact, if I did not believe that something like this is the prevailing tendency of my countrymen. I must walk toward Oregon, and not toward Europe. . . . We go westward as into the future, with a spirit of enterprise and adventure."

They came through Fort Laramie in Wyoming Territory, north of Cheyenne, which is now a federal monument off Interstate 25. From there, they chose one of five major trails that fanned out from the fort like the spokes on a wheel.

The Oregon Trail, which intersected what is now I-25, attracted the most traffic. Sometimes hundreds of cooking fires lit the wilderness sky as wagon trains camped out in fine summer weather all the way from Fort Laramie to South Pass, near present-day Lander. When the California gold rush exploded, the road to Sutter's Mill led in the same direction.

Rough-edged drovers who pushed their longhorns up from Texas toward the railhead in Montana turned northwest out of the fort, along the Bozeman Trail, which hugged the leeward side of the Rockies. The "Bloody Bozeman" snaked on past Buffalo, Wyoming, the northern terminus of modern I-25, and then forked west across Montana, past mountains called Beartooths and Crazies, before ending in the cow town's stockyards.

Rambunctious remittance men, the scoundrel younger sons of English gentry, pounded up and down the Wyoming portion of the old warpath on their imported thoroughbreds, commuting between vast open-range ranches and the fledgling settlement of Cheyenne, where politicians, gamblers, and bawdy women caroused.

Persecuted followers of an ailing Brigham Young christened their own route the Mormon Trail as they followed him out of Nauvoo, Illinois, in search of a Promised Land. They stopped to stay beside the Great Salt Lake, another five hundred miles on beyond Fort Laramie.

Grizzled traders and trappers, spiritual sons of Jim Bridger and John Colter, the men who discovered Yellowstone, were the first deal-makers in the virgin territory. More often than not, they headed south out of Fort Laramie, riding the old Indian trail to Taos, Santa Fe, and the surrounding pueblos of the Tewa Indians. Shrewd merchants with goods to sell could make handsome profits if they evaded marauding Indians, bribed local Spanish officials charged with keeping Americans at bay in Mexican territory, and didn't squander their profits in cantinas.

Always a mecca, this slice of the continent marked "desert" on early maps unceasingly attracted those with a yearning spirit. It was a time, author W. O. Clough later wrote, when

" 'Powder River!' men cry, a wild surge in their throats. For this is the land of the few against the unpersonal much; of uncommunicative spaces and stoic horizons, and the consciousness of holding on.''

Into the Powder River country, thirteen years after Colonel George Armstrong Custer and most of the Seventh Cavalry were wiped out by Sitting Bull and Crazy Horse on June 25, 1876, came a young man named Alexander Dooley Kirkbride. Not quite twenty-four years old when he disembarked from a Union Pacific train at Archer, Wyoming, four hundred miles south of the massacre site and just a few miles east of modern-day I-25, Kirkbride brought with him his dainty wife, Mary, and their two daughters. The young parents carried Eden, who was three years old, and baby Sarah, and set out walking the four miles to the Wilkinson homestead.

It was the fourteenth of April, an uncommonly fair spring day, and it marked the end of a journey that began in Liverpool and included two weeks at sea and a train ride two thirds across the continent from Boston. When they got to Wyoming they had five dollars. They spent half of it on a rocking chair—a symbol of faith and permanence—and saved the rest for emergencies.

The Kirkbrides, whose surname traced back to Scotland and meant "bride of the church," were Yorkshire tenant farmers who knew livestock. Brother James and the Wilkinsons, neighbors in England, had emigrated two years earlier. They wrote home praising the endless open range: the blue gramma, needle-and-thread, big bluestem, and buffalo grasses; the plentiful thread-leaf sedge; the clear streams, the beckoning opportunity in an untrammeled country.

The land suited the Kirkbride clan. As a bonus, James wrote to his kinsfolk back in the Old Country, it was safe because the Indians had been shoved onto reservations and nearby

Fort D. A. Russell had nearly 1,000 troopers—23 percent of the territory's labor force. When Cheyenne became the capital in 1888, 500 servicemen led the parade, and the local newspaper raved that "the 17th Infantry, together with its officers and band, did magnificently in their marching and evolutions and no finer looking body of soldiers had ever been seen under arms in Wyoming."

Only two decades earlier, U.S. Army General C. C. Auger, Union Pacific Railroad chief engineer Granville M. Dodge, and Jacob Blinkensderfer, Jr., an official representative of President Andrew Johnson, had gathered at Crow Creek Crossing on a blistering hot Fourth of July to create a town, a military post, and a railroad station in the same place by a single act. It was on their authority that Cheyenne evolved, illustrating from the beginning that Wyoming's future depended on a military-industrial-political partnership.

Along with James and his older brother Barnard, who also came to Wyoming, Alex D., as he was known, filed on a homestead on Horse Creek thirty-six miles northeast of Cheyenne that first summer. With meager savings, the brothers bought sheep in Nebraska and hired themselves out as extra hands at a dollar a day for badly needed cash. Soon they were proving up prairie on neighboring Cattail Creek, the spot Alex and Mary chose for their home place. Frugal Scotch habits and hard work allowed them to buy a few cows in 1893, and the partnership began an expansion trend that continued for four generations.

In 1912, the brothers split up their joint venture, but each kept buying land. Barnard stayed a bachelor; James married and adopted a daughter and fathered one son, who died young. Alex and Mary produced five more children, ending with the birth of Dan Kirkbride on November 11, 1898.

Although they'd intended to stay in America just six years and earn enough money to go back to England and buy their

Schoolboys in shorts at the Los Alamos Ranch School in 1939.

A young Peggy Pond Church on her horse, Dolly.

The Church family at the Los Alamos Ranch School. From left: Hugh, Allen, Ted, Peggy, and Fermor.

Peggy Pond Church at age 82 in Santa Fe, New Mexico.

The Church brothers. From left: Allen, Ted, and Hugh.

(courtesy of Los Alamos National Laboratory)

Oppenheimer is flanked by Dorothy McKibbin and scientist
Victor Weisskopf at a Los Alamos party in 1944.

Dorothy McKibbin in 1985.

(courtesy of Tad Bartimus)

(courtesy of Los Alamos National Laboratory)

J. Robert Oppenheimer.

Air Force General John ("Pete") Piotrowski.

Manhattan Project scientists. From left: E. O. Lawrence, Enrico Fermi, and I. I. Rabi. Fermi and Rabi were Nobel laureates.

Actor Marlon Brando (fourth from left) with U.S. military extras on the set of the movie *Sayonara* in Kyoto, Japan. Pete Piotrowski is behind Brando, to the actor's left.

Rocky Flats worker Don Gabel in 1976 with his wife, Kae, and his children: Nathan (age 2), Brenna (5), and Ronnie (7).

Anti–Rocky Flats activist Jan Pilcher.

Don Gabel during the spring of 1980, shortly before his death, his head partially collapsed.

Kae Gabel Williams at Don's grave in Arvada, Colorado.

Rancher Kenneth Kirkbride.

Lindi Kirkbride at the MX missile silo on the Harding-Kirkbride ranch.

Missileers Jack Hall and Anne Struckman inside Quebec-1, their MX silo in Wyoming.

(courtesy of Tad Bartimus)

A security door at the MX silo.

Francis Dellenbach in the Atlas silo he bought from the Air Force for $3,116.66.

(courtesy of U.S. Air Force)

own farm, the Yorkshire natives never returned. Their first house at Cattail Creek was a fourteen-by-sixteen-foot log cabin. Water came from the stream, heat from sheltering cottonwoods. As soon as they had a roof over their own heads, they built a second log cabin for a school. All of their children were educated on the homestead.

Alex and Mary started with $2.50 and a rocking chair, but counted themselves rich with freedom and opportunity. They never locked a door, never bought a dollar's worth of insurance, never had a theft or a fire. Their ranch weathered the blizzard of '20, which buried half their herd in snowdrifts higher than a man's head, and they learned harsh lessons when the First National Bank of Cheyenne went under four years later, taking all their savings and operating capital with it.

Alex D., a stubborn man who believed in the Constitution and the Bible with equal fervor, tested the tenets of his adopted land by challenging avaricious cattle barons who were arrogantly fencing in vast stretches of open range in 1906. It was a dangerous time for small operators.

Just three years earlier, Tom Horn, a lawman turned hired gun, had spent several nights with the Kirkbrides without their knowing his true identity. In those days, offering food and shelter to a stranger was a clause in the code of the West, so it was not unusual for strangers to seek bed and board for a few days with settlers isolated by great distances. Personal questions were seldom asked, and free hospitality was taken for granted in an environment where getting lost could kill you and loneliness was a bigger threat than wolves.

Horn and other renegade gunslingers had been hired by cattlemen to intimidate, run off, or eliminate squatters and small-time homesteaders encroaching on the vast public lands the big operators peremptorily used as their private fiefdoms. Horn was eventually hung for his vigilantism.

Alex D., who had to go through two gates to get to grass to graze his cattle and whose brother Barnard was completely fenced in from water and open range, got his dander up and decided to fight back—but within the system. In defiance of the all-powerful cattle barons, he filed an affidavit with the Department of Interior, demanding immediate relief. President Theodore Roosevelt responded by issuing a decree requiring removal of all illegal fences by April 1, 1907. When the land barons defied him, the old Rough Rider sent in the Army to tear them down.

That action marked the first time the two major western factions—soldiers and stockmen—had clashed along the Wyoming portion of America's Nuclear Highway. The lesson learned prevails today: the government always gets its way, by force if necessary. The outcome also convinced Kirkbride men that the United States government stands up for justice, fairness, strength, and protection of its citizens. Roosevelt's, and subsequently the Army's, action sowed seeds of future compliance with the military that would have wrenching repercussions for future generations of Kirkbrides.

As they became established pillars of the community, the immigrant brothers took every opportunity to show their patriotism, a trait they passed on to their heirs. When America entered World War I, they were too old to serve but raised mules for the Army, a venture that almost bankrupted them when mechanization replaced the mules.

During World War II, a six-star flag hung in Alex's and Mary's home to signify the service of six grandsons in far-flung global combat. One of those grandsons was Kenneth Kirkbride, the only child of Dan and his wife, Afra-Aetta, known to all as Peggy.

Kenneth was the issue of two God-fearing, straight-arrow

homesteaders who had known great hardship and depriva-
tion but considered it "character-building."

Peggy was a Harding and hailed from Missouri. Her
people came on the train, crowded into an "immigrant car"
along with what the railroad would let them take—six cows,
three horses, a passel of chickens, a few pots and pans, and
a trunk of clothes. The year was 1916, and Peggy was fourteen. She boarded in town to finish high school, but during
the summer she went to the homestead and looked after her
brothers, hauled water and coal, cooked, made soap, boiled
laundry, tended the garden and canned its bounty, stocked the
root cellar, helped with the accounts, and learned to be a
lady.

Of her parents, she wrote in her privately published book,
From These Roots: "Earnest toil was their way of life and
they expected their descendants to follow suit. . . . The
business interests of the family were built on the principles
that 'Unity Gives Strength.' "

At the age of eighty-eight, her eyesight slipping but her
mind as sharp as a girl's, Peggy Kirkbride saw the past as
yesterday: "We were frugal; we didn't buy things we couldn't
pay for. I think a lot of homesteaders who went broke wanted
to live better, live like the Joneses. We didn't mind going
down the road in a buckboard even if our neighbor passed
us in a car."

She met Dan Kirkbride, who'd come to town to learn to
play the guitar, when she was sixteen and going to a first
dance. He courted by buggy, and they married when she was
seventeen. Kenneth was born twenty months later, in November of 1920, and the family settled three miles east of the
Cattail Ranch, where Dan had been born.

"I'd get up and bake six pies before breakfast during sheep-
shearing time. A lot of military people from the fort came

217

out to our place to hunt and fish. They spent a lot of time on our land; we just took them for granted."

In her book, she wrote: "The big land grab was on! Government land was scarce; therefore vigilant eyes were on homesteaders to ascertain if they were remiss in fulfilling the legal requirements. . . . Unforgettable was the 14-by-16-foot [one] room papered with newspapers! Straightaway an order went to the mail order house for proper wall paper. Great was the transformation. In the fall of 1941 the Dan Kirkbrides rebuilt for space and convenience."

That was twenty-two years after they were married. Twenty-one years after Ken was born. The Kirkbride family never acted precipitously. Change was undertaken slowly, cautiously. This was, after all, a family to whom unity represented strength. Which meant consensus, peer approval. Altering the home was not a project to be lightly undertaken.

By the time Peggy and Dan remodeled their house, the Harding & Kirkbride Livestock Company was seventeen years old. Founded by Elvy Wayne Harding, Peggy's brother, and Dan, it was built on an investment of eight hundred ewes, which cost six dollars apiece. Of the daring business venture, Peggy recalled: "They walked by faith and not by sight, and winning results were by no means certain."

But that stubborn streak saw them through to the end of their stewardship and enabled them to pass on a dynasty to their sons. It wasn't a famous outfit like the King Ranch in Texas or even the Swan Land and Cattle Company, a vast spread just north of the Kirkbrides at Chugwater, which dated from remittance-men days. But it was several thousand acres, carefully accumulated, with good grass, plentiful water, sturdy fences.

In a country where half the homesteaders went bust and bailed out in the first five years, the Kirkbrides and the Hardings had not only survived but also prospered. Their roots were burrowing deep in the sod, and they were in Wyoming to stay.

That legacy was bequeathed to Ken by Peggy and Dan. But like all parents who struggled, they wanted their son to have more, so Ken also became the beneficiary of his parents' reverence for education. When he was a youngster, his mother taught him the first and second grades at home. Then he rode his horse ten miles a day to a bigger school. He went to high school in Cheyenne, living with friends in town and going to the ranch on weekends. After graduation, it was a given that he would enroll at the University of Wyoming. With Hitler haranguing the world on the radio and the Japanese invading Manchuria, young Ken was sworn into ROTC—the Reserve Officers Training Corps—in the fall of 1940.

"It was mandatory for the last two years; I had to take it," Ken recalled. "You could go into the advanced program and get a commission, and that's what I did. I was commissioned in the infantry, but I never served in it, because as soon as I went on active duty I was assigned to the amphibian engineers. Growing up in the Rocky Mountains, I never had anything to do with water, but that's all I did for three and a half years of war, serve on landing craft and live on boats."

A month after graduation—eight months after Pearl Harbor—the young second lieutenant married Shirley Beeson, a fair-haired liberal arts major from Sheridan, Wyoming. Although these children of pioneers drove cars and lived in houses with indoor plumbing, they'd turned out about the same as their parents and grandparents. Their lives were centered on family, livestock, and land. These were third and fourth generations of Wyoming settlers. Ironically, like the Indians they'd run off or exterminated, their days also ebbed and flowed with the seasons. But just as war had shattered the Indians' routine, so too had it disrupted the future of Ken and Shirley Kirkbride.

In July of 1942, he shipped out for Massachusetts to join the engineers and wound up at Camp Edwards for basic training. Plymouth Rock, landing site of the Pilgrims and a revered symbol of freedom, was nearby. Kirkbride was stirred by the monument and all it stood for. Like his father and grandfather, he believed in standing up for a just cause. Now his life was on the line for his principles.

After fleeting stops in Florida and California, his unit sailed for Australia, where it was supposed to meet up with landing craft. Except the boats never arrived.

"We had to build our own. They sent them in kits, in pieces, and we set up a boat factory and manufactured them on an assembly line. I was on the northeast coast, up by Cairns, right off the Great Barrier Reef. A beautiful spot. The boats were made of three-quarter-inch plywood; you'd be surprised how tough they were. When I first saw them, I thought: Oh, boy, these boats are nothin'. But they held together."

Kirkbride arrived in Australia in February 1943, and by July his outfit was getting mauled in New Guinea.

"We were fighting island to island all the way up to the Philippines. The Japanese were dug in, and we were in combat almost constantly. I took over a boat, one of the new ones made out of metal, a forty-five-foot cruiser. Now remember, I'm in the Army, but we've got our own boats because we're carrying cargo. We also rigged up some rockets on them so our boats could attack a beachhead, but mostly our weapons were for defense against planes."

Eventually Kirkbride commanded more than three hundred men. His troops hit the beaches in waves, and many of them died. The fighting was vicious and unrelenting. Then came the bulldozers, the jeeps, the food and medical supplies. From island to island, the pattern never changed.

"You had to see that all this was timed right; whatever had to be done, you did it, but the timing would get off, somebody'd mess up, there'd be a terrible traffic jam, the Japanese would just keep firing, the tides would go out on us, and people would get stuck on the beach."

He was learning the hard lessons of war, and he didn't like them. Closer and closer loomed the specter of invasion of Japan. Like most Allied soldiers, Kirkbride believed that the only way to force the Japanese into surrender was to strike at their home islands and fight them in hand-to-hand combat.

"We were scheduled to hit the mainland on A-minus-four, that meant like D-day in Europe, only A for Japan. We were supposed to go in four days *before* the full invasion. It was top secret, supposed to be sometime in November of '45. We were never told a specific date. Our mission was to go to an island and set up an artillery base and bombard the beachhead for A-day. We were supposed to land a combat regiment and supply them. We were constantly working on the timing and the details. And then we heard about the Bomb."

The Bomb. Ken Kirkbride's faith in atomic energy was consecrated when Little Boy fell on Hiroshima and broke the Japanese will to fight on.

"We didn't understand the atomic bomb's capability at first, the scope of it, how large it was. But right off I knew it was tremendous, that a city had literally been destroyed. It was hard to realize how one little old lousy bomb could do all this. I got the full realization when they bombed Nagasaki. That's when we all got the message.

"All the time we'd been planning the invasion, we figured we could have up to a million casualties on our side, because the Japanese were desperate. We always figured that when we went into Japan they were going to take everything, including pitchforks, and throw them at us. I saw the kamikazes dive on ships and how lethal one guy in a single plane who didn't amount to two rows of beans could be. Those guys could shoot. You'd see the tracers go, and you'd think

221

you could walk on them. And that little plane wouldn't vary off course a single degree. I mean, it was just *boom!* and the ship was either badly damaged or even sunk, and by one measly little guy.

"So I learned they could do a lot with very little."

Ken Kirkbride was convinced the atomic bomb saved his life and the lives of hundreds of thousands of fellow soldiers. He believed the United States did the right thing when it exploded two nuclear weapons on two major Japanese cities and ultimately killed nearly 400,000 people, maiming many thousands more. He was sure in his heart, as millions of other Americans were sure, that the bombs brought peace and stability to a dangerous world.

But Kirkbride's personal war wasn't over when Emperor Hirohito surrendered to General Douglas MacArthur aboard the battleship USS *Missouri* on September 3, 1945.

"They sent me to Korea. We went to occupy it, to get American troops in there quick. We'd already given half of it to Russia, for gosh sakes; they just walked in there and took North Korea without firing a shot. When I got there, the Cold War had already started, because Stalin was tough, he never yielded on anything, nothing. All the concessions were made by the Allies. Between [Allied summit meetings at] Yalta and Potsdam, we gave away half the damned world."

The unsophisticated ranch boy from Wyoming had turned into a wiser man on all those bloody beachheads, had matured into a battle-hardened veteran whose experiences, coupled with the Kirkbride trait of slow and deliberate decisions, had instilled in him a new outlook on a world much bigger, more entangled, than the one he'd grown up in.

Kirkbride men always took responsibility for their actions. When it came to the Soviet Union and its threat to the United States, Ken made up his mind and never looked back. The Bomb was good for America, and therefore good for the world.

It had defeated the old enemy and held new ones at bay. Without it, we would lose the Cold War.

Those were his cosmic views on cosmic issues; but in the fall of 1945, all he wanted to do was get home and get on with the mundane.

"I'd about decided I was going to be in the Army for the rest of my life. Everybody else was going home but me. I was at Inchon, about thirty miles out of Seoul, unloading ships in a place with one of the most extreme tides in the world. We'd only been there a little while when South Korea ran out of coal. And what do the North Koreans have? Coal, and lots of it.

"This was when I learned about the Russians and the Cold War. The Russians were in North Korea, so we told them we needed coal. And they said, 'We don't have any trains.' Well, South Korea had trains, so we sent a train to North Korea to get coal. And that was the last we ever saw of the train. We never got it back. It didn't take long to figure out that the United States wasn't working with a cooperative group.

"That's the way the Russians have operated everywhere in the world. Even though I was a lowly officer, I was involved with enough things that I knew what was going on, I had access to quite a bit of intelligence. From that day on, I believed the Russians were a direct menace to the world and no one was stopping them. We were asleep at the switch."

Kirkbride carried that attitude home with him in time for Christmas of 1945. But global politics soon faded into the distance as more immediate needs demanded his attention. He settled down with Shirley to start a family, expand the ranch, carry on a tradition that was preordained for the only child of a pioneer couple who'd devoted their lives to building up something to pass on.

Postwar America was a prosperous place, a time of

economic growth and national self-confidence. Ken signed up for the Army reserves because "it was a simple, easy deal. We never trained. But then they called us up for the Korean War. I kept getting deferred because I had two little kids. It was nerve-racking. I got deferred a month at a time for fifteen months. Finally, it was over."

By October 1957, Ken and Shirley Kirkbride were raising three sons: Jon Howard, born in 1947; Alan Arthur, born a year later; and Dan Richard, who came along in 1952. They were living in a white clapboard house shaded by precious cottonwoods beside Horse Creek, pronounced "crick" if you were a cowboy. The Harding & Kirkbride Livestock Company was growing at its usual steady, cautious rate, and beef prices were up. Home on the range was good.

And then, a hemisphere away at Tyuratam, an engine ignited and lit up the whole world:

"The clear tones of a bugle were heard above the noise of the machines on the pad," Soviet historian Evgeny Riabchikov was quoted as saying in . . . *the Heavens and the Earth,* by Walter A. McDougall. "Blinding flames swirled about, and a deep rolling thunder was heard. The silvery rocket was instantly enveloped in clouds of vapor. Its glittering, shapely body seemed to quiver and slowly rise up from the launch pad. A raging flame burst forth and its candle dispelled the darkness of night on the steppe. So fierce was the glare that silhouettes of the work towers, machines, and people were clearly outlined. . . .

" 'She's off! Our baby is off!' People embraced, kissed, waved their arms excitedly, and sang. Someone began to dance, while all the others kept shouting. 'She's off! Our baby is off!' "

Sputnik went into orbit five hundred miles above the earth. To the "free world," its steady "beep . . . beep . . . beep" was like the ticking of a time bomb.

Kirkbride remembered the reaction of his neighbors:

"People are provincial. There was very little reaction. Nothing much wakes people up. They didn't have much to relate to Sputnik. Besides, we were living near a military town, and it was always full of rumors. There's one every Saturday night if you don't get two in between."

The next year, the rumors got wilder and closer to home: the Air Force wanted some of the ranchers' land to put missiles in the ground. But this time the gossip was true and the missiles were real: enter the Atlas, a single-warhead rocket that was buried on its side but had to be raised to a forty-five-degree angle for launch. The dinosaur of ICBMs, it needed ten acres for its underground cocoon and was obsolete almost as soon as it rolled off the assembly line.

The government appealed to the ranchers' patriotism and offered a fair price for the missile sites. The Kirkbrides weren't directly involved, but all the ranchers watched closely. Ken distinctly remembered that no one turned down the government. It was just like the old days when the soldiers tore down the stockmen's fences: what Uncle Sam wanted, Uncle Sam got.

"I don't know anybody who said no to the missiles. I'm not saying whether you could have or not; I don't know. But they had their areas picked out, they had prior surveys, they knew right where they wanted to put 'em, and that's where they went.

"One of the reasons they picked this area was because you could drill down to 150 feet and not hit any water. It was dry. And the angle of launch was supposed to be good. It would go right over the top to Russia. The Atlas brought jobs, but they'd no sooner got started than the whole thing was outmoded anyway."

Four years after the Air Force installed three Atlas sites around Cheyenne and set up the control center at old Fort

D. A. Russell, renamed Francis E. Warren Air Force Base, the government men showed up at Ken Kirkbride's house. Finally, it was his turn.

"It was the Minuteman rocket. We got four of them on our land. The Air Force was reasonable. Our roads were so poor that most of them had to be rebuilt. We had this little old bridge that washed out twice a year, and the government spent fifty thousand dollars on a new bridge—and that was twenty-five years ago!

"They only wanted two acres for each site, and the road advantage, frankly, was tremendous. We just didn't have any roads before the missiles came."

Did he realize his ranch would become a direct target for incoming Soviet nuclear weapons when the American ICBMs went into his ground? Did he comprehend that his family had become a bull's-eye at ground zero?

"I figured we would be. But I also figured the missiles had to be someplace. It didn't seem like too much of a contribution; somebody had to have them. And if things went right, we'd never have to use them. If the Russians knew they were there, it would be a better deterrent. You just felt you had to do this; it was part of the world makeup. And anybody that knew anything about the world would realize that once you started something like this, the damage would be unbelievable and nobody would escape.

"I've always considered these missiles a poker game. It's not what you have; it's what you make somebody think you have. That's the key. And the longer I've watched them, the more I've realized it's a close call. I know they can be devastating if they hit, but what you don't know is the ratio of the good ones to the bad ones. There are errors in all phases of the military, I don't care if it's planes, artillery, ships, or missiles.

"But the average person didn't realize how devastating

nuclear weapons can be. The average Joe didn't comprehend it. 'Course, there's a lot of things the average Joe doesn't comprehend. But our leaders knew. And I think that's why we've had this peace for as long as we have. World leaders were well aware of the devastation of nuclear war, and that's why we haven't had one.''

Like civilians around the country, Kirkbride was wooed by the Air Force on a "fact-finding" junket to California to watch a Minuteman III missile launch at Vandenberg Air Force base. He wasn't impressed.

"It fired OK, and everything went fine for a while. We could see it. But when it got out to sea, the direction mechanism went haywire and they had to blow it up. About halfway to Hawaii, I think.''

Except for a few construction stories in the newspaper and speculation by local economists on how much money the deployment might mean to the area, there was little interest in the original installation of the Minuteman I rockets and the conversion a few years later to their offspring, the three-warhead Minuteman III. Two hundred missiles were scattered over 12,600 square miles of Wyoming, Colorado, and Nebraska. Eventually the rockets were controlled by four thousand men and women assigned to the 90th Strategic Missile Wing—the Mighty 90—at Warren AFB, one of the few Air Force installations in the world without a runway. Military aircraft bearing troops and cargo bound for the base have to land at nearby Cheyenne Municipal Airport.

For decades there was no public protest against the missiles along the I-25 warpath. During the Vietnam War pacifists kept a low profile around Cheyenne, a military stronghold where enlisted men, officers, and their families commingled at every level of society and were integrated into all facets of life.

In 1981, Reagan rode into the presidency with a pledge to

beef up America's defenses, especially its nuclear arsenal and missile capability. Warren Air Force Base was squarely in the spotlight when the administration announced it would deploy fifty MX missiles—Reagan called them "Peacekeeper" missiles—to replace fifty of the Minuteman III rockets in Wyoming. Each MX carries the power of three hundred kilotons of TNT—twenty times the power of the bomb dropped on Hiroshima.

Suddenly, protesters were storming the Capitol steps in Cheyenne, calling press conferences, rallying in the streets. Cowboys and housewives were forming grass-roots antinuke groups. In Wyoming, for God's sake!

Much to Ken Kirkbride's surprise and dismay, the protest movement was organized by his own daughter-in-law.

"I always thought the Air Force was very stupid in the way they handled it. When they went from Minuteman I with one warhead to a new one with three warheads, nobody even knew it happened. I mean, a few of us around knew what was going on, but the rest of the country didn't have any idea. With the MX, all you did was add seven more warheads and a little different method of propulsion. It was just modernization as far as I was concerned.

"But the press got ahold of it, and people got all wound up, and God a'mighty, it got turned into a holocaust. It was just ridiculous, all those peace marchers. If you wanted PR that was poor, that's the best model I've ever seen. If the Air Force could have just done it the way they did the Minuteman, then people wouldn't hardly have known what was going on."

Ken Kirkbride—patriot, veteran, macho cowboy, host to four nuclear missiles on his ancestral ranch, a private person who firmly believed in keeping family business in the family and never airing dirty linen in public—found himself the patriarch of a family divided.

"My theory was every family has to have a Carry Nation, so there she is, she's ours," Kirkbride said of Lindi, the forty-one-year-old wife of his middle son, Alan, and the mother of three of his grandchildren. "Did she upset the operation of the ranch? No. Did anybody tell her to stop protesting? I don't know. I never did tell her that. I let her go her own way; she had a cause, and she believed in it."

Neighbors whispered. Fellow parishioners talked. The local newspaper editorialized, intimating Lindi was a Commie red pinko traitor when she went to the Soviet Union on a peace tour with other American women who believed in disarmament.

Kirkbride's reaction to that trip?

"I thought it was nice she had the opportunity to go."

Lindi tried to talk about her two weeks of living among Russian women. In fact, she went on television and told millions of *Nightline* viewers about her experiences. But when she got together with her husband's family for Sunday dinner the first week she was home, no one asked her about the trip. Not a single question.

"It was like I'd just been gone to the store—for a long, long time," she said.

So the Kirkbride family harbored their own beliefs in their hearts and held their tempers when they were together. When they were apart, they followed their own course: Lindi was the "front man" of the Wyoming peace movement, founding Wyoming Against the MX with her husband, Alan, a group of nuns, and a handful of college professors. Initially Alan Kirkbride spoke at rallies and testified at hearings, but he withdrew gradually into the background as his articulate wife gained national attention with her impassioned speeches and her flair for the sound bite on the ten o'clock news.

Meanwhile, Ken's other sons, Jon and Dan, along with their

wives, kept silent on the controversy, ducked interviews, and stuck to raising cattle and kids.

The next Thanksgiving, when the whole God-fearing clan was together around a festive table, holding hands and thanking the Lord for their bounty, two blessings were offered to the heavens: one from Ken, who asked that America be kept strong and free, and one from Lindi, who prayed for peace and goodwill among all men. On the face of it, not incompatible supplications. But the undercurrents were understood by everybody but the babies. For the first time since the Kirkbride Yorkshiremen came to the new land, there was a schism in the clan.

Throughout the '80s, the MX missiles continued to divide the family. Ken remained as adamant as ever that they were good for America, just as the atomic bomb had been good for the country. Hell, it had saved his life. Lindi was indefatigable in her opposition to the MXs, first fighting their deployment and then, when they were in the ground, *in her own backyard,* testifying against their continued presence and the proposed expansion of the arsenal with railroad cars based at Warren AFB.

Shirley Kirkbride—wife of Ken, mother of Alan, mother-in-law of Lindi, grandmother to the next generation—was always the family peacemaker. Like her mother-in-law, Peggy, before her, Shirley baked the pies, tended the sick, baby-sat, and took care of her own aging mother as well as Peggy after Dan died. Hers was always the voice—the polite voice—of reason.

"We discuss all this in our family, and we disagree," Shirley said. "But we all love each other. We've got a lot of thinking folks among the kids. It's hard to know who's right. We love Lindi. She's always been a lady about it; she's never been anything but gracious. She's respectful, and she studies a lot about it. She doesn't just lash out emotionally. This is her thing, and I support her right to do it."

Even Ken talked to Lindi about the missiles—once.

"One time we discussed it a little bit, and I told her it was a poker game, and she didn't agree with me. Trouble is, when you understand all that but start to talk to people about something they don't understand, you're just wasting your time. It takes a lot of backgrounding for people to understand. Lindi didn't understand."

With the crumbling of the Berlin Wall, the election of Václav Havel as president of Czechoslovakia, the triumph of Solidarity in Poland, perestroika in the Soviet Union, and the decreases in the defense budget in the United States, Kirkbride grudgingly admits to rethinking his position—maybe.

"I'm a Doubting Thomas kinda guy, but when you see all these things happen, all this change, without hardly anybody getting killed—well, a few in Romania, of course—then you kinda have to start believing a little. Disarmament would be tremendous, because we've been putting all this money into weapons and it's just wasted, absolutely wasted. Think of all the things you could do that would be good, like health care."

But for now, until the Soviet Union completely rids itself of nuclear weapons, Kirkbride believes the MX should stay. And that means stay on his ranch.

"It took me quite a while before I trusted the Russians at all. And that was just as far as I could see 'em. But that isn't very far."

10

LINDI'S PEACE OFFERING

I believe in the brotherhood of man and the uniqueness of the individual; but if you ask me to prove what I believe, I can't.
ALBERT EINSTEIN

In the bleak crevasse of the calendar between Thanksgiving and Christmas, the treeless tabletop that is eastern Wyoming is simply the place where the wind keeps going. There is more night than day, and gray is the shade of the season. Cattle stand with their backs to the west, or the north, but never to the south, where the warmth has fled. Horses lie down, deer paw at the snow, hares burrow to hide from hawks. The harvest moon is past, the hunter's moon gone too. It is that rare time of year when even distant stars hold no promise.

It was on such a day that Lindi Kirkbride pulled on her old goose-down parka, bulky boots, and heaviest mittens to drive the four miles on a narrow gravel road to the place where Evil dwells.

"Please God, let the angels hold down those warheads," she prayed.

"Please God, let the angels hold down those warheads. . . .

"Please God, let the angels hold down those warheads. . . .

"Please God . . ."

And then she was there.

The surface of an MX missile site looks like a child's playground without toys. In the center, there is a big concrete slab. The perimeter is surrounded by a chain-link fence as common as the ones sold at Sears. The ground is buried in gravel to keep out the weeds. All of the missile sites are nicknamed according to the military's radio alphabet: A for Alpha, B for Bravo, C for Charlie, P for Papa. The nicknames are given to prevent confusion when relaying messages.

Except for posters warning that deadly force is the deterrent of choice, the only telltale signs that Papa-10 is a dangerous place are the black masks. Mounted on tall poles at each corner of the cement square of Papa-10 are ornaments that look like the decapitated heads of Darth Vader and his three identical brothers. Those black masks, negative images of Georgia O'Keeffe's skulls, are the acoustical periscopes—the electronic ears—of Papa-10. Lindi Kirkbride did not say hello.

Standing like her Herefords, her back hunched to the west out of habit, to ward off the wind, Lindi felt the tears snatched from her eyes by the marrow-chilling gusts. Why did they have to hide the missiles here? she thought. Why were those instruments of death poised to blast out of such a serene place?

The ridge lines and gullies of the Harding-Kirkbride Ranch are not the meadowed hills and dales of fairy tales. But the undulating landscape is carpeted with wildflowers in springtime, rich with summer's abundance of grasses, and a self-renewing seedbed in autumn. Even in winter, when streams dry up and pastures lie fallow under the ferocious blizzards that always come, Lindi Kirkbride finds a subtle beauty in her home ground.

What led Lindi Kirkbride to this place to launch a crusade that often alienated her family, caused dissension with her husband because of the consuming passion she brought to the cause, triggered criticism from her own children, and divided the Thanksgiving table even as everyone joined hands, bowed their heads, and beseeched the Lord's blessing?

Ignoring her tears, Lindi briskly set about the business that had brought her to the MX missile site.

They weren't much, the gaily wrapped packages. In one box there were photographs of Lindi, Alan, and the children, Ryan, Rhonda, and Anduin. Nothing formal, just a few happy snaps of smiling adults and children romping in the yard, and three little school pictures like the ones the kids traded back and forth and sent to Grandma and Grandpa.

In a second plastic bag, Lindi could tell with a gentle shake, the homemade Christmas cookies already were starting to crumble. The sugar crystals had fallen off Santa's face; icing was hardening in subzero weather; the stars' tips were snapping off in the cold. Never mind. The crumbs would be delicious.

Two smaller parcels were stuffed with chocolate fudge and divinity, candy canes and mints.

Finally, there were the letters.

"Our wish this holiday season is for peace. We know you want the same goal. Even though we disagree on ways to achieve peace, we send Christmas greetings from our family to yours."

Each letter said about the same thing, although they were penned according to the individual thoughts of the writer: Lindi wrote, and Alan and the children helped. It was the Kirkbride family's way of reaching out, beyond the chain-link fence, past the concrete slab and Darth Vader and his clones, to the men and women of the 90th Strategic Missile Wing, the four thousand Cold War warriors charged with overseeing one hundred and fifty Minuteman III and fifty MX missiles, the most powerful land-based weapons ever invented.

Her fingers, awkward in their mittens, carefully dropped each gift into a big garbage bag, then closed the top with bright yarn. Satisfied the plastic sack was as secure as she could make it, Lindi took another swatch of yarn and tied it to the fence. No alarm sounded. No soldiers rushed up, machine guns at the ready. No helicopters swooped down from the sky. Just as the jackrabbits who brushed against the metal knew, just as the cows who scratched their backsides on the rough corners knew, Lindi Kirkbride knew that she was safe from assault as long as she stayed on her side of the fence. But she was sure that if she tried to scale the barrier, if she tried to tie her offering to the other side, the warriors would come with a terrible swiftness.

Tugging at the yarn harness one more time, Lindi knew her Christmas offering would have to withstand the buffeting wind for just a few hours before sentries made their rounds in big blue vans with tinted windows and aerials bristling from the fenders.

"They'll probably throw the pictures away," thought Lindi, watching the garbage bag flap in the gale. "I'm sure they'll turn in the bumper stickers and the peace buttons. They already tell so many stories about me, call me 'Old Lady Kirkbride,' say I carry a rifle in my car, make me out to be the enemy."

The hostility of some personnel at F. E. Warren Air Force Base toward Lindi Kirkbride made her sad, and more tears silently flowed down her chapped cheeks. So she talked to her Friend, as she always did when sadness engulfed her.

"Well, Lord, this act was really inspired by You, so maybe

You'll direct them to at least eat the cookies, try some fudge, look at the pictures, read one letter. I'm sure they'll probably think I'm trying to poison them, but maybe they'll test it on a dog. All I'm trying to do is reach out in this season of goodwill.''

With the black masks listening for any whisper of treason, with the gusts of wind drowning out her words, the middle-aged housewife whose conscience led her to take on the nation's entire military-industrial complex sang "Silent Night."

With a final whispered prayer ("Please God, let the angels hold down those warheads . . . Please God, let the angels hold down those warheads . . . Please God . . ."), Lindi got back into her car and drove to a private service of prayers and singing with anti-MX friends who'd also made protest pilgrimages to various missile sites that day. Then she went home to fix lunch for her husband and the hired hand.

Her journey to Papa-10 symbolizes the duality of Lindi Kirkbride's life since 1980. She is a wife, a mother, a homemaker, a church leader, an overcommitted civic volunteer, a crafts-maker, a canner of pickles, and a gardener of flowers. That was the traditional role she chose when she married her college sweetheart in 1970 and moved with him to his family's ranch thirty-five miles northeast of Cheyenne—thirty-five miles from the nearest shopping mall or chain grocery store.

The ranch is part of the 65,000 acres of the Harding & Kirkbride Livestock Company, a business owned entirely by the descendants of Hardings and Kirkbrides. They are not the richest, or the most powerful, and certainly not the most flamboyant or high-profile ranchers in the Cowboy State. But the Kirkbrides and the Hardings are right up there among the most important stockmen in Wyoming.

Respected for their conservative business acumen, which has consistently helped them prosper, even during lean times,

Kirkbride and Harding men are also admired for their dili-
gence, for being good stewards of the land, and for being
raised up to be pillars of their communities. In this family
corporation, only the men have a vote or draw a salary.

In a self-published history of the company, titled "What
Makes Harding & Kirkbride Work," Lindi's brother-in-law
Dan Kirkbride wrote that the most important ingredient was
that "we get along. It's a combination of liking, respecting,
and appreciating the other partners and family members. These
positive relational feelings keep the organization oiled and
working."

The next important requirement, wrote Dan Kirkbride, was
perseverance.

"Ranching is a character builder in that it not only takes
perseverance, but it develops it. A child on the second day
of trailing yearling steers from the East Pasture to Wiley
Warner's gets exhausted. But he learns that he can't quit the
project three miles from the destination. So he pushes on to
the finish—building on his heritage of perseverance."

The fifth generation is being readied to carry on that tradition in the twenty-first century, learning their parents' standards, which are just as high as old Alex Dooley Kirkbride's
were when he arrived in Wyoming Territory in 1889—a year
before statehood—to start a new life with old values.

Lindi Kirkbride didn't know any of this when, as a perky
college freshman with a stop-traffic figure and a smile that
would light up a city block, she fell in love with Alan Arthur
Kirkbride, a sophomore at the University of Wyoming at
Laramie. Wyoming was like an exotic, wonderful country to
the coed from Texas. She chose it because she'd been to
Laramie to visit relatives many times, and because she liked
the feel of the place, the way it looked, the kind of open,
friendly, unpretentious people who lived there.

Alan was a bigger-than-life, recruiting-poster image of what a cowboy ought to be. Broad-shouldered, blue-eyed, with sandy blond hair and a complexion to make a Miss America envious, he could rope a steer, mend a fence, dig a well, or build a house if you wanted him to. But he could also dance and sing and play the Autoharp, he liked to read about far-away places, and above all, he made Miss Linda Lamoreaux of Lubbock laugh.

She smiles when she remembers the first time he took her home.

"You had to drive several miles on gravel before you actually got to Kirkbride land. I can remember going across the cattle guard and Alan said, 'Now!' and I got a shiver, a rush, thinking: Oh my gosh, what an honor, I am in such awe that this is your land, that you will be in charge of it for just a brief time, what an honor, what a privilege. I've always thought that stewardship of the land was part of the adventure. I didn't understand the economic aspects of ranching for years, but from the beginning I understood the importance of being a good caretaker."

For three years of college, they laughed together and dreamed together and planned the life they would share on that wonderful ranch that seemed to stretch forever, where only blizzards and big winds disrupted its peace.

In June 1970, Alan was awarded a degree with honors in agricultural business. He'd been student body vice president and an outstanding campus leader. Lindi was graduated with a major in social work in 1973 after commuting from the ranch to UW to finish her senior year. After their big wedding on August 29, 1970, at Saint Mark's Episcopal Church in Cheyenne, the handsome couple moved above the garage of Alan's parents' home on Sprager Creek, but Lindi didn't carry a full load of classes that year, nor the next, so it took extra time to get her college diploma.

Kenneth and Shirley Kirkbride had settled in the valley in

1945, soon after Ken got back from his three and a half years in the South Pacific. It was just four shacks and a cowshed back then, and Ken remembered the house had four rooms, a porch, a closet, "the roof leaked and you could throw a cat through the walls."

The senior Kirkbrides patched and painted and built a new barn first, as prudent ranchers always do—successful ones always seem to have a big, fancy barn and a small, plain house—then erected a new home in 1948. A workshop and a chicken house followed, and the little garage apartment was added in 1952, when son Alan was only four years old.

By the time Lindi and Alan moved in, the garage apartment was cozy and comfortable . . . but it was still next door to her in-laws. And Shirley Kirkbride—sweet, kind, a nurturer who always put everybody else in the family first— was a tough act to follow if you were expected to be bucking for ranch wife of the year.

"Shirley is the crown jewel in the entire operation," Ken wrote of his spouse in the 1989 booklet commemorating the Harding & Kirkbride Livestock Company's sixty-fifth anniversary. "She cooked for hired hands on the coal stove, washed clothes by hand, pumped water, ironed with flat-irons, patched clothes, made shirts, and taught the boys to read before they went to school. She also helped me feed cattle in the winter. She basically held us all together. Without her, things would have been a fiasco."

That was the young bride's role model, the image she was expected to emulate. Those expectations came not only from the Harding and Kirkbride families but also from neighbors and friends whose womenfolk did the same thing, day in, day out, without thinking twice about it.

In her first act of modest rebellion, Lindi Kirkbride got a job in town. She was hired as a part-time counselor with Cheyenne Youth Alternatives and drove seventy miles round

239

trip every other day. In 1973 she was named Wyoming's Outstanding Young Woman. She joined the League of Women Voters and eventually served on its state board. She got involved in the Cheyenne Safe House for battered women. She eventually was named to the Wyoming Council for the Humanities. She filled up twenty-five hours every day while Alan settled into the ranching operation with his dad, older brother Jon, and younger brother Dan.

In 1972, Ken and Shirley moved to town to take life easier in retirement; Jon and his wife, Dianne, moved into their old house, and Alan and Lindi soon vacated the garage apartment and moved across the road to a new split-level house they'd designed. In 1974, their son Ryan Alec arrived, followed by Rhonda Kapri in 1976. The circle was unbroken. By then Lindi was back home full time, juggling family and church, expertly doing many of the chores she'd learned from her mother-in-law and Alan's "Grandmother Peggy," whom she consulted nearly every day by telephone—baking bread, putting up preserves, getting ketchup out of football jerseys—as well as taking food to the needy, planting crocuses in the fall, chauffeuring kids to piano and swimming lessons, and cheering on the home team at Little League games.

Her house was a jumble of kids and dogs and cats, stray socks, piles of books and magazines, photos and odd scraps of paper nearly obliterating the refrigerator, and folks coming and going constantly through the unlocked doors. Laughter, music, prayers at mealtime and bedtime, bickering children, and ringing telephones seldom surrendered to silence in that house that was truly a home.

Lindi Kirkbride presides over all this while Alan tends to the cows and the land beyond the crabgrass. An almost-beautiful coed who grew into a lovely woman with a sense of her own style, Lindi is bright and shiny as a freshly minted Krugerrand. Brimming with charm, that elusive quality so hard to describe but so easy to spot, she is a lady in the most arcane, exemplary definition of the word. Even when she is pulling weeds in the garden or shuttling kids to volleyball practice, her curly brown hair is always combed, her freckled cheeks dusted with a touch of blush, and her generous mouth tinted with lipstick.

A weight watcher who's partial to chic sports clothes and pretty dresses her mother's generation called frocks, she is fashionable enough to wear shoes to match each outfit and keep up with changing hemlines, even if she does live thirty-five miles out of town on a gravel road. An inveterate reader, she belongs to a literary club and a Bible study group. Among her friends is Alan's cousin Mae Kirkbride, who first told her about the mishap that crippled Ken Kirkbride's Aunt Betty and left her in constant pain from an amputated right leg and a mangled left side.

Everybody thought what happened to Betty Kirkbride was a shame and a travesty and shouldn't have occurred at all. It had almost happened to her sister-in-law Peggy Kirkbride, Ken's mother, only two hours earlier, although she got lucky and saw the hazard in time to stop. There was still daylight then. (Mae said Peggy blames herself for not warning neighbors of the danger of an open trench on a deserted, unmarked, but heavily traveled road.) For a hundred miles around, every rancher and his wife condemned the Air Force for being negligent and ruining a good woman's life.

It happened in May 1964, on a warm spring night, about nine o'clock. Mae remembered:

"The Air Force was in the middle of construction on the Minuteman missile sites. Morrison-Knudsen was the contractor, working for F. E. Warren Air Force Base, putting in the roads. Betty lived at the old Cattail Ranch, the old home place. She was going to town when it happened. They were preparing to rebuild the road, to put in culverts, and they'd dug a trench, ten feet wide and five feet deep. The road was just an old gravel road on private land, but it was one everybody used, a main road. The road crew had just put up a little string of flags, like the kind they use at service stations to advertise gas, and then they'd gone home without telling anybody what they'd done.

"The road went up a little hill and then took a turn, and the trench was right there, where nobody could see it. Betty hit it hard, and her car nosed down and slid into the trench. Her feet were trapped under the pedals, and she hit her head. They found her at 6:00 A.M. the next morning. She'd managed to drag herself out of the car and was laying down in the trench, in and out of consciousness. She was in the hospital for two months. There was a lawsuit, it went to trial, but they settled out of court for $65,000. Everybody said that was the biggest settlement that had ever been handed out in Wyoming. Of course, the lawyers had to get paid. Betty got about $40,000, which I don't think covered her medical bills.

"She got an artificial leg, but she was pretty crippled up. She and Slim [her husband, James William Kirkbride] had to move to town. She had to take painkillers for the rest of her life. She died in 1979. It made her bitter, I think, and left a bad feeling toward the Air Force."

Mae's husband, Rod, Betty's son, said of the days when cable was being laid to connect the deadly web of nuclear deterrence:

"They had two thousand miles of ditch and we [local ranchers] lost about two thousand cattle in it. A cow a mile. But they paid for the cattle. Probably got as good a price as we'd have got at the market. Angus were worse about gittin' in the ditch than Herefords. . . . I think I lost a cow and a half. I didn't have the average, see. I had ten miles of ditch and only two head who died. I lucked out. . . . It's going to go on, life is. As long as they don't blow 'em up. If they blow 'em up, that'll be the end."

Before Betty Kirkbride's accident, the ranchers' complaints were kind of like gripes about the weather: they were constant, but nobody did anything about them. Gates were accidently left open, allowing livestock to stray; sentries drove down the middle of farm roads in defiance of good manners, local customs, and safety standards; young airmen littered with beer bottles and cigarette packs; the Air Force didn't usually help farmers and ranchers plow out during blizzards, but never turned down a reciprocal offer.

But after Betty Kirkbride lost her leg and her way of life, attitudes changed.

"It affected the whole community; everybody was upset, " said Mae Kirkbride. "Nobody ever came to apologize. That's when some of us first started to realize we didn't want those missiles, that it was wrong to have them anywhere. That accident shouldn't have happened to Betty, and nobody ever said they were sorry."

The year after Betty died, Mac and Lindi Kirkbride went together to Cheyenne to hear anti-MX speakers from Utah and Nevada when they were touring the West protesting the proposed placement of the nuclear weapons in those two states. To Lindi, the issue was becoming more complex, and sometimes she felt that the more she knew, the less she knew.

"I was aware of the MX battle in the Great Basin of Utah and Nevada, but most of what I knew I'd learned from *Newsweek*. There was no antinuclear group in Wyoming. I knew we had missiles on our land, but I was so naive, I didn't know anything about them, and they had gone in in the '60s, long before I ever got to the ranch, so to me they'd always been there."

But the summer before the Soviet Union invaded Afghanistan, the Cheyenne Chamber of Commerce and the League of Women Voters sponsored a debate between former U.S. Ambassador Paul Warnke and the Committee for the Present Danger on SALT II. Lindi asked for, and received, a huge packet of information on the issue from the Department of Defense.

"It was that experience which galvanized and primed me for the coming MX battles. I was horrified at the pace of nuclear weapons development and despaired that SALT II did not cut back but allowed for a much greater number of missiles," Lindi said.

Then Reagan decided to put MX missiles in Lindi Kirkbride's backyard.

"When Reagan got into office, I knew he was going to make a decision about where to put them. I can remember watching the evening news, and it came on television that [Wyoming] Governor Ed Herschler had decided to invite the Air Force to put the missiles into existing silos around Cheyenne. Alan and I were flabbergasted. We looked at each other and said, 'Did you hear what I heard?'

"I called Mae, who told a TV station that if Governor Herschler wanted the missiles, why didn't he put them on *his* ranch?" (He didn't.)

Lindi dates the gestation of her activism to that night, but it took a while before her public protest was born in the full glare of television floodlights and clusters of microphones. First, she had much more to learn about the MX missile and what it would do. Each MX missile carries ten nuclear warheads, which can each be aimed at separate targets. The MX can deliver its payload more than six thousand miles in less than thirty minutes. Lindi became immersed in tomes about nuclear weapons and U.S. defense policy.

"Until then I was on the fence about speaking out or organizing public opposition. I didn't like it that we had these missiles on our land, and I already felt compromised by having them be there, but that had not been my decision to make. I thought: What can I do about it? How can I speak out?"

That's when she met three nuns who were actively campaigning for peace and against the MX.

"We talked, and I came to see that although I'm not grateful the missiles were on our land, at least it woke me up because it was in my backyard. Maybe that's why they were put there, to force me to speak out."

Already deeply religious in a traditional sense, Lindi felt herself undergoing "a spiritual awakening. That's how I could do it, get off the fence."

Sister Paula Hirschboech was the first to challenge Lindi's commitment, and Sister Frances Russell soon followed.

"At my first peace retreat, Sister Mary Luke Tobin of the Thomas Merton Peace Center in Denver asked me how deep I wanted to get into it: did I just want to get my toes wet on the edge and feel how cold it is, or was I going to be in it for the long haul? The euphoria of a proposed nuclear freeze had captivated a lot of us at the same time, and it was really exhilarating. But the nuns kept pressing me, challenging my commitment. They made me think while supporting me with their love. Initially I came at the anti-MX from a land issue: I wanted to protect the land, our land, because that's how I'd learned about these terrible weapons and that's how they affected our lives. But it soon grew into a social justice issue for me. Later, when the defeats and disappointments came as the MX moved inexorably toward its eventual deployment, it was that true belief in disarmament and peace that kept me going during all those burnout times."

Alan and Lindi Kirkbride and Alan's cousin Mae were among the handful of people opposed to putting the MX missiles in Wyoming. Theirs was not a popular position. Cheyenne had always loved having the missiles, ever since the

Atlas D, America's first ICBM, arrived in the late 1950s. Even though the Atlas fleet's active-duty life was short, it had a major economic impact on the area and paved the way for Minuteman I missiles in the mid-1960s and an upgraded contingent of Minuteman IIIs in the 1970s.

The sweetheart relationship between Cheyenne and Warren AFB leached into all aspects of life in southern Wyoming. One of the capital's streets is called Pershing Boulevard, after General John J. "Black Jack" Pershing, General of the Armies during World War I, who'd served a tour of duty there. There's also a Missile Drive and an Atlas Motel. The students at Central High School called their literary magazine the *Armageddon Express*.

A citizens' coalition with a large rural element successfully battled to keep the MX from being deployed in Utah and Nevada after the Mormon Church finally, after months of official foot-dragging, put the full force of its opposition behind the effort. Soon after it became clear the multiwarhead weapons weren't going to the Great Basin, a prominent group of Cheyenne businessmen and military boosters lobbied Washington to relocate them to Wyoming, in hopes their arrival would rejuvenate a faltering economy hard hit by recessions in the mining and oil industries. Never mind that the $15 billion spent to build the MXs went to out-of-state contractors.

Lindi had no intention of being a leader in the fledgling opposition to the new missiles. Instead, she tried to push her husband to the forefront. But Alan Kirkbride balked. He was uncomfortable in the limelight, it went against the family grain, and his opposition was narrowly focused on the missiles' disruption of the land, rather than on broader issues such as disarmament, a nuclear freeze, or the moral efficacy of having weapons at all.

"It wasn't that he didn't want to help; he just wasn't comfortable being a spokesman," Lindi said. "I really felt like he ought to be the one, not me. Alan and I and others already had written up a petition and gathered a lot of information, because we'd assumed that most of the people who would come to our first meeting would be against us.

"It was difficult for me that first time. I believe people listen more to men; it's the culture we live in. I value women's voices, but I didn't have confidence that I could do it. We called the meeting [to be in] the post office cafeteria in the federal building in Cheyenne—you can bet that's the last time they ever let us meet there!

"About thirty or forty people came, and we wondered what we wanted to call ourselves. . . . Somebody wrote 'Wyoming Against the MX' on the chalkboard, and that's what we became. Later, we wrote a mission statement, founded the Tristate MX Coalition with folks from Colorado and Nebraska, and later still another organization, Western Solidarity, an eight-state group.

"But in the beginning it was just us, and then, as Alan withdrew into the background, it was me out there in front with the Kirkbride name, and my two dear friends who were nuns. I was scared to death because I was breaking the family rule by speaking out, by going against the views of my father-in-law, who was very much in support of the missiles and was the patriarch of the family. I didn't want them to hate me, but I was bucking the women's role because I felt I was telling the truth—my truth—and following my conscience. That meant going against Ken's views. To me, that was the scariest thing of all—scarier than the missiles."

But of course, it wasn't scarier than the missiles. Nothing was. That was just the hyperbole of the moment, a sentence without deep thought behind it, honest at the time but not the whole truth, nothing but the truth. So that's why Lindi kept protesting, kept putting herself in the public spotlight despite all the dissension it was causing in her home life.

Later, she would marvel at the spiritual growth that occurred in her during that period, reflect on why and how she kept going, every day, despite the disapproval.

And what about her husband?

"Alan was there, trying to run the ranch, keep things smooth, and basically hoping that nobody was reading the newspaper."

Paula Hirschboech was a Dominican nun who'd met Lindi through the Wyoming Church Coalition when she moved to Cheyenne in late 1979. She used to go alone to the gate of the Air Force base, which is only ten minutes from downtown, and sit under a tree on Sunday afternoons.

"I was horrified by the missiles," Ms. Hirschboech remembered. "As you drive into the base, they have models of the Minuteman I, Minuteman III missiles [and now the MX], and I would sit under a tree across the road and stare at them and pray. Gradually, a few people joined me, then more and more. It became a regular Sunday event."

Through those early years of Wyoming antinuke protesting she kept a diary:

[March 9, 1980] Wyoming Against the MX has been born with Lindi and is growing! . . . the culmination so far! . . . I keep going to the base to pray.

[May 17, 1980] Earth Week—we had a whole group go out to the base, and then we had a festival. . . . went to Lindi's ranch and we picked dandelions and all ate them for supper. . . . the Bishop called me to say he didn't want the church to be scandalized by me praying at the base.

[January 20, 1981] We founded Siena House today, our peace and justice education center. . . . it is a protest to the dismaying event in Washington today, Reagan's inauguration.

[November 22, 1982] Invasion! Attack! Bombed! Blasted! Ripped away from hope . . . maybe. We awoke to the news of the MX coming to Cheyenne. It feels like life is totally ripped away. The phone began to ring immediately and continued all day . . . frustration and anger as the horror of the MX [is] taking over our lives.

Eight days later, the beleaguered nun withdrew from an active role in Wyoming Against the MX. The following year she left Cheyenne and in the late 1980s left the Dominican sisterhood. But her memories of that time are bright.

Of Alan Kirkbride, Ms. Hirschboech recalled that "he was always cautious, always on the fringe. He seemed to want to protect his freedom by not taking any risks. But he was a fine man, supportive and kind."

Of Lindi, her recollections are vivid and kaleidoscopic:

"She was always the solid, committed person of passion. In our early days, before we knew the missiles were coming to Wyoming, we wanted to be a consciousness-raising group. But to me it always felt like events overtook us. Because of pressure from the press, and other national peace groups that wanted us to be the center of the action, we got catapulted into the limelight. I was a Dominican, not a native Wyomingite, and not as committed because I always viewed myself as an educator. But Lindi had her feet on that soil, and her whole heart was in what she saw as preservation of sanity. She was our true spiritual leader, and I never saw her sit on the fence, never saw her doubt or waver," said Ms.

Hirshboech, who ultimately returned to Wyoming as chair of the humanities and fine arts department at Central Wyoming College.

"What I will always carry with me about Lindi was her absolute conviction that she can accomplish her dreams."

And there is another memory, bright as a summer afternoon.

"Lindi's little girl Anduin is my godchild," Ms. Hirschboech said. "She invited me to the ultrasound to see the baby for the first time, and I was deeply awed. This was right in the middle of our organizing, and so the child became a symbol of hope to all of us, even before she was born." She came on May 15, 1981, and that summer she was baptized in a clear mountain-fed stream flowing through Kirkbride land, not far from where the missileers sit buried in their bunkers waiting for war, not far from the warheads themselves.

"The minister had his boots on and he carried her into the stream. Lindi and Alan named her Anduin, after the great river flowing through Middle Earth in J. R. R. Tolkien's trilogy *Lord of the Rings*. They gave her the name Hope for a middle name. It was a glorious moment."

Sister Frances Russell, a founder of the Tristate MX Coalition, is now a social worker in Topeka, Kansas. Along with Lindi and Paula, she formed the triumvirate of leadership opposing the missiles.

"I was a lot freer than Lindi," Sister Frances said. "That's part of what being a religious woman is about—you don't have family or contingencies like married people do. Lindi had to constantly weigh her actions against the reactions of her in-laws, who were very reserved people. As she became more public, it became harder and harder to live with those people, who were not for this protest. She had a lot more to struggle against, had a lot more constraints. I always saw her as being very courageous, and constantly growing."

Cheyenne, then as now as always, is rigidly conservative. Its social strata are based on land ownership, longevity in the state, political connections, or military rank if the resident is stationed at Warren AFB. Although it is the state capital and—until the oil and coal boom of the late 1970s and early 1980s, when it was outranked by Casper—was always the biggest town in Wyoming, its population is still just under sixty thousand residents. Many longtimers are related to one another, and everybody of any local or regional importance knows everybody else's family tree.

Birthed by the railroad, the cavalry, and Washington's visions of expansionism, Cheyenne still reflects its roots. Union Pacific trains roar through the heart of town day and night, directed on throughout the West by switchmen in a huge, elevated control center which towers over downtown viaducts. The Albany Hotel near the old railroad station is still one of the hottest spots for a power lunch—the cowboy aboard the bucking bronco on the side of the sporting goods store never gets thrown off—especially during Frontier Days, a rodeo with the slogan "The Daddy of Them All."

Frontier Days is to Cheyenne what the Kennedy Center Honors are to Washington, D.C., the Oscars are to Hollywood, and the opening of the Metropolitan Opera season is to New York: it is simply *the* social event of the year.

When Lindi Kirkbride started protesting against missiles, her invitations to Frontier Days parties evaporated.

"It seemed that 99.9 percent of the people in Cheyenne either didn't know about the MX or didn't care," Sister Frances said. "I always felt Lindi was more courageous than the rest of us because she was stepping out of her family circle, and Alan was always quietly observing this. I know it was tough for him. But I believe he loves her very much."

Throughout 1981, when it still looked as though the MX, if it was deployed, might go to Nevada and Utah, and then in 1982, when the Reagan administration bowed to vehement opposition from friendly senators in those states and, casting about for the missiles' new home, chose Wyoming, Lindi Kirkbride was in a whirlwind. That year she was thirty-four years old, the mother of three, including a baby girl. And as the Christmas season approached, she was about to embark on the most incredible journey of her life. She was going to Russia. She would be part of a people-to-people delegation whose only purpose was to get to know one another better and talk about peace.

"There were seven of us, from five western states, under the Ranchers for Peace program. There were two women at first, but the other one had to drop out because she couldn't afford to go. I was getting desperate because I didn't want to be the only woman on the trip, and I happened to sit down next to another lady at a farm economics meeting, and we got to talking, and the conversation came around to MX issues, and finally, I asked her, 'Do you like to travel?' " Her new friend from Colorado, Doris Williams, ironically had just gotten a passport, so she joined Lindi on the journey.

Lindi's decision to become part of a "citizens' détente" mission to the Soviet Union stunned friends and family, especially her in-laws, who found out through a press release because she didn't have the nerve to tell them face-to-face. Her daddy took to calling her "Jane Fonda of the Plains," and she didn't think he was joking, although in hindsight she realized he was proud of her. Alan's parents simply wouldn't talk about it. It became an issue of control in a family that built all relationships on control. Swallowing her pride, Lindi asked her mother-in-law to look after baby Anduin while Alan kept the older two children. Shirley Kirkbride, loving her grandchildren and ever mindful of her son's welfare, agreed. Alan helped Lindi pack. But the marriage was strained by conflict and dissension. Lindi remembered:

252

"It was such a strange time in our lives. Some people would come up to me on the side and tell me, in a low voice, they were real supportive but they didn't want to show it publicly. Some friends didn't want to talk about it. It was a huge, but nonverbal, issue. They knew Alan and I were doing these things, but they didn't know how to react to us. They didn't know if they should respect us or if we were just weird.

"We weren't scorned, exactly, because the Kirkbride family is too well-respected, and they couldn't write us off, because we were part of the old guard in Wyoming. If we'd just been newcomer upstarts, they could have written us off, or lashed out at us. But because we were who we were, they just acted like everything was normal. And of course, nothing was."

In the period before she left, Lindi remembered getting only three hours' sleep a night, driving herself harder and harder to make her absence easy on her family while easing her own guilt at the same time.

Sister Frances Russell described Lindi as being "tireless" in that hectic period leading up to her departure.

"She worked for weeks to make sure her family would be well provided for while she was gone. She prepared enough meals for the entire two weeks and bagged and labeled them and put them in the freezer. She wrapped all the Christmas presents and decorated the house and baked endless batches of cookies and cakes. She didn't want her absence to be Alan's burden, so she tried to leave it in what she thought was normal condition while she was gone. Her trip was such a daring, bold thing for her to do. And yet there was that domestic, loving, nurturing side of her that insisted everything be left perfect so her family wouldn't suffer."

Lindi's determination to go conquered her guilt about leaving. She left for the Soviet Union right after Thanksgiving, after Kenneth Kirkbride had offered a blessing at the festive holiday table that thanked God for allowing his family to live in such a strong, free, and patriotic country, and after Lindi had countered with her own grace, imploring the Lord to bring peace to all the world and dwell in every heart.

The travelers met with ordinary Soviet citizens and learned of a great universal commonality. Lindi discovered that Russians wanted good health care, good educations, and plenty of food and shelter for their children, just as she did. Despite the language barrier, the Americans and the Russians reached out to one another and agreed their countries spent too much money on guns and not enough on butter. Exhausted but exhilarated, Lindi and the other ranchers flew home to interviews on the *Today* show and the demands of hordes of print journalists, each trying to get a piece of the story. Requests to speak at chamber of commerce meetings, schools, senior citizens' centers, and a myriad of other groups swamped the travelers.

When she finally arrived in Cheyenne, a local editor denounced Soviet sympathizers and talked about people who were "Lenin's ripe fruit." Except for Alan and Mae, not one of the Kirkbrides asked Lindi a single question about her trip. And even Alan "sort of drew his lines and told me where they were," Lindi recalled.

"He let me know there were certain things he didn't want. He made it clear he would do the dishes and take care of the kids as I went here and there, but he didn't want to be used by press people, and he didn't want my commitment to try and block deployment of the MX to take away from our family, because we have to get along with our neighbors, the kids have to get along in school, and we have to try and have a normal life. Alan really believes that if this is what makes me happy, that's fine. But I had to realize that although I'm all for peace, if it doesn't start here in the family, then forget it."

And so Lindi performed a daily juggling act, balancing her increasing activism and growing public profile with what she saw as her obligation to be an exemplary wife and mother. In March 1983, she appeared on *Nightline* with Soviet spokesman Vladimir Posner, Democratic senator Joseph Biden of Delaware, and administration official Richard Perle, to respond to President Reagan's announcement to proceed with research on his multibillion-dollar Star Wars initiative. Nervous but determined to get her point across, Lindi debated those diplomatic and political heavyweights ("Ted Koppel was really nice to me—he let me speak first and have the last word"), but her appearance was largely ignored or denigrated by the folks of Cheyenne.

At the same time she was appearing on national television as the eloquent spokeswoman for a national movement, she was cooking huge lunches every other day for Alan and the hired hand, alternating with her sister-in-law across the road. She testified at MX oversight hearings and traveled to Washington to buttonhole congressmen for support for her cause, but still religiously canned vegetables from her garden. As a woman intimate with the land, who sends homemade chokecherry syrup to friends at Christmas and even coaxes pretty weeds, Lindi turned to a domestic analogy to explain the years of growth and almost schizophrenic change that followed her irrevocable decision to climb down off the fence and fight the MX.

"I began to get the feeling that life is a bunch of jumbled threads and all the time you are weaving them together, but most of the time you only get to see the backside, you don't get to see the pattern. We know there are lots of colors, and some threads keep weaving in and out, so we know a lot's going on, but we still don't have a clue about what the front looks like until, perhaps, we get beyond this life. But there have been moments during this crusade when I feel like I've

255

sort of gotten a quick glimpse of the other side, and it all fits together. I got a tiny peek at the pattern, and it's beautiful. I've gained so much positive energy from this—even the death threats haven't bothered me—that I know I was meant to do this. Why else would God have brought this Texas girl to Wyoming and put me down on a ranch with three missile silos?''

Only occasionally discouraged by constant setbacks and the relentless progress of MX deployment, Lindi persisted in writing letters of protest to the pro-MX Wyoming congressional delegation. She continued to be the target of editorials and letters to the editor.

But by late 1988, when all fifty of the country's MX missiles were armed and poised for launch in remodeled Minuteman III silos surrounding Cheyenne, another mortal threat invaded the Kirkbride family and began to consume the energies and emotions of every member.

"There are good stories of roundups, rattlesnakes, and rodeos yet to be told, but they'll have to wait," wrote Lindi's brother-in-law Dan in the July 1990 issue of the *Wyoming Stockman Farmer*. "We have cancer at our house."

Dan's wife, Pam, the mother of two little girls, was stricken at age thirty-five. "We've been on a life detour ever since. Almost every family takes its turn at such things. Divorce, accidents, infirmity, bankruptcy, chemical dependency. You don't have to seek them, they have a way of finding you," her husband wrote. ". . . With life a mixture of great trial and great grace we continue the detour, in the distance the wolves are howling. At times the wail would be almost unbearable if it weren't for the whispering of the prayers and the smell of the chocolate chip cookies."

Together, Pam's mother, Shirley Kirkbride, and her daughters-in-law Lindi and Dianne were baking those cookies, tending to Dan's and Pam's little girls, cleaning house, shopping, and comforting them and each other. Aunt Mae and a hundred neighbors, relatives, and friends also took turns helping Dan and Pam and their daughters, Hannah and Abby.

Cancer in the house and nuclear weapons in the pasture. Probably unrelated. But plutonium in your backyard raises your consciousness. The continued presence of nuclear weapons has influenced many farmers and ranchers throughout missile country to now read reams of government documents, always searching for clues about whether their patriotism could affect their children's health. But technical jargon and Environmental Impact Statements that ignore people to concentrate only on air, water, and plants yield few clues of future or even present dangers.

"The impact on threatened and endangered species is moderate in the short term and long term due to impacts on the Colorado butterfly plant and the wooly milkvetch." So reads a portion of the Final Environmental Impact Statement, Peacekeeper in Minuteman Silos, 90th Strategic Missile Wing, F. E. Warren Air Force Base, Wyoming.

But there was no amount of homework that could have prepared the Kirkbrides and their neighbors for the fear they experienced when something went wrong inside a silo on June 15, 1988. An MX missile just west of the tiny town of Chugwater, where Dan and Pam Kirkbride live, collapsed in its underground silo after dropping eight inches from its braced position sometime during the previous three days. During the collapse, the MX gave a "missile away" signal. Air Force officials attributed that false signal to the breaking of the rocket's umbilical cord when it settled to the base of its silo. They did not say how long it took to determine that the signal was erroneous. The missile did not ignite.

But the Air Force's final accident report indicated that ignition inside the missile's silo, if it had occurred, could have scattered plutonium around the site. The government said the odds of an accidental ignition were one chance in ten million.

All that official reaction came two and a half years after the accident. Initially, when word began leaking around Cheyenne several days after the accident that something had gone badly wrong at a missile site, the Air Force and the state's congressional delegation stonewalled or denied any knowledge of the accident. No one was officially alerted to any possible danger from contamination or explosion of the missile itself.

The first word Lindi and Alan Kirkbride got was an anonymous telephone call from a man who said he worked for a contractor converting the old Minuteman silos to hold MX missiles. He warned Alan that something terrible had happened and asked him to pass the word because, he said, the military was trying to keep the mishap secret as it figured out what to do. And yes, he added, the broken MX was still out there, in the ground.

Lindi called the offices of Wyoming's governor, Mike Sullivan, its senators, Malcolm Wallop and Alan Simpson, and Dick Cheney, the state's sole congressman, who was tapped in 1989 by President Bush to become secretary of defense.

"I'd had a lot of contact over the years with all of the politicians, and except for Sullivan, who was new in office, they'd all treated me very patronizingly and never taken me very seriously," Lindi said. "When I went to Washington once to lobby against the MX, I dug up dirt from my garden and filled big fruit jars with it as a symbol of why I was fighting to save my land—their land too. I gave the jars to their aides, then heard later that all those impeccably dressed gentlemen, who were so courteous to my face, rushed to their trash cans and dumped the dirt. I guess they were scared it was radioactive because the odor had changed in D.C.

"I remember the first meeting with Cheney, in his office in Cheyenne, I had Anduin as a tiny little baby in my backpack. He had his feet on his desk, and he was eating a hamburger. We were so naive, all ten of us meeting with him to protest the missiles. He did the 'us and them' kind of thing, really put us in our place, and we walked out of there with our tails between our legs, really humiliated. He was very condescending, like 'You people don't understand; if you knew half of what I knew, you wouldn't be in here.' We were the enemy, not the missiles.

"All of them—Cheney, Wallop, Simpson—when you meet them in Wyoming they're so arrogant and grandiose and feeling their oats you can't get near them, but back in Washington, D.C., I think they feel they're part of the pack, so they're real polite and accommodating, like maybe they don't have quite the power and influence there they have when they're back home. But no matter where you talked to them, they didn't really hear us."

Throughout the rest of June 1988, Lindi attempted to get an explanation of what had happened at Quebec-10. None was forthcoming. Only Sullivan's office returned her calls, and a spokesman for the governor said he didn't know much more than what he read in the papers. She tried to track down the tipster based on the name he'd given Alan over the phone. When she went to the Cheyenne house of a man with the same name, it was empty. She bought the address change he'd left behind from the post office for a dollar and called Seattle after tracking his new telephone number.

"When a man answered, I said, 'Did you used to work in Cheyenne with the missiles?' and he said, 'Nope, wrong guy,' and hung up. If that missile had ignited, we wouldn't have been vaporized; we would have been exposed to this incredibly toxic chemical and nuclear materials spewing out. Dan

259

and Pam would have been immediately downwind. But I guess they figure it's an expendable area, there aren't too many people around, you know? So why should they tell us?"

Pam Kirkbride's cancer rallied the family around a common enemy, reunited them, but no one has put aside political and moral differences. Rather, said Lindi, "we respect one another and can disagree respectfully." From Pam's illness, and the sheer passing of time, came a gentle healing of old wounds and a better understanding of the bonds that tie.

"The family has been stretched, maybe even sometimes to the limit, but it's never been divided," Lindi reflected. "There's been tension, but why wouldn't there be on such an incredible issue? That has never meant that I didn't love them all. And I never doubted, in my heart, that they cared about me too."

Lindi spends a lot of time, as all women do, looking out her kitchen window. What she sees is a wide horizon where newborn calves nurse, where her husband rides by on his horse and waves, where her children bob up and down on the trampoline in the flower-filled front yard. It is to that window that she has taped a prayer by Thomas Merton which guides her journey:

My Lord God, I have no idea where I am going. I do not see the road ahead of me. I cannot know for certain where it will end. Nor do I really know myself, and the fact that I think I am following Your will does not mean that I am actually doing so.

But the path Lindi Kirkbride has chosen is her own, nobody else's, and she has vowed to follow it to the end.

11

LIFE IN THE SILOS

Dig a hole, cover it with a couple of doors, then throw three feet of dirt on top. . . . It's the dirt that does it. . . . if there are enough shovels to go around, everybody's going to make it.

T. K. JONES, *deputy under secretary of defense for Strategic and Theater Nuclear Forces during the Reagan administration, commenting on projected nuclear war survival*

The solid-steel door clangs shut with finality. An instant later, the big box begins to move, inexorably downward. The military policeman at the controls looks straight ahead, silent, his hand resting ever so carefully at his side a fraction away from the loaded gun riding square on his hip. The lights make the walls of the shaft scrolling upward outside the elevator's bars look like softened vanilla ice cream. Within two minutes, the whine of the motor quits, and the elevator stops with a gentle bump. The policeman is firmly in command, ordering interlopers to stay behind the yellow line painted on the concrete floor until he gives permission to cross it. His hand still rests near the gun. Everyone obeys.

Beckoned forward, his troop crosses the yellow line just as it would cross the median in the road—carefully, looking both ways, then looking again. It is ten steps into an antechamber dividing two rooms. The left fork leads to a cavern crammed with generators, diesel engines, metal boxes carefully labeled in jargon only insiders would understand. There's a smell of grease and mold and old water left too long in corners.

The right shaft is blocked by a thirteen-ton steel door. The guard moves to the telephone on the wall and picks up the receiver, mumbles a few words into the mouthpiece, then hangs up and waits. Slowly, as though it was the sepulcher itself, the door swings open. A handsome lieutenant in a starched blue uniform topped off with a jaunty cravat smiles at the strangers clustered around the door, but he blocks entry into the inner sanctum until he has read from a list of rules attached to his clipboard.

Reduced to their simplest definition, the rules are: Don't touch anything and do exactly what the officers with the guns tell you to do, instantly and without question.

"Welcome to Quebec-1," says the lieutenant, turning sideways at last to grant the first glimpse into the Oz of Armageddon, the command capsule that controls some of the most powerful weapons on earth. This is the domain of the missileers, the men and women who are empowered to turn the keys on World War III. These are the wizards behind the curtain.

They are an elite fraternity, smart and quick, with excellent eyesight and finely toned bodies. Their personal grooming habits would make a mother proud. They are our sons and daughters, some of the best, smartest, and most attractive young people in America. And they are young: most are in their late twenties. They debunk the myths of Dr. Strangelove, and they are certainly not the ideologue children of the late General Curtis LeMay, who wanted to bomb an Asian enemy back to the Stone Age. But neither are they flower children, the descendants of peaceniks who hung out on the corner of Haight and Ashbury. The missileers are the patriotic offspring of the Silent Majority, the new cold warriors in a warmed-up world of crumbling Berlin walls, splintered Eastern European alliances, and the inevitable unrest of a volatile, explosive Middle East.

Just as millions of workers do every day, these fraternal companions, bonded by training and dedication, carpool and commute to work. When they get there, a color TV, a microwave, and an exercise bike are available. There's even a chef on duty to cook up popcorn in the middle of the night if they get a sudden craving. Everyone wants them to be comfortable at work.

But this fraternity's hazing is a little skewed: pledges are required to watch films of the vaporizing blast at Hiroshima and the aftermath of the bombing of Nagasaki, burned bodies, skeletons lying in the street, a city suddenly crushed. They are put through psychological tests and required to sign a pledge that if they are ordered to launch nuclear weapons, they will obey. Just as there are no cowards in foxholes, so there is no room for second thoughts in a nuclear control bunker. The military wants to be damned sure its missileers know exactly what they are committing to do. Anybody with doubt is cashiered out.

Once they are accepted into their elite band, work rules are also unorthodox. They are forbidden to take any medication stronger than aspirin without asking their commanding officer to temporarily relieve them of duty. All members are encouraged to goldbrick if they are even slightly depressed, and to snitch on each other if there's a personal problem interfering with their work.

It is the work that truly defines them. Their mission, should they be ordered to carry it out, would be to launch nuclear weapons against an enemy and contribute, without question, to the end of civilization and the destruction of the planet as mankind has known it.

Besides the nuclear weapons aboard submarines and Air Force bombers, there are one thousand land-based intercontinental ballistic missiles in the United States arsenal. They are positioned around Malmstrom Air Force Base, Montana; Minot and Grand Forks Air Force Bases in North Dakota; Ellsworth Air Force Base, South Dakota; Whiteman Air Force Base, Missouri; and F. E. Warren Air Force Base at Cheyenne, Wyoming, home of Quebec-1. All but fifty of the ICBMs are Minuteman II and Minuteman III models dating from the 1970s.

The remaining ICBMs are designated "MX," for "Missile Experimental," the ones christened "Peacekeeper" by President Reagan, and all are assigned to Warren. They were planted in south-central Wyoming throughout 1988 in old Minuteman silos redesigned and "super hardened" for the bigger missile.

It is the missileers' job to train for Doomsday while holding steadfast to the motto "Peace Is Our Profession." Over their left breasts—over their fiercely beating hearts—are sewn badges showing a mailed fist clutching a flash of lightning and an olive branch. It is a schizophrenic emblem for the young men and women—kids, some of them—who live in buried bunkers at the business end of man's bargain with the devil. For unlike the bombardiers of all previous wars, they are also known direct targets. Quebec-1 is the command center for outgoing, but it is also a bull's-eye for incoming. No place on the face of the earth can withstand the impact of a direct hit from a nuclear warhead. Quebec-1 and its crew could not survive ground zero of a Russian missile. And popular scuttlebutt has it that the Pentagon is sure the Russians have every single missile silo and its command post double-targeted.

If the world's atomic journey began with the Trinity blast in the Jornada del Muerto of New Mexico only four decades ago, it could end at any time in the rolling high plains of Wyoming. The journey along America's Nuclear Highway during the Cold War led from the deserts of White Sands and the first burst of Oppenheimer's apocalyptic vision north to Los Alamos and its continuous quest to create a bigger bang for the buck, to Cheyenne Mountain and the U.S. Space Command in Colorado Springs, on past the flawed Rocky Flats nuclear weapons plant with all its deadly hazards, straight into a vast missile field the size of Belgium. MX MIRVs are the latest man-made mutants to evolve from the atom's secrets.

Today's missileers are part of that evolution too. They are young enough that the Vietnam War happened to their parents and is just something else to be studied in history class. Their rigid training in electronics, physics, chemistry, and navigation teaches them that harnessing atomic energy to make "better" weapons has been America's best insurance against the outbreak of another war. They believe, as generations of their national leaders have believed, that carrying the biggest stick—carrying thousands of them—is the best way to maintain peace.

Quebec-1 is only half a mile off Interstate 25, within sprinting distance of a clapboard farmhouse and a barn full of hay. Except for the sign on its front gate—USE OF DEADLY FORCE AUTHORIZED—and the bristling antennas, the main building is innocuous, perhaps the headquarters of a prosperous well-drilling company or a farmers' co-op.

As one stands at the chain-link entrance, waiting for the guys in fatigues and berets to shoulder their M-16s and open the gate, a glance over the shoulder reveals a steady flow of traffic going both directions along I-25. The unmarked Quebec-1 turnoff is less than thirty miles north of Cheyenne. Another twenty miles up the Nuclear Highway there's Tango-1, and across the roadway to the east are Romeo, Sierra, and

Papa command capsules and their flocks of MXs. Each control site monitors ten MX missiles, or one hundred warheads. The "Peacekeepers" buried along a sixty-mile stretch of I-25 constitute the entire MX arsenal in the United States.

Every day, thousands of cars barrel along I-25, and undoubtedly thousands of transients, many of them tourists headed for Yellowstone National Park, seven hours northwest, or Mount Rushmore, seven hours northeast, complain about the treeless, windswept landscape. About how boring it is, how dull life must be, speculating that nothing except a blizzard or a rattlesnake ever crosses those empty hills.

But to those under that endless horizon, beneath the wild grass, the snowpack, the prairie flowers, daily life is seldom dull, because they keep themselves psyched for action. No, life is not boring to the missileers, to their guards, or to their bosses back down the highway at Warren. Monotonous, perhaps. But never boring. Every day when they go to work, deep in the recesses of their highly trained brains there is bound to be one tiny, nagging doubt floating in their subconscious like the first grain of sand intruding into the oyster shell: Will today be the day? Will I have to do it today? Will I be ordered to launch? If George Bush or Mikhail Gorbachev, or their successors, decide that today is *the day*, then yes, the missileers will have to unlock their red boxes, insert their keys, and turn them.

The women missileers pass the time reading *Redbook* and *Glamour*, riding the exercise bike to tone up their thighs, and, if they are pregnant, boning up on baby care. Females may continue working until the delivery of their child, but they may not work in the actual command capsules after their sixth month of pregnancy. Instead, they practice in the simulator and staff the missileers' office on the Air Force base.

Men, who are never confronted with such interruptions in their careers, theoretically could advance more quickly up the promotions ladder. But like their feminine counterparts, they, too, combat boredom in the capsule with stacks of *Sports Illustrated, Golf Digest,* and *Popular Mechanics.* Both sexes share *Business Week, Forbes,* and *Fortune,* because of the missileers' propensity for getting advanced degrees in business management, a specialty field that will hold them in good stead if they decide to leave the military early, or even after formal retirement in mid-life.

But all those mundane accoutrements of ordinary life aboveground, transported into "the hole" to provide a semblance of normality, are merely distractions to pass the time as the crews sit, waiting, for the one klaxon that would call them—literally—to arms.

That's what the free higher education, good medical benefits, thirty days annual leave, fast-track promotions, and all that training, over and over and over, has been about. Unlock the box, turn the key, do the dirty work.

Missileers such as Ann Struckman, a petite, red-haired lieutenant who wears discreet eye shadow and the trendy perfume Knowing by Estée Lauder. A newlywed who married missileer Dana Struckman, Ann was graduated in 1987 from Pace University in Manhattan with a degree in computer science. Her father was a banker, but he often talked about his days in the Marine Corps and what a great experience it had been for him before he went home to Staten Island to settle down. When the Air Force recruiter came around during her senior year, Ann was curious.

"The more I talked to them, the more it appealed to me. I didn't know what I wanted to do when I graduated. I didn't much want to commute into the city every day, and finding a place to live in New York is next to impossible, so the thought of leaving, of going away, was good."

Born in 1965, Ann was only ten when Saigon fell and America turned its back on the Vietnam War and the draft.

Having come of age in the era of the all-volunteer force, the savvy college graduate with good grades and an ambitious eye decided to sign up and try for officers' training school (OTS).

"What convinced me was the traveling and the benefits," Ann recalled. "But I'd also gone up to West Point once, and what appealed to me was the overall attitude. It was like it was a big family. I figured going to California with the Air Force was easier than going to California on my own. There's also something else driving you to do this. It's not the money. I really felt I would be serving my country, and that was important to me from the beginning."

Ann waited a year, working in a bank and at Macy's on Staten Island, before a slot opened up in OTS. And then, when she got to Lackland Air Force Base in San Antonio, "it was a shock."

"There was a lot of emphasis on physical fitness, but I felt I couldn't give up. The first six weeks were terrible, the worst, but I kept going." She was commissioned on August 10, 1988, then went home on a four-day pass. "My mother made me wear my uniform around the neighborhood." Pride and patriotism were on the rise in the eighth year of Ronald Reagan's presidency.

Although Air Force is synonymous with pilot, Ann didn't want to fly. So she visited with a career development specialist. In the Air Force? Yes. Today's military is borrowing all kinds of jargon and jobs from civilian companies, including human resources management, job counselors, and screening tests to find out what person is right for what job. After counseling, Ann applied to be a missileer and was sent to Vandenberg Air Force Base in northern California, where all missile operators undergo their training. For her, as for the vast majority of her fraternity brothers and sisters, the decision was mostly based on the Air Force's pledge to entirely pay for her master's degree in human resources management. And being a missile officer meant a job in "operations"—an active position as opposed to being a disdained "desk jockey."

"To make general, it helps having operations experience. It's good for promotions to be in missiles."

Missileers work in pairs in their control capsules buried eighty feet beneath the ground near Chugwater, Rawhide, Little Bear, and other dots on the Wyoming map. This is Cowboy Country, where "Real People Eat Real Beef" and the rodeo is the highlight of the summer. But it is also the heart of great fishing, hunting, and winter sports, and those attractions were bonus perquisites to Ann, her spouse, who is also a lieutenant, and her capsule partner, Captain Jack R. Hall. It certainly isn't the money, which is decent but not great: Ann earns about $22,000 a year; Hall, who outranks her, takes home about $36,000. On the "outside," their training and expertise could probably net them two to three times that much tomorrow.

A coed missileers corps was unthinkable at its inception.

"The problem is," said a former Warren public affairs officer in 1987, "there are only two members in a missile crew, and only the crew can open that locked door from the inside. If you had a crew of one man and one woman, the spouses of those two individuals would have to be extremely strong people not to imagine some illicit activities, whether there were any or not. So we do not have mixed crews."

On January 1, 1988, reality outdistanced imagination, and that myth, too, fell, like the old ones that had claimed women couldn't be in the Army because there weren't any bathrooms for them, or couldn't be in the Air Force because they didn't have good enough eyes to fly, or couldn't be in the Navy because, after all, where would they sleep in a crowded ship?

269

Jack's young bride, Michele, and Ann's husband help their spouses pack for the twenty-four-hour-plus shifts at Quebec-1. The two couples are off-duty pals and socialize together. While not exactly family to one another, they are close friends.

So what really goes on "down in the hole"? Nothing but work, says the missileer team indignantly. There's too much of it for anything else. These are, after all, professionals. Their focus is lasered on their careers.

Hall is in charge of the shift. Handsome and athletic, he has an engaging smile and an easy manner that invites conversation. A native of Antioch, California, Hall is the son of a chemical engineer who retired from the Navy as a commander after three years on active duty and seventeen in the reserves. Knowing a little bit about the rigors and rewards of military service, Jack Hall started aiming for an Air Force career early. He was a high school football star and was eager for an Academy appointment and collegiate stardom on the gridiron. When he got to the Air Force Academy, he wasn't quite big enough or strong enough for football, so he played only one season in Falcon Stadium before switching to lacrosse, at which he excelled for the next three years. When he graduated, in 1986, he entered flight training, another long-nurtured dream. But he washed out, saying only, "I made it one third of the way through T-38s. My final report said I landed too fast," in tight-lipped response as to why he wasn't wearing pilot wings above his left breast pocket. Dissatisfied with being a navigator—"it's just not the same as being a pilot"—Hall entered missileers training and again, just as he did at lacrosse after his short-lived collegiate football career, excelled at his second choice.

He and Lieutenant Struckman teamed up at Warren in 1990. Both of them claim it's a good match and that their jobs suit their goals. Throughout the Air Force, the prestige of that service is linked to pilots and the fancy planes they fly. For a "ground pounder" in the Air Force, there weren't many leavings if you didn't have wings on your breast. But at Warren, there are no obvious reminders of the Air Force's chief mission.

"Warren is the only Air Force base without a landing strip or airplanes," said Hall. "The mission here is missiles. We *are* the mission."

Their shifts begin with a briefing for all outgoing missileers at headquarters. Then the crews drive to their remote battle stations. Although all five MX crews are within a sixty-minute commute to their command capsules, many of the Minuteman III officers must travel up to two hours—much longer in bad weather—to reach their assignments. One crew holds a record of being stuck more than three days in a command capsule because their reliefs couldn't make it to work.

Once inside the gate of the Launch Control Facility (LCF), the crew checks in with the enlisted man, usually a senior sergeant, who is the flight security controller and runs the aboveground operation. They are briefed on anything out of the ordinary, including weather, intruders (nearly always of the four-legged variety, but occasionally a rancher strays into the area), or VIPs headed their way. Then they fill out meal requests with the full-time cook, who fixes and delivers four squares a day, including a midnight snack. Each crewman pays a nominal charge for food: $1.25 will buy a macaroni and cheese dinner with green beans and salad. Fresh apple pie is another quarter.

Sometimes they rummage through the facility's supply of videotapes to run on the capsule's VCR, and often they filch a magazine or two. They decide among themselves and the LCF officer what the day's entry code into the capsule will be, and then it's time to take the elevator down to the "basement." Because only the officers inside the capsule can open the blast door, there is never a moment when the missiles are not "on alert."

The egg-shaped container is balanced on shock absorbers as tall as a man, so that theoretically it can withstand the impact of a near miss. The high plains were picked for the silos because the mile-high altitude gives missiles a greater range, like standing on a hill to throw a ball instead of trying to lob it up from a gully, and also because the ground is springy, like a sponge. Pentagon planners claim the prairie around Cheyenne can absorb more impact from incoming missiles than rocky ground.

The capsule's interior is about the size of a skinny budget-motel room. There is one bunk, a toilet shielded by a flimsy curtain, and a sink. But there, except for the color television set on brackets high above a control chair, the resemblance to a Motel 6 abruptly ends. Across the tiny aisle from the bed there are blinking lights, a chattering teletype, ringing phones, and the buzzers and klaxons and bells that disrupt the illusion of a cozy office. And certainly, the red box with the padlock, the sliding executive chairs bolted to the floor on miniature railroad tracks, and most of all, the sealed key-holes, which would be used to launch the missiles, dispel any notion of an ordinary workplace.

The unmanned missiles fan out like spokes in a wheel, with the command capsule responsible for a "flight" of ten. The two capsulemates begin their work underground by inspecting all the delicate seals on their launch equipment: if any of them are accidentally broken, they are immediately reported and repaired. Each missile stands upright in its own silo, tethered to the capsule by an intricate web of underground cables that constantly relay its physical "health" while electronic sensors stand guard against intruders. Every forty seconds, computers ask each missile, "Are you OK?" and in an optimum situation, the missile answers back in byte talk: "Yes, I'm OK." If it's "sick," a fault light is supposed to appear on crew consoles, and repairmen are dispatched to "penetrate" the silo, disable its launch capability, and fix the problem. Just as computers can get viruses, so nuclear weapons can get sick. Their power supplies can be interrupted by storms and short circuit. The temperature fluctuations of the outside air, from thirty-below-zero winters to hundred-degree summers, affect all man-made apparatus.

Millions of pieces of hardware are strung together in an MX missile: the potential for a malfunction, or multiple parts failures, is enormous, probably incalculable given the various combinations. The electrical lifeline from the command capsule to the missile silo is the umbilical cord through which all this vital information on the MX's "health" is conveyed, and it is the missileers' job to constantly check the vital signs.

Each capsule crew member gets one rest period in twenty-four hours, with the commander usually pulling rank and claiming the five or six hours that would be nighttime if the officers could look out at the sky. The officer who remains awake continues to watch over electronic systems while getting in a little extracurricular reading, studying for his or her advanced-degree classes, and even catching a favorite TV show, if all equipment is operating normally. A favorite is *Star Trek. Gilligan's Island* reruns are also popular.

Critics of the missiles' safety and efficiency claim their Achilles' heel is antiquated hardware and the rural power supply that keeps the whole apparatus running. The same electric lines that feed a remote windmill supplying water to Herefords on the range are also powering the lights and heat at MX command capsules. The Air Force responds that redundancy—diesel engine backup, and giant batteries to backstop the diesel—will protect the integrity of the missiles and their launch capsules in case the rural electricity system collapses.

The officers of the missile squadron and their public affairs experts are always quick to tell you about the things their superiors insist will work. What they don't tell you is about the time, back on January 10, 1984, when guards resorted to parking an armored car on top of Minuteman III silo Hotel-10, just ten miles northwest of Sydney, Nebraska, in an attempt to stop what appeared to be the launch of a malfunctioning nuclear missile.

Blinking lights in the command capsule and a failed guidance system on the missile mistakenly caused Warren officials to think a launch sequence had started. An Air Force spokesman said later: "If the President gave the command to launch, it would go through light changes: 'launch in progress,' 'missile launched,' 'missile has left the silo.' " He said the light sequence followed that pattern, an ART (alarm response team) was summoned and drove a big armored car on top of the silo, then got the hell out of there. The ART team's theory was: in the event of a launch, the Minuteman III's concrete cover would open and the heavy vehicle would fall in the hole, damage the missile, block its path, and prevent its launch. The Air Force said the three nuclear warheads on the missile were not activated because they can only be armed automatically after they are launched. But the *what if?*s were haunting. If the missile had indeed managed to spring out of its silo, if it had been able to arm itself, if it had somehow exploded, in the silo or out, if . . . if . . . if . . . Any variation on that theme would have been disastrous, both from a national defense posture and in view of the possible environmental and human consequences.

An investigation immediately determined that the missile was in no danger of firing, but the probe also revealed the inadequacy of stopping an actual malfunctioning missile from launching.

Problems with the Minuteman III guidance system were only a hint of the problems to come with the Peacekeeper's aiming apparatus. The MX's electronic brain is a basketball-sized beryllium ball chockablock with 19,401 delicate parts costing about $6 million. Built by Northrop Corporation, the inertial measurement unit (IMU) has been afflicted with production and testing problems from drawing board to silo. Congressional investigators have heard allegations of fraud, financial mismanagement in fulfilling the contract, and shoddy workmanship. Testing the IMU in the first two years of production was a crapshoot. If it didn't blow up, its creators considered themselves lucky. Of the first sixty-six IMUs Northrop delivered, there was a 68 percent failure rate among the guidance systems. That meant that either MXs already installed in silos had questionable guidance mechanisms or the whole guts of the basketball were off somewhere being repaired, leaving the missile sitting idly in its hole.

Congressman Les Aspin, the Wisconsin Democrat who chairs the House Armed Services Committee, said of the MX guidance system: "We are dealing with a decidedly unguided missile." His House colleague Jim Cooper, a Tennessee Democrat, said during a hearing: "What we're really talking about is the probability of launching a nuclear attack perhaps against ourselves."

But the missiles' accuracy and projected performance are staunchly defended by the missileers, even though they spend a good part of their day behaving like the little Dutch boy who stuck his finger in the dike to prevent a flood. Their statistics come right out of the manuals and off the public relations sheets. And they will brook no argument. The young officers "in the hole" also point out to all visitors that there is redundancy built into their world: there are five separate

275

communications systems flowing in and out of the command capsule, including regular commercial phone lines, satellite connections, and a link with Air Force planes that fly overhead. Critics doubt that any would work in the confusion and destruction of a nuclear war.

On any given day, crews can spend an entire shift just juryrigging a thirty-year-old system of nuts and bolts inside the capsule in order to keep track of the most sophisticated weapon ever deployed. Within the capsule itself, for instance, twenty varieties of light bulbs are needed. Nothing is standardized. The outmoded toilet is the kind installed in prisons in the 1960s. To describe the hardware inside the capsule as old-fashioned would be like saying a Model T is outdated. Being a missileer charged with keeping equipment in MX and Minuteman command capsules running is the equivalent of being full-time Apollo 13 astronauts, who wound up using a sock and some tape to hold together a multimillion-dollar space capsule long enough to limp home from the moon.

The only outstanding feature at a silo site is the huge concrete door on the ground, which would be blasted off by compressed gas if the missiles were launched.

That order would come in a spoken command over two loudspeakers in each control capsule. Known as an EWO— Emergency War Order—it consists of a series of codes, such as "Foxtrot, Yankee, Alpha . . . ," broadcast very loud and slowly direct from the Strategic Air Command (SAC) headquarters at Offutt Air Force Base near Omaha. Lieutenant Struckman and Captain Hall are attached to the 400th Squadron, the nation's only MX unit. That squadron is part of the 90th Strategic Missile Wing, based at Warren, which reports to SAC.

"Every transmission that we receive could be an EWO, so

we have to decode each one to find out," said Hall, adding that it takes only a few seconds to decipher. "If we got a transmission to launch, we would next open the locked red box here on the wall. It holds documents telling us whether or not the message is actually from the President."

During rehearsals, the sound of a bell like the one in a boxing ring is what missile crews hear when they practice getting the right signal to launch.

When it is received, the "enable code" has to be dialed into the console. There are six dials, with sixteen numbers on each dial. That means the chance of randomly hitting the correct code without actually knowing it is approximately one in sixteen million. Without that exact code, the missile supposedly cannot be armed and therefore cannot be fired.

Those codes are carried at all times in a slim black briefcase, nicknamed "the football," by a military officer who's always near the President. The briefcase also holds specific war options. The President himself carries an authenticator system about the size of a credit card, which would ensure that launch orders came directly from him. When President Reagan was shot, in March 1981, doctors had to cut away his clothing in the emergency room. FBI agents immediately impounded his authenticator as evidence in the assassination attempt and reportedly refused to return it for days.

Missileers in the bunkers stoutly insist that only their Commander in Chief or his constitutional successor can authorize a launch of nuclear weapons. That successor includes not only the Vice President, the speaker of the House of Representatives, and the president pro tem of the Senate, but the cabinet in order of rank, starting with the secretary of state. When all officers of the government are assembled in one place, such as for the President's State of the Union speech to Congress, at least one cabinet officer—usually the secretary of education or the head of the Department of the Interior—is always "uninvited" and asked to stay away from Washington in case the Bomb goes off.

Although the White House won't confirm it, authenticator code cards are believed to be possessed also by the secretary of defense, the deputy secretary, the chairman of the Joint Chiefs of Staff, and perhaps one or two other persons in the chain of command.

The whole nuclear defense apparatus rests on the premise that so many safeguards are layered, one atop the other, that it would be impossible for an accidental or "madman" missile launch to erroneously trigger World War III. For years, admirals and generals have paraded before congressional committees, assuring U.S. lawmakers that the fail-safes against a monumental nuclear mistake are foolproof. Many, in fact, have complained that the precautions are so stringent they could hamper retaliation in a surprise attack.

Within an MX (or Minuteman) command capsule, the two officers sit twelve feet apart, at individual consoles. Each has a launch key sealed in a lockbox. In the past, each wore a handgun, in case the "buddy" system got corrupted and a rogue missileer suddenly went crazy. But in early 1991, without fanfare or official furor, that regulation was quietly rescinded.

If the crew of Quebec-1 ever gets an "enable code," then both officers must turn their launch keys simultaneously, within five seconds. When that happens, they initiate a "launch vote." Such action requires two separate crews. That means another crew, in another capsule—a captain and a lieutenant at Tango-1, Romeo-1, Sierra-1, or Papa-1—must simultaneously be turning their keys within the same "window" in order for an MX to blast out of its silo.

"There is no way a single capsule can launch a missile alone," Hall said. "That capsule must have assistance. If everybody else is gone, then it will have to have airborne assistance.''

Which comes from "Looking Glass," a flying command post that mirrors the capability of SAC's underground bunkers. For twenty-nine years, a Looking Glass plane—an EC-135, which is a converted Boeing 707—was in the air round the clock, ready to take over retaliation in case ground-based launchers were wiped out in a BOOB attack: a Bolt Out Of the Blue. In the jargon of the U.S. military, nobody ever dies; people are merely "rendered inoperable." If Captain Hall and Lieutenant Struckman and all their counterparts were "rendered inoperable," Looking Glass would be their backup.

But in July 1990, in a cost-cutting binge that might save $25 million annually in fuel and repair bills, and in a gesture of relaxed tensions with the Soviet Union, SAC announced that America's flying nuclear command post would no longer stay continuously in the sky but would be relegated to ground alerts and fly at random several times a week.

Looking Glass planes are based at SAC headquarters but fly secret patterns over long distances, carrying three crewmen and about twenty-eight experts in intelligence, communications, and maintenance. The general who's always on board sits next to the double-locked code box. The pilot must wear a black patch at all times to protect one eye in case the glare of an exploding nuclear weapon blinds his other one. Looking Glass can stay aloft, its internal air system blocking dangerous fallout, for thirty-six hours if it gets refueled. But its high-powered engines must then get oil or burn up. And that means the plane must finally come down to join whatever—and whoever—would be left.

When it practices, Looking Glass flies an evasive pattern, always playing its deadly serious war game of eluding the enemy. Driving along I-25, with nary a sheep's silhouette between sky and soil, one sees a huge metal bird occasionally roaring up out of a draw near the rust-red cliffs of Hole-in-the-Wall, or leaving a telltale vapor trail in the vast blue canopy above Buffalo, Wyoming, the northern terminus of the thousand-mile interstate that begins near the Texas-Mexican border. Unsuspecting travelers often are transfixed by the sight, curious but unconcerned. And then, because it is practicing, the plane is gone. Is it Looking Glass, or just some other mysterious metal avian? Who knows? Only SAC and the missileers.

Sometimes, with its engines throttled back to near stall speed to conserve fuel and its altitude down to just above treetop level, if there were any trees to top, Looking Glass's decorated SAC pilot gets on his microphone and visits with the missileers buried in the ground below his wings.

They talk business, they talk about the weather, and, if they've built up a verbal rapport over time, they ask about each other's health. Missileers and Looking Glass pilots are very rational people who view their work as important and necessary. Every day, they practice acts some consider insane. They have more power at their fingertips than all the generals combined who've ever waged war. Ask them, and they'll tell you, yes, they've weighed the consequences of what they may one day be called upon to do, and yes, they are fully prepared to do it. But in the interim, the men and women responsible for unleashing the horrors of nuclear war go about their daily routines just like folks who work for the phone company or check out groceries at Safeway. They do not dwell on the inevitable consequences of their actions. Instead, they focus on training, on professionalism, on competing with their peers, on getting ahead.

In their own way, they each will say they cannot possibly force themselves to think, day in, day out, about what they are charged to do if the United States is under nuclear attack. It is, they each say, in a slightly different way, beyond human comprehension. That is not to say the consequences are not always in their subconscious; that is to say they do not consciously dwell on them. So instead of staring death in the eye when they get to the "office," every missileer becomes a technocrat, fussing over lights and buzzers and encrypted messages and checklists. There is security in minutiae, danger in the Big Picture.

"The job is deterrence," Ann Struckman said. "To even get the job you have to have an extensive psychological interview. Yes, I've thought about it, and yes, I can do it."

The lieutenant speaks in a quiet, authoritative voice, her posture relaxed, her face unlined by doubt or anxiety. Beside her, Captain Hall nods in agreement.

Other missileers exchange solemn glances, then reaffirm that they, too, are in accord.

"If the message comes down and we're told to launch, we will do it because somebody higher than us has told us to, and we have complete trust in that," said Lieutenant Jeff Stein, a career veteran who enlisted in the Air Force in 1973 and earned his officer's commission fourteen years later.

His capsule partner, Lieutenant Ken Boschert, concurred.

"My justification for launching nuclear missiles is our country's policy of 'No First Strike.' To me, it's like a revenge policy. If somebody's going to kill my family, then I'm going to kill theirs."

Their enthusiasm is high. But their stress level is stretched.

Hall adds, "When I come off alert I'm pretty tired. It's a subtle fatigue, not so much from what's riding on the bombs but from being alert all the time."

Lieutenant Struckman summed up a missileer's life: "You're constantly waiting for something to happen."

Everybody knows what that "something" is. And yet missileers, like B-52 bomber pilots and the crewmen of nuclear submarines, talk in euphemisms. They don't call them bombs; they call them "reentry vehicles." They don't say kill; they say "carry out our duty." They don't say war; they say "something." Oh, yes, it's something, all right.

Lieutenant Struckman and Captain Hall and Lieutenant Stein have helped launch an unarmed nuclear test weapon at Vandenberg AFB, and they each said it was the biggest thrill of their career. Occasionally an MX or a Minuteman missile is removed from its silo, disarmed, and shipped to Vandenberg. To see if it still works, the missile is fired down the Pacific range toward Kwajalein atoll. Ann said watching the unarmed rocket soar into the sky on its test flight was her most exciting moment in the military.

There is a vigorous esprit de corps among missileers, such as is seldom found outside fighter squadrons or special forces units. Their pride shows in the way they wear their uniforms, in the cravats in distinguishing colors: white scarves signify evaluators, missileers who are trained to test and inspect the performance of their peers; orange is worn by instructors; and blue-and-white scarves are donned by officers actually on duty in the capsule. Most of them also wear little buttons that aren't regulation.

The pins are reminders of another war in another age, a time before Hiroshima, when men fought hand to hand and dueled against each other, one on one, in the sky.

In World War II, Colonel Art Rogers was the first commander of the 90th Bomb Group, flying B-24s up the chain of South Pacific islands as Americans like Ken Kirkbride pushed the Japanese back toward Honshu. When Rogers's men designed embroidered patches for their leather flying jackets, they made a pun on his name, using the old "Jolly Roger" pirate symbol with a skull and crossed bombs instead of bones. Rogers commanded the 90th's original four squadrons—400th, 319th, 320th, 321st—until the war ended and the bomb group became the 90th Bomb Wing, transferred to B-29s, and trained for the Korean War.

Over the decades, the wing kept shifting into more sophisticated aircraft, until it became the 90th Strategic Missile Wing when two hundred Minutemans were deployed at Warren. The base's missile squadrons retain the same numbers as Rogers's, and each round pin bearing the skull and crossed bombs also has printed on it the name of a lost pilot from Rogers's command.

Missileers who wear the pins with a dead stranger's name say they feel a kinship to the fallen flier who was killed long before they were born. They see no incongruity in the fact that those long-ago pilots died in individual combat, staring down their enemy even as he killed them, either from a ship firing ack-ack or in another airplane coming straight on with guns blazing. The missileers' mission is a lonely one, performed in antiseptic isolation, in what most likely will be their own coffins if nuclear war erupts. There may be no one left to wear pins with their names on them.

There's a small museum on the base, with displays chronicling the evolution of Colonel Rogers's old outfit. Even his flight jacket is there. The museum is a hodgepodge of memories, a receptacle for leftover artifacts not meaningless enough to throw out, not valuable enough to enshrine in a more prominent setting. Dwelling only briefly on the short period when Warren AFB was the first and only ICBM base in America, there are still pictures left of that tense time during the Cuban missile crisis, in October 1962, when all the base's Atlas missiles were raised out of their coffins into the firing position and stayed that way for a full month.

Eventually the Air Force put four of its obsolete and abandoned Atlas missile sites up for sale. In 1966, Francis Dellenbach bought one about four miles east of I-25 mile marker 47. He paid $3,116.66 for it and pronounced it perfect for his screw-making business. After three years of "renovation," Dellenbach moved in.

He lives and works in the control area, accessible from an outside tunnel, where the missile crew used to enter. He painted the topside entry hot pink as a favor to his late wife and added an elevator to take him down to his home. The power and equipment room that used to pump out 34,000 cubic feet of air a minute now shelters a washer and dryer, an exercise bicycle, and extra parts for his business. Dellenbach converted the empty space that used to hold huge fuel tanks into an automobile storage area: a '67 cherry-red soft-top Camaro, a '24 Model T Ford, a couple of Edsels, a '51 Kaiser—eleven cars in all. He mostly stores the vehicles for other people who want to protect them from the harsh Wyoming weather. Because the silo was built into a sloping hillside, the cars could be driven in and out, just like in the garage of a split-level house.

In 1990, the seventy-one-year-old Dellenbach told an Air Force officer he prefers solitude, and that living thirty feet belowground in the old Atlas bunker and launch tunnel is just perfect for him. But he does complain that the rubber roof, half a football field long, which used to roll back to allow the Atlas to stand upright, leaks.

"You'd never think it would," he said, "but my dog, Blackie, sits up there on the roof for hours, barking at the coyotes and digging holes in the roof with his claws."

As far as the Air Force knows, Dellenbach is the only human inhabitant of an abandoned Atlas missile silo.

Along with the Atlas photos in the museum and the dramatic snapshots of an MX launch, there are artists' renderings of what the Air Force thinks its next mission will be—putting MXs on railroad cars and shuttling them around the country to evade detection.

If the "MX Rail Garrison" is implemented, six more states would get MX missiles besides Wyoming. The Bush administration wants to put fifty Peacekeepers on twenty-five trains, each carrying two MXs. The trains would be kept on Air Force bases and moved onto civilian railroad tracks in times of crisis. Warren AFB would continue to be the main MX operating base. Pesident Reagan wanted fifty more MXs for his trains, but with Pentagon belt tightening and a $300 billion deficit, President Bush proposed taking the fifty MXs from their Wyoming silos and using them on the trains.

"This dispersal will offer enhanced missile survivability in the event of an enemy attack, providing the potential for prompt retaliation vital to the successful deterrence of war," said the Air Force in its usual khaki-speak. The cost of taking the fifty MX missiles out of their silos and building new "garrisons" as shelters is expected to be at least $5.6 billion, according to a Pentagon mathematician. Work has progressed to the point of construction of a mock train capsule, in which eighteen crewmen lived for a month-long test. Four of the trains were slated to be based at Warren by 1992, but the Middle East crisis and the slack economy intervened. The Air Force said that once the trains are sent out, they'll have access to more than 120,000 miles of commercial railroad track.

So far the concept has failed to get beyond the planning stage, because of its multibillion-dollar price tag and because powerful congressional critics remain unconvinced it will work. The two primary problems usually cited by critics are the ability of the train to withstand the powerful launching of the MX and also the reliability of the missile's delicate guidance system after the MX has been jostled around on railroad tracks for several days during a crisis. As one Wyoming farmer said at a public hearing in Cheyenne: "I can't even get to San

Diego safely on Amtrak, so how the hell are you going to protect a nuclear weapon on an American railroad track?'' His comment was greeted with thunderous applause; the Air Force colonel flown in from the Pentagon to answer questions stood silent on the stage as the audience's ovation for the skeptical farmer continued for a full minute.

But the bomb-makers are always at the drawing board, tinkering with the heart of life to make bigger, faster death for our side. From the slingshot to Star Wars, mankind has strived to create a better weapon than the one it's got. The missileers are the spiritual offspring of David if not Goliath, of William the Conqueror and Charlemagne, of George Washington and Robert E. Lee, of ace Eddie Rickenbacker, Medal of Honor winner Sergeant York and all the fallen at Flanders Field, of John F. Kennedy's PT-109 crew and Lieutenant Colonel Paul Tibbets and the boys of the *Enola Gay*. They are the shock troops of tomorrow's war, beyond Grenada, beyond Panama, beyond Iraq, the true children of Oppenheimer and his clan.

So the journey is complete. The highway has taken us from the birth of the Bomb in southern New Mexico to its latest legacy in the Wyoming grass, from creation to deployment. In a crease of the country where mountains and plains collide, where water is scarce and land is cheap, where vistas and dreams seem to last forever, the atomic bomb has altered the landscape and changed the people. It has robbed some of their way of life and their life savings, it has made fortunes for others. All the research and all the gizmos may cure cancer someday; they surely have already caused it. The Bomb changed the course of history. It leveled two cities, it poisoned people downwind of tests, and it helped keep the peace. Like Los Alamos itself, the legacy is mixed, the choices never simple. And what the Bomb also did was mold and shape and change a part of the country—the Nuclear Highway.

As the nation closes the books on the first half century of nuclear weapons, it can tally the lessons of the Nuclear Highway. America can be certain that the weapons will always get bigger, that there will be new discoveries and bigger booms and more toys of mass destruction, that there will someday be Star Wars and Stealth Wars and inevitably the next generation after that. Maybe there might even be a counter-countermeasure to it all, but a sure lesson of the Nuclear Highway is that that day is doubtful. The people of the Nuclear Highway have learned that no army ever retreats, that living next to the Bomb can be hazardous, that you can never put the genie back in the bottle. They have seen that the critics probably never win, even though sometimes they are proved right, and that even today we don't know all the environmental and safety dangers. Yet at the same time, the people of this place on the front lines of momentous history have learned that there is always a silver lining in nuclear weapons work. It sure helps pay the bills, it can stretch the frontiers of science, and it probably helps keep us out of World War III.

With a little more exposure to each other, those on the outside may learn that those on the inside are dedicated believers and not Dr. Strangelove kooks, and those on the inside may find that the protesters and "antis" are not close-minded ideologues but mothers and fathers and neighbors. Someday we all may realize that the generals and the bomb-makers actually share many of the same concerns as the ranchers and the peaceniks.

The time line that began in 1945 in the empty desert known as the Journey of Death, where the sand turned to green glass as Trinity exploded and thrust the world into the shadow of the mushroom cloud, does not end forty-six years later and a thousand miles northward, beneath the waving prairie sand reed and buffalo grass of the open plains of Wyoming. The place of Peacekeeper and Looking Glass is simply the edge of a precipice on which we all stand, poised, waiting for the next mile marker in our nuclear journey. For we are all Trinity's Children now.

ACKNOWLEDGMENTS

This book would never have been possible without the trust of the men and women of the Nuclear Highway who opened their lives to us. They were more than sources; they were each an inspiration, and some have become valued friends. We would especially like to acknowledge Mary McDonald; G. B. and Yvonne Oliver; Ted, Hugh, and Allen Church; General John L. "Pete" Piotrowski, USAF (Ret.), and his wonderful wife, Sheila; Jan Pilcher; Kae Gabel Williams; and Ken, Shirley, Alan, and Lindi Kirkbride.

The idea would never have come together without our Associated Press colleague Mort Rosenblum, who finally convinced us that if he could do it, we could do it. Carol Mann, our agent, showed us how to do it and believed that we could. We would also like to thank our editor at Harcourt Brace Jovanovich, Claire Wachtel, whose enthusiasm buoyed us, and her assistant, the patient Ruth Greenstein, whose hard work and keen eye kept us on track.

Wisdom, sustaining humor, and support were offered by colleagues and friends at the AP, especially Kristin Gazlay, Fred Bayles, George Esper, Sharon (Aren't you done yet?) Cohen, David Breslauer, Tim Gallivan, Susie Hoffmann, Bill Ahearn, Marty Thompson, Mary Campbell, Horst Faas, Eileen Murray, Andy Lippman, John Lumpkin, Paul Stevens, and Sylvia Wingfield.

No one could have better compadres than Jo Jones, who kept us laughing; Carol Graham, who kept us fed; Carol and Jim Crain, who kept us in fudge; Paula Steige, who kept us in books; Kay Cody, who drew the map; Tammie Hastings, who arrived in the nick of time; Carole Page, Shauna Duell, and Chris Moody, who always came through on logistics; Tay and Lowell Thomas, Jr., Steve Craig, Hank Waters III and Vicki Russell, Bob and Beverly Blumenthal, Pat Ashworth, and Lynda Hoffman, who were always there when needed; Laura Palmer, who warned of pitfalls and steered a true heading; Nick Lyons, who offered wonderful advice; George and Lucile Moses, Catharine Hamm, and Bill and Ellen Hoch, who kindly read rough drafts.

Public affairs officers, historians, sources, and researchers up and down the highway were a tremendous help, especially Jim Eckles at White Sands; Nigel Hey at Sandia; Rich Garcia at the Air Force Weapons Lab in Albuquerque; John Webster and Roger Meade at Los Alamos National Lab; Hedy Dunn and Theresa Strottman at the Los Alamos Historical Society; John and Nancy Bartlit of Los Alamos; Richard Salazar at the state archives in Santa Fe, N.M.; Sam Ballen of the La Fonda Hotel in Santa Fe and the Oppenheimer Memorial Committee; Martha DeMarre and John Harney at the Department of Energy records warehouse in Las Vegas, Nev.; Diana Stein of La Galeria de los Artesanos in Las Vegas,

N.M.; Don Hancock of Southwest Research and Information in Albuquerque; Major Thomas A. Niemann, U.S. Army, and Colonel James Moore, USAF, at Peterson AFB; Bill Baugh at Falcon AFB; Will Ketterson at the Air Force Academy; Bruce DeBoskey of Denver; Daniel Sheehan of the Christic Institute, Washington, D.C.; Samuel Day, Jr., at Nukewatch; Professor Charles Wilkinson of the University of Colorado – Boulder; and Airman Karina Keinanen at F. E. Warren AFB.

We would also like to recognize the importance of two people very close to us who died during this project: Colonel James L. Bartimus, USAF (Ret.), and Dr. Pam Blumenthal. Both of them always set the highest standards and spent their lives making the world a better place. We loved them deeply, and we miss them very much.

Most of all, we would like to thank our spouses, Dean Wariner and Karen Blumenthal, who kept us on course and kept us going. They were our best editors and our truest believers.

TAD BARTIMUS
SCOTT MC CARTNEY
Shining Mountains Inn
Estes Park, Colorado
January 1991

GLOSSARY

atom   A particle of matter, the fundamental building block of chemical elements. Splitting an atom, called fission, or fusing two together, called fusion, yields tremendous energy, thus the power of atomic bombs.

atomic bomb   A weapon whose energy comes from splitting the atoms of uranium or plutonium.

background radiation   Radiation in the natural environment, including cosmic rays and radiation from naturally radioactive elements. Standing outside under the sun, or flying in an airplane, exposes a person to background radiation.

Brilliant Pebbles   A proposed Strategic Defense Initiative antimissile system, made up of independent, computerized interceptors in space that would detect a nuclear missile and then crash into it to destroy it.

chain reaction   A reaction that stimulates its own repetition, crucial to nuclear reactions and explosions. See *critical mass*.

CINC   Commander in Chief.

critical mass   The amount of fissionable material that, under certain conditions, is capable of sustaining a chain reaction. When critical mass is achieved, atoms begin splitting, releasing energy.

deuterium   An isotope of hydrogen that is about twice as heavy as normal hydrogen. It is nonradioactive and is a component of hydrogen bombs.

DOE   Department of Energy.

electromagnetic pulses (EMP)   Electric and magnetic waves that are produced in a hydrogen bomb explosion and travel at the speed of light, disrupting normal radio and electrical operations.

fallout   Airborne particles containing radioactive material that fall to the ground following a nuclear explosion.

Fat Man   Nickname of the atomic bomb dropped on Nagasaki, Japan. Fat Man was a rotund implosion device, a copy of the gadget tested at Trinity.

fission   Splitting the nucleus of an atom, accompanied by the release of large amounts of energy that had been binding the nucleus together. An atomic bomb uses fission.

fusion   Forming a heavier nucleus from two lighter ones by fusing them together. The process releases huge amounts of energy. A hydrogen bomb uses fusion.

glove box   A sealed plexiglass box in which workers, protected by gloves, can handle radioactive materials.

half-life   The time in which a radioactive material decays to half its potency.

hydrogen   The lightest element. It has a natural nonradioactive isotope, deuterium, or heavy hydrogen. Another isotope, tritium, is produced in reactors. Both deuterium and tritium are used in hydrogen bombs.

hydrogen bomb   A nuclear weapon that derives its energy primarily from fusion.

ICBM   Intercontinental ballistic missile, a weapon capable of traveling thousands of miles, from continent to continent, and delivering a payload of nuclear warheads.

implosion   Compressing a quantity of fissionable material with a shell of regular chemical explosives so that a supercritical mass is produced—thus a nuclear explosion. The world's first nuclear explosion, the Trinity test, was an implosion device, as was the bomb dropped on Nagasaki, Japan.

isotopes   Different forms of elements with the same atomic number but different atomic weights. That is, the nuclei of isotopes have the same number of protons but a different number of neutrons. Deuterium is a heavier isotope of hydrogen because its nucleus has a neutron and a proton, and normal hydrogen has only a single proton.

kiloton   A unit of measure of the force of a nuclear explosion, equivalent to 1,000 tons of TNT.

laser   An acronym from *l*ight *a*mplification by *s*timulated *e*mission of *r*adiation. A laser puts molecules in an excited energy state, causing them to emit light of a precise wavelength in an intense, narrow beam.

LCF   A missile launch control facility, where the signal would be given to launch a nuclear missile.

Little Boy   Nickname of the first atomic bomb used against Japan. Little Boy was a uranium gun device dropped on Hiroshima.

Looking Glass   A Strategic Air Command EC-135, a converted Boeing 707 airplane, based outside Omaha, Neb., crammed full of equipment and flight crews capable of launching retaliatory nuclear missile strikes in the event the President and his normal chain of command are incapacitated.

Manhattan Project   War Department program during World War II that produced the first atomic bombs. The term originated with the secret code name: Manhattan Engineering District.

megaton   Explosion equivalent to 1 million tons of TNT, or 1,000 kilotons.

MIRV   Multiple independently targetable reentry vehicle, the warheads of an ICBM. Each ICBM can carry several MIRVs, or thermonuclear weapons, which separate in space and head for separate targets.

MX   A four-stage, 71-foot ICBM, which can carry ten independently targetable nuclear warheads. There are fifty in the U.S. arsenal, all deployed around Cheyenne, Wyo. Each MX is 8 feet in diameter, weighs 97 tons, and can travel 6,000 miles. Dubbed "Peacekeeper" by President Reagan.

NORAD   North American Aerospace Defense Command, a joint

U.S.-Canada command created in 1957 for the common defense of the North American continent.

nuclear bomb Collective term for atomic and hydrogen bombs. Any weapon based on a nuclear explosion.

nucleus The small, positively charged core of an atom.

plutonium A radioactive, man-made metal. Its most important isotope is fissionable plutonium-239, the material used in the Trinity and Fat Man devices and still used in today's hydrogen bombs.

rad, rem, roentgen The basic units of measurement for doses of radiation.

Sputnik World's first satellite, launched October 4, 1957, by the Soviet Union.

Star Wars Nickname, after the popular movie, for the Strategic Defense Initiative.

Stealth Capable of evading radar. The Stealth fighter, or F-117, was a star of the Persian Gulf War.

Strategic Air Command, SAC Omaha-based command of the nation's airborne defenses.

Strategic Defense Initiative, SDI A military program launched by President Reagan to develop lasers, rockets, and other weapons to intercept and destroy incoming nuclear missiles.

thermonuclear bomb A hydrogen bomb.

Trinity Code name for the test of the world's first nuclear device, which occurred in southern New Mexico.

tritium A radioactive isotope of hydrogen with two neutrons and one proton in the nucleus. It is man-made, heavier than deuterium, and used in hydrogen bombs.

uranium A radioactive element found in natural ores. Uranium is the basic raw material of nuclear energy.

uranium gun Bomb assembly used in the Hiroshima atomic bomb. A plug of uranium was shot into a matching hollowed-out sphere, producing the critical mass and nuclear explosion.

NOTES

Chapter 1

The authors would like to note that the inception of the book and many of the original interviews came from an Associated Press series of newspaper stories they wrote in 1988 called "The Nuclear Highway." The series was released nationally to AP member newspapers and radio and television stations in June 1988.

Information on the selection of the Trinity Site came from a Los Alamos National Laboratory publication, "Trinity," #LA-6300-H.

Descriptions of the bomb assembly and the McDonald ranch house came from a White Sands Missile Range publication, "Trinity Site, a National Historic Landmark." Additional detail can be found in Richard Rhodes's Pulitzer Prize–winning book, *The Making of the Atomic Bomb*, Simon & Schuster, 1988, especially p. 659. The Rhodes book is a monumental work of science and history and is commended to readers.

The anecdotes about the accidental bombing of the Trinity base camp came from David Hawkins's official history of the atomic

296

bomb project, *Project Y: The Los Alamos Story*, Tomash Publishers, Los Angeles (reprinted in 1983 in anticipation of the fortieth anniversary of Trinity), 238, and from a Los Alamos National Laboratory publication, "Los Alamos 1943–1945: The Beginning of an Era," LASL-79-78, reprinted in July 1986.

It should be noted that no one recorded the actual second of the Trinity explosion. Historians working with the scientists involved have estimated the time at 5:29:45 A.M., although no more specific note was made than 5:29 A.M.

The McDonalds were interviewed numerous times in Alamogordo and Carrizozo, N.M., including May 1990 and September 1990.

The Martins were interviewed May 1990 at Alamogordo, N.M.

A secret memo prepared for Major General Leslie R. Groves on the day of the Trinity test by Captain T. O. Jones lists places where the explosion could be seen, including Amarillo, Texas, as well as towns where it was heard, where the air shock was felt, and where public reaction was observed. This memo, declassified in 1987, also includes the account of the forest ranger reporting the blast to the Associated Press. The memo was obtained by the authors from the Department of Energy archives in Las Vegas, a warehouse established to make declassified documents regarding nuclear testing available to the public.

The Georgia Green story is found in University of New Mexico historian Ferenc Morton Szasz's 1984 book on Trinity, *The Day the Sun Rose Twice*, University of New Mexico Press.

Raemer Schreiber was interviewed April 1990 in Los Alamos, N.M.

The accounts of radiation levels and the various studies of contamination from Trinity are taken from numerous declassified documents found in the DOE archives. Another good source is a 1983 Defense Nuclear Agency publication, "Project Trinity 1945–46," #DNA 6028F.

Today's allowable radiation levels were tightened by the Nuclear Regulatory Commission December 13, 1990, for the first time in more than thirty years. The new levels were reported by H. Josef Hebert of the Associated Press.

G. B. Oliver was interviewed at his White Sands ranch in 1988, and again in Alamogordo, N.M., in 1990.

Clippings and reports on Project Gnome can be found at the DOE archives in Las Vegas.

———

Chapter 2

The Goddard quotation appears in several U.S. military booklets, including booklets for the White Sands Missile Range and the U.S. Air Force Phillips Laboratory.

Bush's comments on the Patriot missile were made before a group of Raytheon workers in Massachusetts. A transcript of the speech was transmitted by the Associated Press.

Frank Borman was interviewed by telephone in 1988.

Replay of the Patriot test firing and interviews with Range Control personnel were conducted at White Sands Missile Range in November 1990. Additional reporting was done there in April 1988.

White Sands history is available from several documents issued by the missile range.

The Victorio Peak treasure legend was chronicled by one of the authors in a 1987 Associated Press story, based on a visit to the peak with White Sands personnel and numerous interviews.

Information about current White Sands programs was gleaned from several trips there by one of the authors, including numerous interviews and site visits.

James Wise was interviewed November 1990 at White Sands.

Miracl laser was visited November 1990 by one of the authors, and Gene Frye was interviewed at the time. He has since retired from that post.

Chapter 3

One of the authors visited the New Mexico Institute of Mining and Technology and TERA in Socorro in 1988.

The DOE study that found plutonium in Albuquerque soil was released in August 1990 and actually confirmed results that had been found five years earlier. Gene Runkle was quoted by the Associated Press on August 13, 1990.

It is worth noting that while Albuquerque is the only United States city that has had a nuclear bomb dropped on it, it is not the only place in the country with that ignoble distinction. At least three other nuclear bombs have been accidentally dropped in the country—but in rural areas. As in the Albuquerque case, there was never a nuclear detonation.

Sandia, Kirtland, and the entire "City of Secrets" were visited numerous times since 1988 by one of the authors, primarily for stories for the Associated Press.

David H. Morrissey of the *Albuquerque Journal* wrote a series of stories in March 1986 profiling the "Atomic Economy" in New Mexico, including a rundown of different agencies based at Kirtland.

Richard and Mary Carter were interviewed in 1988 at their home in Four Hills.

The DOE memo faxed to governors' offices around the country was reported by Brendan Riley, the Associated Press correspondent in Carson City, Nev., on March 13, 1990.

Czeslaw Deminet was interviewed in 1988.

Chapter 4

The Churches were interviewed in Albuquerque, N.M., April 1988, February 1990, and March 1990.

The secret submarine project tale was included in a front-page story of the Santa Fe *New Mexican* the day after President Truman announced the dropping of the atomic bomb and where it was created.

The two best sources on the Pond family history are *The House at Otawi Bridge*, by Peggy Pond Church, University of New Mexico Press, 1959, and *When Los Alamos Was a Ranch School,* a booklet written by Peggy and Ferm Church for the Los Alamos Historical Society, 1974.

Information on the graduates of the Los Alamos Ranch School was obtained from the Los Alamos Historical Society.

The Army's search for a Manhattan Project site is recorded in Hawkins, as well as Lieutenant General Leslie R. Groves's 1962 book, *Now It Can Be Told: The Story of the Manhattan Project*, Harper & Brothers.

Condemnation papers were obtained from a federal court warehouse in Denver by the Los Alamos Historical Society.

Fermor Church's papers are stored at the New Mexico State Archives in Santa Fe, where they were reviewed by one of the authors. The collection includes documents concerning the ranch school, personal correspondence, War Department letters, even newspaper clippings on the Manhattan Project.

Peggy Pond Church's poem on her husband, Fermor, was titled "In Memoriam FSC 1900–1975" and published in a collection titled *Birds of Daybreak: Landscapes and Elegies*, Gannon, 1985.

Peggy Pond Church was interviewed by one of the authors in 1985, Santa Fe, N.M.

Peggy's poem "Endangered Species" was also published in *Birds of Daybreak*.

Françoise Ulam was interviewed at Santa Fe, N.M., April 1990.

Hedy Dunn was interviewed at Los Alamos, N.M., April 1990.

Chapter 5

Oppenheimer's oft-quoted remark on sin was made in a lecture at the Massachusetts Institute of Technology, titled "Physics in the Contemporary World," November 25, 1947.

A trip to Los Alamos is highly recommended, even though the town almost goes out of its way to stay isolated from tourists. The historical society's displays at Fuller Lodge are worthwhile, as is the Bradbury Science Museum, tucked away at Los Alamos National Laboratory but open to the adventuresome public.

Hawkins provides a good starting point for the early days of Los Alamos.

Dorothy McKibbin was interviewed by one of the authors before her death for a story on the fortieth anniversary of the bomb. The interview was in 1985 in Santa Fe, N.M. Mrs. McKibbin also gave an oral history to the Los Alamos National Laboratory, dated January 13, 1982.

Oppenheimer's famous nail requisition and his comment about plumbers' salaries are recounted in James W. Kunetka's *City of Fire*, University of New Mexico Press, Albuquerque, 1978, p. 64.

Schreiber was interviewed April 1990 in Los Alamos, N.M.

Robert Wilson's letter to H. D. Smyth was obtained from the Los Alamos National Laboratory archives. Wilson's oral history was also obtained from the Los Alamos archives, document #TR-84-006. It was a 1984 interview with the Los Alamos staff.

The "flop heard round the world" verse was taken from Kunetka, p. 157.

Teller's Cold War strategy letter to Leo Szilard, which included: "The things we are working on are so terrible that no amount of protesting or fiddling with politics will save our souls," was dated July 2, 1945. It was obtained from the DOE records warehouse in Las Vegas.

Groves's response to Oppenheimer on the necessity of dropping at least three bombs on Japan was in the form of a July 19, 1945, teletype, found at the Los Alamos archives.

Oppenheimer's memo on scaling down Los Alamos was addressed to "All Division and Group Leaders" and dated August 20, 1945. It was declassified and obtained from the Los Alamos archives.

Kistiakowsky's memo to Oppenheimer was found in the Los Alamos archives, document #A-84-019, 19-5 memo. It was titled "My Activities During Your Absence," dated September 4, 1945.

Groves's letter to Bradbury in which he outlined his belief that he should go ahead and make long-range plans for Los Alamos was dated January 4, 1946. It was on War Department stationery and classified Secret at the time. In 1985, it was verified unclassified. The authors obtained it from the Los Alamos archives.

The Daghlian and Slotin radiation deaths are examined in several books, including Kunetka and Barton C. Hacker's *The Dragon's Tail: Radiation Safety in the Manhattan Project, 1942–1946*, University of California Press, 1987, which was sponsored by the Department of Energy.

Nancy Bartlit was interviewed September 1990 at Los Alamos.

Joe McKibben was interviewed April 1990 at White Rock, N.M.

Sig Hecker was interviewed April 1990 at the Los Alamos National Laboratory.

Richard Burick, Sid Singer, and other Los Alamos Star Wars people were interviewed April 1990 at Los Alamos. Additional Star Wars–related interviews were conducted at Los Alamos in March and May 1988. Among other helpful publications on work at Los Alamos used by the authors were the annual "Research Highlights" booklets.

Dick Slansky was interviewed April 1990 at Los Alamos.

Defense Secretary Dick Cheney's concern for the safety of the W-79 nuclear artillery shell was revealed by the Washington *Post* in May 1990.

Data on Los Alamos and DOE pollution were gathered from several sources, including studies, interviews, and a General Accounting Office report, "Nuclear Health and Safety: Need for Improved Responsiveness to Problems at DOE Sites," GAO/RCED-90-101, March 1990.

Wayne Hansen was interviewed April 1990 at Los Alamos.
John Bartlit was interviewed September 1990 at Los Alamos.

Chapter 6

Miscellaneous anecdotal information concerning Seymour Cray came from numerous periodicals, including *Time, Newsweek, Business Week, Forbes*, and *Fortune*, and many newspaper articles, including stories in *The New York Times, The Washington Post*, the Colorado Springs *Gazette Telegraph, The Denver Post*, the *Rocky Mountain News*, and others. Cray refuses, almost always, to be personally interviewed or to have any contact whatsoever with the press. He made an exception by granting *Gazette Telegraph* writer Russ Arensman an interview on March 31, 1988. Cray had agreed to a thirty-minute interview; he abruptly broke it off after just fifteen minutes, declining to answer any more questions. Other information on Cray and his firms came from promotional materials supplied by Cray Computer Corporation and from two telephone interviews with the company's president and CEO, Neil Davenport, in January 1991.

The quotes by J. Robert Oppenheimer were drawn from a transcript of his testimony before the Atomic Energy Commission's Personnel Security Board hearings in April 1954, "In the Matter of J. Robert Oppenheimer, Transcript of Hearing Before Personnel Security Board and Texts of Principal Documents and Letters," MIT Press, 1971, and from *Science and the Common Understanding*, by J. Robert Oppenheimer, BBC Reith Lecture, 1953; Oxford University Press, 1954.

Miscellaneous facts and figures regarding Colorado Springs and El Paso County statistical profiles, as well as the effect of the savings and loan crisis on the area, came from the Colorado Springs Chamber of Commerce, the Greater Colorado Springs Economic Development Council, the Board of Realtors, and numerous interviews with business and professional people in the area, conducted in person and by phone from January 1988 through January 1991. The authors have written extensively about the S&L crisis in Colorado, Texas, Arizona, and California for the Associated Press.

Tales of the early days of Colorado Springs and its environs were drawn from numerous old newspaper clippings and from

Marshall Sprague's 1987 revised edition of *Newport of the Rockies*, Swallow Press/Ohio University Press, 1961.

Also helpful for background on Colorado's colorful early-day pioneers was *The Rocky Mountain Herald Reader*, edited by Thomas Hornsby Ferrill and Helen Ferrill, William Morrow, 1966. Also contributing to background were numerous histories of the area available through Colorado public libraries.

Every military installation in the Springs area has its own public affairs office, and each supplied an official history of its facility. Particularly helpful was the staff at Peterson Air Force Base, especially Major Thomas Niemann and his boss, Colonel Jim Moore, who found information on Ent Air Force Base, which preceded Peterson. Fort Carson, the Air Force Academy, and Falcon Air Force Base also provided their own histories.

Much of the material on President Eisenhower came from the Eisenhower Library and Museum, Abilene, Kan., as well as Colorado Springs sources.

Data on Martin Marietta came from the public relations office of the company's Denver facility, from interviews with Martin Marietta executives in 1988, and from numerous periodicals.

Anecdotes about Frank Aries came from interviews with several of his Colorado Springs business associates, especially H. Pike Oliver, at the company's offices in Colorado Springs in 1988, and from numerous periodicals and newspaper articles.

Astronaut Jim Irwin was interviewed in Colorado Springs in 1988 and again in 1989, and the office staff of his High Flight Foundation also provided assistance.

Attorney Newman McAllister was interviewed in Colorado Springs in 1988 and several times by telephone in 1989.

Chapter 7

The public affairs offices of the U.S. Space Command, the North American Aerospace Defense Command, and the Air Force Space Command provided much of the unclassified details of construction and operation pertaining to Cheyenne Mountain and its worldwide network.

Also contributing information on the Space Command and NORAD were numerous periodicals, especially *Aviation Week and Space Technology, Air & Space, United States Space Foun-*

dation bulletin, *High Country News, Time, Newsweek, Scientific American*, and major national newspapers as well as local newspapers.

Information on the false missile attack alerts that occurred at Cheyenne Mountain in November 1979 and June 1980 were obtained in interviews with military and civilian personnel, from the official Air Force response supplied by NORAD's public affairs office in October 1990, and from *The Button*, by Daniel Ford, Simon & Schuster, 1985.

General John L. "Pete" Piotrowski graciously spent more than fifty hours over three years answering tape-recorded questions about his life and career, which climaxed with his retirement as commander in chief of NORAD and the U.S. Space Command in April 1990. Also extensively interviewed throughout 1988, 1989, and 1990 for details of his life were his wife, Sheila; his former commander, General W. L. "Bill" Creech, USAF (Ret.), of Las Vegas, Nev.; his military buddy Vaughn Lancaster, of Midwest City, Okla., who served with him in Japan; his brother-in-law Harold "Hal" Frederickson, of Mesa, Ariz.; and numerous subordinates who served with General Piotrowski over the years.

Especially helpful in providing historical context to the general's first Vietnam tour was *A Bright Shining Lie*, by Neil Sheehan, Random House, 1988.

Government publications provided by the Strategic Defense Initiative Organization and the General Accounting Office in Washington, D.C., as well as publications provided by Nukewatch of Madison, Wis., and Public Citizen of Washington, D.C., were also helpful in writing about various elements of Star Wars.

Chapter 8

Over nearly five years, and especially in 1988, 1989, and 1990, Jan Vittum Pilcher consented to more than one hundred hours of taped interviews and conversations about her life and social activism pertaining to Rocky Flats and provided many contacts that led to more information garnered for this book. The American Friends Service Committee in Denver, especially Steve Graham and Tom Rauch, supplied historical files for background on Rocky Flats.

Information on the first protests against Rocky Flats is contained in "Local Hazard Global Threat," jointly authored by ten members of the Rocky Flats Action Group—including Jan Pilcher—in August 1977.

Cass Peterson's takeout on Rocky Flats in *The Washington Post* offers extensive information on the history of the plant's problems. It was published in December 1988, and again in the December 26, 1988–January 1, 1989 "Washington Post Weekly Edition." Peterson obtained copies of the documents sealed in the lawsuit settlement and offered a thorough account of why Rocky Flats should never have been built where it was.

The Atomic Energy Commission report on the 1969 fire was obtained by the authors from the Department of Energy records warehouse in Las Vegas, Nev. The report was dated November 18, 1969.

The EPA study on cattle contamination was reported in the *Rocky Mountain News*, Denver, Colo., on December 5, 1974.

Dr. Carl Johnson's work was detailed in several news accounts. In addition, a June 3, 1987, paper by Johnson was consulted.

The *Rocky Mountain News* reported the Adolph Coors Company involvement in the waste at Rocky Flats on March 10, 1990.

A General Accounting Office report in October 1988 detailed some of the issues. It was titled "Nuclear Health and Safety: Summary of Major Problems at DOE's Rocky Flats Plant."

The Associated Press has covered the Rocky Flats issue extensively. Among other reports from which information was drawn were October 9, 1989, and June 1, 1990, explorations of the sixty-two pounds of plutonium in the air ducts.

The raid by FBI and EPA agents was widely reported at the time, including the *Rocky Mountain News*, June 7, 1989. The unsealed 116-page FBI affidavit was reported by the *Rocky Mountain News* and *The New York Times*, June 10, 1989, and *The Wall Street Journal*, June 12, 1989.

For a comprehensive account of Wellesley, Mass.–based EG&G and its takeover of Rocky Flats operations, see John Holusha's account in *The New York Times*, Sunday Business section, December 3, 1989.

A Public Citizen publication, "Nuclear Legacy," details radioactive waste in the United States and notes that the DOE and weapons programs provide four times as much waste as commercial power plants.

The quote "We have one hell of a legacy to clean up" was made by Leo Duffy, top adviser on long-term environmental issues to Energy Secretary James Watkins, and was reported by Robert Burns of the Associated Press on July 15, 1990.

Bruce DeBoskey's work was chronicled, among other places, by Keith Schneider in *The New York Times*, November 18, 1989.

The story of Don Gabel's life, illness, and death came from several interviews with his widow, Kae Gabel Williams, in 1991, as well as from his attorney, Bruce DeBoskey, of Silver & DeBoskey of Denver, and from numerous periodicals and newspaper stories.

Also interviewed by telephone in January 1991 was Chris Beaver, a San Francisco–based independent documentary film-maker, who, along with his colleague Judy Irving, produced *Dark Circle*, about Rocky Flats. The film was released in 1983 and contains the last known photographs of Don Gabel before his death in September 1980. The authors are grateful to Beaver and Irving for permission to use a still photograph taken from their movie that they had given to Kae Gabel Williams, who made it available for this book.

Rockwell International's position, voiced by lawyers and public relations employees throughout the 1980s, was found in numerous periodicals and testimony records.

Don Gabel's courtroom testimony was contained in hearing transcripts and also quoted in numerous periodicals. It was also reconstructed by his widow in an interview with one of the authors.

The medical theories of Dr. Alice Stewart of Birmingham, England, who testified on behalf of the plaintiff at the Gabel hearing, were paraphrased for one of the authors by attorney DeBoskey, and excerpts from Dr. Stewart's comments at the Gabel hearing were contained in numerous periodicals, especially *The Denver Post* and *Rocky Mountain News* of June, July, and August 1980.

Chapter 9

Historical information and background on settlement of the American West surrounding the Nuclear Highway came from dozens of publications, and a list of those can be found in the bibliography. The authors are especially appreciative of the help offered by Charles F. Wilkinson of the School of Law at the University of Colorado at Boulder. Dr. Wilkinson offered time and insight in an interview on the CU campus in October 1989, in Jackson, Wyo., in May 1990, and in several phone conversations. His *The American West: A Narrative Bibliography*, published by the University Press of Colorado, Boulder, 1989, was an invaluable resource tool.

The story of Black Elk, the Sioux Indian holy man, is told in *Black Elk Speaks*, by John G. Neihardt, University of Nebraska Press, 1961.

The story of the immigration of the Kirkbride clan from Yorkshire, England, was told in "From These Roots," by Mrs. Dan "Peggy" Kirkbride, Pioneer Printing and Stationery Company, Cheyenne, Wy., 1972.

Peggy Kirkbride was interviewed at her home in Cheyenne in July 1990.

Ken Kirkbride was interviewed at his home in Cheyenne in January 1990.

The eyewitness account of the launch of Sputnik I on October 4, 1957, by Soviet historian Evgeny Riabchikov was contained in . . . *the Heavens and the Earth*, by Walter A. McDougall, Basic Books, 1985.

Chapter 10

Lindi Kirkbride, her husband, Alan, and her children, Ryan, Rhonda, and Anduin, were first interviewed in 1988 for the AP series on America's Nuclear Highway. Lindi subsequently gave more than one hundred hours of taped interviews and informal conversation to one of the authors, at the Kirkbride ranch near Meriden, Wyo., in Cheyenne, Wyo., and in Estes Park, Colo.

Anecdotal material on the Kirkbride and Harding families is contained in Peggy Kirkbride's self-published book, "From These Roots," cited in Chapter 9, and in "Still on the Trail: 65 Years of Harding and Kirkbride," published privately in 1989 by the Kirkbride and Harding families and edited by Dan Kirkbride.

Mae Irene Kirkbride was interviewed by telephone from her home outside Cheyenne, Wyo., in November and December 1990. Further information about Mae Kirkbride's activism and comments made by her husband, Rod, about the deployment of nuclear weapons in Wyoming came from periodicals, especially *The Denver Post*, and Wyoming newspapers.

Paula Hirschboech was interviewed by telephone from her home in Riverton, Wyo., in November and December of 1990, and provided access to her personal diaries.

Sister Frances Russell was interviewed by telephone from her home in Topeka, Kan., in November and December 1990 and January 1991, and gave the authors access to all her personal diaries and scrapbooks pertaining to the deployment of Minuteman III and MX missiles in Wyoming.

Historical background on deployment of all Air Force weapons in Wyoming came from the Strategic Air Command, especially the public affairs office of F. E. Warren Air Force Base, Wyo., Offutt Air Force Base, Neb., and Norton Air Force Base, Calif. Among their most useful publications for this book were "From Snark to Peacekeeper: A Pictorial History of Strategic Air Command Missiles" and "SAC Missile Chronology 1939–1988." Also helpful was the U.S. Department of Defense's 1990 publication "Soviet Military Power."

Other background information was obtained in numerous environmental impact statements, public hearings, transcripts of congressional hearings, General Accounting Office reports, and interviews. Especially helpful were articles in *High Country News*, the *Observer* of London, England, a 1981 series by Bill Prochnau in the *Washington Post Magazine*, and *Northern Lights*, a publication of the Northern Lights Research and Education Institute.

Information on the accident in the MX missile silo on June 15, 1988, came from official press releases from the Air Force, numerous reports in magazines and newspapers from 1988 through 1990, and interviews with the Kirkbride family.

Chapter 11

The description of life inside an MX control capsule came from numerous interviews conducted since 1988 by one of the authors, who also spent time in an actual MX control capsule—Quebec-1—in December 1990 and in a simulator capsule on F. E. Warren AFB, Wyo.

Lieutenant Ann Struckman was interviewed at F. E. Warren AFB and at Quebec-1 in December 1990; Captain Jack Hall was interviewed at the same places at the same time. Captain Jeff Stein and Lieutenant Ken Boschert were interviewed at Quebec-1 in December 1990.

Information on the history of the 90th Bomb Group came from the museum and public affairs office at F. E. Warren AFB.

The story and photograph of Francis Dellenbach and his residency in an old Atlas missile site were provided by the public affairs office at F. E. Warren AFB and were based on an interview Dellenbach gave to Air Force Lieutenant Amy K. Sailer in 1990. The Air Force made them available to the authors.

Information on the MX Rail Garrison project came from public hearings and government publications, as well as interviews with public officials and ranchers.

BIBLIOGRAPHY

Bragg, William F., Jr. *Wyoming: Rugged but Right*. Pruett Publishing, 1979.

Broad, William. *The Star Warriors: A Penetrating Look into the Lives of the Young Scientists behind Our Space-Age Weaponry*. Simon & Schuster, 1985.

Buchholtz, C. W. *Rocky Mountain National Park: A History*. Colorado Associated University Press, 1983.

Church, Peggy Pond. *Birds of Daybreak*. William Gannon, 1985.

———. *The House at Otawi Bridge*. University of New Mexico Press, 1959.

———. *New & Selected Poems*. Ahsahta Press, 1976.

———. *The Ripened Fields*. The Lightning Tree, 1978.

Church, Peggy Pond, and Ferm Church. *When Los Alamos Was a Ranch School*. Los Alamos Historical Society, 1974.

Cochran, Thomas B., et al. *Nuclear Weapons Data Book*. Ballinger, 1984.

Connell, Evan S. *Son of the Morning Star*. North Point Press, 1984.

Daniel, Joseph, and Keith Pope. *A Year of Disobedience*. Daniel Productions, 1979.

Day, Samuel H., Jr., ed. *Nuclear Heartland*. Nukewatch/The Progressive Foundation, 1988.

DeVoto, Bernard. *The Journals of Lewis and Clark*. Houghton Mifflin, 1953.

Duncan, Dayton. *Out West*. Viking Penguin, 1987.

Ferrill, Thomas Hornsby, and Helen Ferrill. *The Rocky Mountain Herald Reader*. William Morrow, 1966.

Ford, Daniel. *The Button*. Simon & Schuster, 1985.

———. *The Cult of the Atom*. Simon & Schuster, 1982.

Fradkin, Philip L. *Fallout: An American Nuclear Tragedy*. University of Arizona Press, 1989.

———. *Sagebrush Country*. Alfred A. Knopf, 1989.

Frazier, Ian. *Great Plains*. Farrar, Straus & Giroux, 1989.

Frey, Rodney. *The World of the Crow Indians*. University of Oklahoma Press, 1987.

Gage, Jack R. *The Johnson County War*. Flintlock Publishing, 1967.

Goetzmann, William H., and William N. Goetzmann. *The West of the Imagination*. W. W. Norton, 1986.

Goodchild, Peter. *J. Robert Oppenheimer: "Shatterer of Worlds."* British Broadcasting Corp., 1980.

Groves, Leslie R. *Now It Can Be Told: The Story of the Manhattan Project*. Harper & Brothers, 1962.

Hacker, Barton C. *The Dragon's Tail: Radiation Safety in the Manhattan Project, 1942–1946*. University of California Press, 1987.

Hansen, Chuck. *U.S. Nuclear Weapons: The Secret History*. Aerofax/Orion, 1988.

Hawkins, David. *Project Y: The Los Alamos Story*. Part I: *Toward Trinity*. Tomash Publishers, 1983 (reprint).

Horgan, Paul. *The Centuries of Santa Fe*. William Gannon, 1976.

———. *Of America East & West*. Farrar, Straus & Giroux, 1935.

Jette, Eleanor. *Inside Box 1663*. Los Alamos Historical Society, 1977.

Jungk, Robert. *Brighter Than a Thousand Suns*. Harcourt, Brace, 1958.

Kirkbride, Mrs. Dan "Peggy." *From These Roots*. Pioneer Printing & Stationery, 1972.

Kirkbride Family and Harding Family. *Still on the Trail*. Edited by Dan Kirkbride. Printed privately, 1989.

Klotz, Marcia. *A Citizen's Guide to Rocky Flats*. Rocky Mountain Peace Center, 1988.

Kunetka, James W. *City of Fire*. University of New Mexico Press, 1979.

Lamont, Lansing. *Day of Trinity*. Atheneum, 1965.

Larson, T. A. *Wyoming: A History*. W. W. Norton, 1977.

Laurence, William L. *Dawn Over Zero*. Alfred A. Knopf, 1946.

Leydet, François. *The Coyote: Defiant Song Dog of the West*. University of Oklahoma Press, 1977.

Lowie, Robert H. *The Crow Indians*. University of Nebraska Press, 1935.

Lyon, Fern, and Jacob Evans, eds. *Los Alamos: The First Forty Years*. Los Alamos Historical Society, 1984.

McAdow, Beryl. *Land of Adoption*. Johnson Publishing, 1970.

McDougall, Walter A. *. . . the Heavens and the Earth*. Basic Books, 1985.

McPhee, John. *Basin and Range*. Farrar, Straus & Giroux, 1980.

——. *The Curve of Binding Energy: A Journey into the Awesome and Alarming World of Theodore B. Taylor*. Farrar, Straus & Giroux, 1974.

——. *Rising from the Plains*. Farrar, Straus & Giroux, 1986.

Mojtabai, A. G. *Blessed Assurance: At Home with the Bomb in Amarillo, Texas*. Houghton Mifflin, 1986.

Moran, William T. *Santa Fe and the Chisholm Trail*. Published privately, undated.

Nadeau, Remi. *Fort Laramie and the Sioux*. University of Nebraska Press, 1967.

National Park Service. *Exploring the American West, 1803–1879*. U.S. Department of the Interior, 1982.

Neihardt, John G. *Black Elk Speaks*. University of Nebraska Press, 1961.

Perrigo, Lynn. *Gateway to Glorieta: A History of Las Vegas, N.M.* Pruett Publishing, 1982.

Powder River Heritage Committee. *Our Powder River Heritage*. Powder River Heritage Committee, Kaycee, Wyo., 1982.

Pringle, Peter, and James Spigelman. *The Nuclear Barons*. Holt, Rinehart & Winston, 1981.

Rashke, Richard. *The Killing of Karen Silkwood*. Houghton Mifflin, 1981.

Rezatto, Helen Graham. *The Making of the Two Dakotas*. Media Publishing, 1989.

Rhodes, Richard. *The Making of the Atomic Bomb*. Simon & Schuster, 1988.

Rocky Flats Action Group. *Local Hazard Global Threat*. Rocky Flats Action Group, 1977.

Rosenthal, Debra. *At the Heart of the Bomb: The Dangerous Allure of Weapons Work*. Addison-Wesley, 1990.

Sandoz, Mari. *The Cattlemen*. University of Nebraska Press, 1958.

Scheer, Robert. *With Enough Shovels: Reagan, Bush, & Nuclear War*. Random House, 1982.

Sheehan, Neil. *A Bright Shining Lie*. Random House, 1988.

Smith, Helena Huntington. *The War on Powder River*. University of Nebraska Press, 1966.

Sprague, Marshall. *Newport in the Rockies*. Swallow Press/Ohio University Press, 1961, revised 1987.

Stegner, Wallace. *The American West as Living Space*. University of Michigan Press, 1987.

Stewart, Edgar I. *Custer's Luck*. University of Oklahoma Press, 1955.

Szasz, Ferenc Morton. *The Day the Sun Rose Twice*. University of New Mexico Press, 1984.

Truslow, Edith C., and Ralph Carlisle Smith. *Project Y: The Los*

Alamos Story. Part II: *Beyond Trinity*. Tomash Publishers, 1983 (reprint).

United States Atomic Energy Commission (1954). *In the Matter of J. Robert Oppenheimer*. MIT Press, 1971.

United States Atomic Energy Commission. *Nuclear Terms*. Undated.

Utley, Robert M. *Custer Battlefield*. National Park Service, U.S. Department of the Interior, 1988.

Van Every, Dale. *The American Frontier, 1804–1845: The Final Challenge*. Quill/William Morrow, 1964.

Wagner, Glendolin Damon, and William A. Allen. *Blankets and Moccasins*. University of Nebraska Press, 1987.

Wilkinson, Charles F. *The American West: A Narrative Bibliography and a Study in Regionalism*. University Press of Colorado, 1989.

Worster, Donald. *Rivers of Empire*. Pantheon, 1985.

Wyden, Peter. *Day One: Before Hiroshima and After*. Simon & Schuster, 1984.

INDEX

315